# SELF-STUDY

# BIBLE

# COURSE

## ON

# ROMANS

## REVEALING THE
## RIGHTEOUSNESS OF GOD

# DEREK PRINCE

WHITAKER
HOUSE

## SELF-STUDY BIBLE COURSE ON ROMANS:
*Revealing the Righteousness of God*

Derek Prince Ministries
P.O. Box 19501
Charlotte, NC 28219-9501
www.derekprince.org

ISBN: 978-1-64123-954-7
eBook ISBN: 978-1-64123-955-4
Printed in Colombia
© 2023 by Derek Prince Ministries–International

Whitaker House
1030 Hunt Valley Circle
New Kensington, PA 15068
www.whitakerhouse.com

Library of Congress Control Number: 2023934617

1 2 3 4 5 6 7 8 9 10 11 ⊔ 30 29 28 27 26 25 24 23

# CONTENTS

# INTRODUCTION: INSTRUCTIONS TO THE STUDENT

Read these instructions before answering any questions.

## PURPOSE OF THIS BIBLE COURSE

Whenever I teach on the book of Romans, it is with a sense of excitement and great responsibility. I find the responsibility of interpreting this marvelous book to God's people a very serious one. It is my sincere desire and prayer that I will be both faithful to God's Word and sensitive to His Holy Spirit.

My purpose is to examine the book of Romans on an almost verse-by-verse level to reveal the very important truths that God has hidden in this letter, which was written by the apostle Paul. Repeatedly in this book, we read the phrase *"Do you not know…?"* and my experience is that, when Paul asks that question, Christians do *not* know. But that doesn't have to remain so. God has given us His Word, along with the Author, the Holy Spirit, to teach us *"all things"* (John 14:26; see also 2 Timothy 3:16). Let's open the Scriptures together and discover what God wants to teach us about the fullness of our righteousness* in Christ and how to live the Spirit-filled life.

## SYSTEM OF BIBLE REFERENCES

This course uses the *New King James Version* (NKJV) of the Bible as its main translation, so, if you use a different version, the wording may be slightly different from the verses quoted in the lessons. We encourage you to obtain a copy of the *New King James Version* for working through this study so that the wording of your answers to the questions will correspond to the wording of the answers in the "Correct Answers with Notes" section, especially where there are fill-in-the-blank questions for Scripture verses. If you have access to the Internet, you can easily look up the *New King James Version* through a Bible search engine. However, the truths taught in this course are equally clear in any reliable Bible translation, such as the *New International Version* (NIV), the *New English Translation* (NET), or the *New American Standard Bible* (NASB). (While Bible paraphrases can be helpful for general Scripture reading and gaining a fresh perspective, they are not designed as study Bibles and thus are not recommended for this course.)

## WORD DEFINITIONS

The glossary at the end of the book provides simple definitions of various theological terms and other vocabulary found in these studies with which you may be unfamiliar. Every word with an asterisk (*) next to it can be found in the glossary. Glossary words are designated only at the first appearance of a word in a lesson or in the "Correct Answers with Notes" section for a lesson. (For simplification, plurals of glossary words are not designated with asterisks, although the glossary entries "Gentiles" and "Jews" are in the plural.)

## HOW TO COMPLETE EACH STUDY

Before attempting to answer any questions, read the introduction to the lesson, which summarizes the teaching content. With nearly every question, there are references to one or more Scripture verses, either from the book of Romans or from related passages in other books of the Bible. Write your answer in the space provided below the question or on the line(s) within the question, or circle the correct answer from either Yes/No or multiple-choice options. Sometimes the answer to one question is divided into two or more parts. In such cases, the individual parts of the answer are listed under lowercase alphabetical letters.

## MEMORY VERSES

At the beginning of each lesson, you will find a key Scripture verse or verses for memorization that you must learn by heart. The process of memorization is invaluable for our spiritual lives. Scripture is called *"the sword of the Spirit"* (Ephesians 6:17) and forms part of the armor of God that enables us to *"withstand in the evil day"* (verse 13).

Psalm 119:11 says, *"Your word I have hidden in my heart, that I might not sin against You."* When we memorize Scripture verses, those Scriptures become always available to us for reference, comfort, correction, and meditation. They become a wellspring that we can draw from day and night.

If you have had difficulty memorizing passages in the past, I would like to encourage you to ask the Holy Spirit for His help. As I indicated in the first section of this introduction, in the gospel of John, Jesus says the Holy Spirit will teach us *"all things"*: *"The Helper, the Holy Spirit, whom the Father will send in My name, He will teach you all things, and bring to your remembrance all things that I have said to you"* (John 14:26). God will be faithful to help you hide His Word in your heart.

In addition, for your convenience, Scripture memory cards are included at the back of this book. Carry these memory cards with you wherever you go. Whenever you have a spare moment, review the verses. Regular review is the secret to successful memory work. In this way, you will learn portions of the Word by heart. God's Word will give you guidance, strength, spiritual food, victory over the devil, and seed to sow into the hearts of others.

If you have a smartphone, you can download Bible memorization apps that can be useful in committing Scripture verses to memory.

## PROCEDURE FOR WORKING THROUGH THE COURSE

For each lesson, after you have read the introduction, worked on memorizing the verse(s), and written your answer to every question, write out the memory verse(s)—with your Bible closed—in the space provided at the end of the "Questions" segment (you may also write them from memory on the back of the Scripture memory cards).

Following this, turn to the "Correct Answers with Notes" section of the book so you can check your work. If your answer to a question does not agree with the correct answer, read the question and the corresponding Scripture(s) again until you understand the reason for the correct answer.

The answers section includes additional notes that will give you deeper insight and information. Read through these notes and look up any Scriptures that are listed.

Finally, mark the points that you earned for each answer. If an answer is valued at more than one point, do not allow yourself the full number of points unless your answer is as complete as the correct answer.

Remember that the points for reciting the memory verses are important!

As you complete each lesson, add up your points and then check the total by the standards given at the bottom of the "Correct Answers" portion for that lesson. You may evaluate your score in this way:

50 percent or more = Pass

70 percent or more = Very Good

80 percent or more = Excellent

While the points will indicate how well you understood the lesson prior to working through the "Correct Answers and Notes" section, they won't reflect how much you understood *after* checking your answers against the model answers. Don't become discouraged if you didn't do as well as you had hoped; but, also, don't be prideful if you did well, because the end purpose of Bible study is not just knowledge but practical application in our lives. The more we read and study God's Word under the direction of the Holy Spirit, the more we will absorb it and be able to apply it.

And no cheating! Always write your own answers before checking the correct answers—including when you are writing out the memory verses.

When you have completed the final lesson, turn to the section entitled "Tally Sheet for Each Lesson" on page 253. Write in your score for each study in the space provided, add the scores for a cumulative total, and discover your overall achievement level.

## FINAL PERSONAL ADVICE

1. Begin each study with prayer, asking God to guide you and give you understanding.

2. Do not rush. Don't try to accomplish the whole study in one sitting. Read through each passage of Scripture several times until you are sure of its meaning. It will often be helpful to read several verses that come before and/or after the given Scripture verse(s) in order to grasp the full meaning of the passage. As is the case for most students, with the amount of biblical material that you will be learning, you should do no more than one study per week in order to absorb the teaching properly. This means that the whole Bible course will take about six months or more to complete.

3. Write neatly and clearly. Do not make your answers longer than necessary.

4. Pay special attention to the memory verses.

5. Finally, pray daily for God to help you apply the truths that you are learning to your own life.

God bless you as you begin your journey through Romans and learn how to become established in Christ's righteousness, walk in faith, and grow in grace.

# PRELUDE TO THE BOOK OF ROMANS

*Read Romans 1:1–17*

## INTRODUCTION

Through this *Self-Study Bible Course on Romans*, you are setting out on a journey in the realm of the Spirit that will both inspire and challenge you. At times, the going will be tough. This journey will take you down into the darkest depths of human depravity* and then up to the glistening heights of God's grace and glory.

Paul's letter, or epistle*, to the Romans is a unique combination of the spiritual and intellectual realms without parallel in human literature. It unfolds the most sublime* spiritual truths in terms of the most flawless logic*. It will not merely challenge your intellect; it will also illuminate your spirit.

For this reason, Romans will not yield its riches to careless or superficial reading. If you are to complete this pilgrimage successfully, you will need two essential items of spiritual equipment: prayer and perseverance.

Following the introductory passage of Romans 1:1–17, the first seven chapters of the book of Romans are divided into ten stages. We need to traverse each of these stages to reach the destination of the marvelous, Spirit-filled life described in Romans 8.

In chapters 9 through 11, Paul focuses on the destiny* of Israel*. Unless we comprehend God's plan for Israel, our understanding of the revelation of the gospel is incomplete. For too long, God's people have been denied the precious truths contained in these three chapters. Yet, without them, the church can never fully understand her own destiny.

Chapters 12 through 16 are where we are challenged to put our faith into action. They include down-to-earth truths on how to live out what we believe. As you face the mounting pressures of evil in these closing days of human history before Christ returns, you will find that these truths are nothing less than your key to survival!

Be encouraged by the words of the Lord to Joshua as he prepared to enter the promised land: *"Be strong and of good courage"* (Joshua 1:6). God went on to say that it would be by meditating on and obeying Scripture that Joshua would make his way prosperous and have good success. (See verse 8.) Let's keep our hearts and minds open to all that God wants to say to us through His Word and by His Spirit.

## MEMORY VERSES: ROMANS 1:16–17

[ ] Check here after memorizing the verses.

## QUESTIONS

### ANCIENT AND CONTEMPORARY LETTERS

Ancient letters, as they are found in the New Testament, are similar to today's business letters. Answer the questions below and use those same answers to fill in the blanks in the sample letter that follows to see how Paul's letter might look in a modern format.

1.  What was the name of the person sending the letter to these first-century believers? (Rom. 1:1)

    [1 point]

    _____

2.  To what particular ministry role was this person called? (Rom. 1:1) [1 point]

    _____

3.  Who was hosting the author of the letter? (Rom. 16:23) [1 point]

    _____

4.  In which city did the recipients of the letter live? (Rom. 1:7) [1 point]

    _____

5.  What were the believers receiving the letter called to be? (Rom. 1:7) [1 point]

    _____

6.  The writer of the letter was *"separated to the* _____ *of God."* (Rom. 1:1) [1 point]

7. Who transcribed the letter? (Rom. 16:22) [1 point]

_____

_____¹, Bondservant and _____²

House of _____³

Corinth, Greece

Circa* AD 57

To all those loved by God in _____⁴, Italy

Called to be _____⁵

Re: The Promised _____⁶ of God

Grace to you and peace from God our Father and the Lord Jesus Christ.

First, I thank my God through Jesus Christ for you all….

—REST OF THE CONTENTS OF THE LETTER—

…to God, alone wise, be glory through Jesus Christ forever. Amen.

Written down by _____⁷

## THE LETTER'S RECIPIENTS

8. To whom was Paul primarily called—to the Jews* or to all nations (the Gentiles*)? (Rom. 1:5)
   [1 point]

_____

9. In Romans 1:5, Paul's particular service is noted as bringing people to "_____ *to the faith.*" [1 point]

10. In Romans 1:6–7, we learn certain facts about those to whom the letter was written:

   a. They were _____ of Jesus Christ. [1 point]

   b. They were _____ of God. [1 point]

   c. They were called to be _____. [1 point]

## PAUL'S GREETING

11. The typical Hebrew greeting is "Shalom!" meaning *peace*. Paul indicated that, in the new covenant*, _____ comes before peace. (Rom. 1:7) [1 point]

12. Paul's greeting was not on his behalf alone but from *"God our Father and the* _____ _____ _____." (Rom. 1:7) [1 point]

13. Paul gave thanks to God because the faith of the Roman believers was spoken of throughout the whole _____. (Rom. 1:8) [1 point]

## THE GOSPEL OF GOD

14. The word *gospel* simply means "good news" or "glad tidings." In the book of Romans alone, this good news is expressed not only as "the gospel" but also as:

   a. The gospel of _____. (Rom. 1:1; 15:16) [1 point]

   b. The gospel of His _____. (Rom. 1:9) [1 point]

   c. The gospel of _____. (Rom. 1:16; 15:19; 15:29) [1 point]

   d. _____ gospel. (Rom. 2:16; 16:25) [1 point]

   e. The gospel of _____. (Rom. 10:15) [1 point]

15. Paul was careful to ensure that no one would think he had improvised this gospel. In Romans 1:2, he reassured his readers that this was the same message of hope that God had _____ beforehand through His _____, recorded in the Holy Scriptures. [2 points]

16. Jesus was *"declared to be the Son of God with* _____ *according to the Spirit of* _____ *, by the* _____ *from the* _____."
(Rom. 1:4) [4 points]

17. Read 1 Corinthians 15:1–4 and then complete the key facts of the gospel below:

    a. Christ _____ for our sins. (v. 3) [1 point]

    b. He was _____. (v. 4) [1 point]

    c. He _____ again the third day. (v. 4) [1 point]

## RESULTS OF THE GOSPEL

18. The gospel of Christ is *"the* _____ *of God to* _____ *for everyone who believes."* (Rom. 1:16) [2 points]

19. The gospel was for the _____ first and then also for the _____ (or Gentile).
(Rom. 1:16) [2 points]

20. According to Romans 1:17, what is revealed from faith to faith? [1 point]

    _____

## MEMORY WORK: ROMANS 1:16–17

Write out these verses from memory: [8 points]

_____

_____

_____

_____

_____

Check your answers on pages 161–63 in the "Correct Answers with Notes" section at the back of the book.

## PRAYER RESPONSE

Heavenly Father, I thank You for the opportunity to spend time with You through Your Word and under the guidance and companionship of Your Holy Spirit. I ask that You would help me to persevere through each lesson and to mine out every truth that You have hidden in the book of Romans for my benefit.

Thank You for the gospel—the wonderful message of reconciliation between You and me, Father—made possible through the priceless sacrifice of Jesus's blood on the cross. Help me to live out this message of surrendering to God, dying to self, being buried through baptism, and being raised to life as a new creation in Christ. Amen.

# STAGE 1: GOD'S SELF-REVELATION: MAN'S REJECTION AND ITS CONSEQUENCES

*Read Romans 1:18–32*

## INTRODUCTION

In the latter part of Romans 1, Paul discusses the opposite side of the coin concerning God's revelation to mankind. He has talked about the revelation of God's *righteousness**; now, he talks about the revelation of God's *wrath*. Both aspects are contained in the gospel, because when we look at Jesus's sufferings on the cross, we must bear in mind that He endured the wrath of God. Why? Because He became the eternal sin offering on our behalf.

He took our sin, and He took the judgment for our sin. He paid the full penalty. Once He became sin on the cross (see 2 Corinthians 5:21), the wrath of God was poured out upon Him. It had to be. The gospel is not a sloppy, sentimental, "Father Christmas" message. Again, we must see the other side of God's revelation regarding His righteousness: the gospel also reveals His wrath against sin.

If anybody could have made sin acceptable to God, it would have been the sinless Jesus when He took our sins upon Himself on the cross. But when Jesus became sin, He underwent God's judgment. There is no way, then, that God will ever condone sin. He will deal with it, and He will forgive it, but He will never tolerate it.

In this lesson, we will look at Paul's description of God's wrath against the whole human race. This is a very important part of the first chapter of Romans, because a lot of people think, "How could God punish harmless, innocent people?" That is not the problem, because there *are* no harmless, innocent people! The Bible says that *"all have sinned and fall short of the glory of God"* (Romans 3:23). The problem is, how can God forgive wicked sinners? In Romans, Paul explains how God resolved this problem. But, to begin with, he describes how God makes the sin and accountability of the whole human race abundantly clear.

## MEMORY VERSES: ROMANS 1:18–19, 21

[ ]   Check here after memorizing the verses.

(Review the verses from prior lessons daily.)

# QUESTIONS

## THE REVELATION OF GOD'S WRATH

1.  What is revealed from heaven against all ungodliness and unrighteousness of men? (Rom. 1:18) [1 point]

    _____

2.  What has mankind done to arouse God's wrath? (Rom. 1:18) [2 points]

    _____

## THE WITNESS OF CREATION

3.  In Romans 1:19, Paul gives us a very subtle piece of reasoning. Note the combination of two realities:

    a.  *"What may be known of God is manifest _____ them…."* [1 point]

    b.  *"…for God has shown it _____ them."* [1 point]

4.  Since when have God's invisible attributes been clearly seen and understood? (Rom. 1:20) [1 point]

    _____

5.  Which two particular invisible attributes of God have been revealed? (Rom. 1:20) [2 points]

    a.  _____

    b.  _____

6.  List four ways that creation demonstrates God's existence and His attributes: (Psalm [Ps.] 19:1–2)

    a.  *"The heavens declare the _____ of God."* (v. 1) [1 point]

    b.  *"The firmament shows His _____."* (v. 1) [1 point]

    c.  *"Day unto day utters _____."* (v. 2) [1 point]

    d.  *"Night unto night reveals _____."* (v. 2) [1 point]

7. In Deuteronomy 4, Moses uses the phrase *"take heed"* or *"take careful heed"* four times when urging the Israelites to watch themselves and be careful that they do not fall into sin.

    a. Which four entities does Moses warn the Israelites to be cautious about regarding how they perceive them, lest they *"feel driven to worship and serve them"*? (v. 19) [4 points]

    i. _____

    ii. _____

    iii. _____

    iv. _____

    b. To whom has God given these four things? (v. 19) [1 point]

    _____

    c. As what has God given them? (v. 19) [1 point]

    _____

8. According to Scripture, is it reasonable to suppose that the physical universe, including the laws that govern it, could have come into being without the Creator? (Job 38:1–11) [1 point]

    _____

9. Whom does Scripture say is the Lawgiver of the spiritual and moral laws that govern us, as well as of the physical ones? (Isa. 33:22) [1 point]

    _____

We hear a lot about evolution, but there is another side to consider: devolution, or degeneration. A lot of things in the world are not evolving; they are devolving. We will see further examples of this reality in this study. It is illogical to talk about evolution as if it were the only possible way that life on earth came into being. The fact is, there is greater evidence for devolution than evolution in the world today, particularly in the human race. And that devolution is related to the effects of the fall and man's continuing rebellion against God and His ways.

10. In Romans 1:21, Paul states the first two downward steps of humanity. What two things did mankind *fail* to do that started the decline? [2 points]

    a. _____

    b. _____

11. First result:

    Despite professing to be wise, what did these people become? (Rom. 1:22) [1 point]

    _____

12. Second result:

    Where Romans 1:23 says, *"And changed the glory of the incorruptible God into an image…,"* it is describing the sin of: [1 point]

    a. Adultery

    b. Covetousness

    c. Idolatry

## GOD'S CONSEQUENT JUDGMENT

13. Three times, Paul uses a similar phrase to denote God's judgment: God _____ _____ up/over to. (Rom. 1:24, 26, 28) [1 point]

14. What sin had Ephraim (Israel\*) committed that prompted God to say, "Let him alone"? (Hos. 4:17) [1 point]

    _____

15. First-Level Judgment: God gave them up to lust and defilement. Read Romans 1:24–25 and fill in the blanks below:

    a. "God also gave them up to _____, in the lusts of their _____…." (v. 24) [2 points]

b. *"…to dishonor their _____ among themselves…."* (v. 24) [1 point]

c. *"…who exchanged the _____ of God for the _____…."* (v. 25) [2 points]

d. *"…and worshiped and served the _____ rather than the _____."* (v. 25) [2 points]

16. Second-Level Judgment: God gave them up to vile passions.

    Answer the questions below based on Romans 1:26–27:

    a. In one word, commonly used today, what sinful practice is Paul describing in these verses? (The word is not found in the text.) [1 point]

    _____

    b. Whom does Paul name first as exchanging *"the natural use for what is against nature"*? (v. 26) [1 point]

    _____

    c. In committing what is shameful, where do such people receive the penalty of their error? (v. 27) [1 point]

    _____

17. In 1 Corinthians 6:18, Paul admonishes us, *"Flee sexual immorality."* He goes on to explain that every sin that a man does, with one exception, is outside the body. But *"he who commits sexual immorality sins against _____ _____ _____."* [1 point]

18. The city of Sodom is mentioned frequently in Scripture. Genesis 13:13 says, *"The men of Sodom were exceedingly wicked and sinful against the LORD."* Genesis 19:1–29 describes Sodom's depravity* and destruction, with the salient sin being homosexuality. However, homosexuality is not mentioned when Ezekiel lists the sins of Sodom. Write down the four characteristics attributed to *"the iniquity of your sister Sodom"*: (Ezekiel 16:49) [4 points]

    a. _____

    b. _____

    c. _____

    d. _____

19. If you have struggled (or if someone you know has struggled) with sexual sin of some description, I want to point you to a verse that Paul wrote to the church in Corinth. How does Paul describe the Corinthian church that he would present to Christ? (2 Cor. 11:2) [1 point]

_____

20. Third-Level Judgment: God gave them over to a debased mind.

    What did these people *not* like to do that resulted in God giving them over to a debased mind? (Rom. 1:28) [1 point]

_____

21. The two *"God gave them up to"* statements in Romans 1:24 and 26 relate to the people's bodies, but the third statement, where it says, *"God gave them over to,"* is in the area of their _____. (Rom. 1:28) [1 point]

In Romans 1:29–31, Paul lists twenty-three sinful behaviors and attributes that we will not analyze in detail, but I suggest you read them and say, "This is the end of people who refuse to acknowledge God, glorify Him, and be thankful to Him."

Let's notice that *"whisperers"* (verse 29) appear on the list. This inclusion is important because gossiping—a sin mentioned alongside murder and hating God—is a sin of churchgoers.

The word translated *"untrustworthy"* (verse 31) refers to people with whom you cannot make a covenant*. This is one of the most conspicuous features of our age: an unwillingness to make and keep covenants. Nations break treaties, governments break promises, and men and women break their marriage vows to one another, but the essence of a covenant is that it lasts until death.

In Romans 1:32, Paul concludes,

> *...who, knowing the righteous judgment of God, that those who practice such things are deserving of death, not only do the same but also approve of those who practice them.*

It astonishes me how people involved in these kinds of sins can approve one another. Perhaps they feel they would be lonely if they stood on their own, so they endorse anybody as wicked as themselves.

In 2 Timothy 3:1–5, we find a historical parallel. There, Paul says that *"in the last days...men will be..."* and then describes nearly all the sins listed in Romans 1. Romans is the logic*, and 2 Timothy is the historical outworking—and we see the same things happening in our own time.

Corruption is irreversible. Understanding this truth is vital. The result of mankind's sin is corruption in every part of our being—spirit, mind, and body. Corruption cannot be reversed in any area of life. God's program is to start over, to make a new creation. But those who do not become new creations must endure the inevitable progress of corruption in their lives.

## MEMORY WORK: ROMANS 1:18–19, 21

Write out these verses from memory: [12 points]

_____

_____

_____

_____

_____

_____

_____

Check your answers on pages 164–67 in the "Correct Answers with Notes" section at the back of the book.

## PRAYER RESPONSE

Heavenly Father, thank You for creation. From the smallest particles of matter to the largest cluster of galaxies, I marvel at the intricacy and the grandeur of Your designs. I also thank You for my senses and my mind, which are able to appreciate the work of Your hands.

I proclaim that You alone are God; You are the Sovereign, and I am the subject. And yet, You have called me Your friend. I am humbled and amazed, and I give You thanks for redeeming me and calling me to establish Your kingdom on earth. May I never suppress the truth about who You are but be courageous to declare Your goodness and Your glory. In Jesus's name, I pray. Amen.

# STAGE 2: MORAL KNOWLEDGE AND PERSONAL RESPONSIBILITY

*Read Romans 2:1–3:8*

## INTRODUCTION

The second chapter of Romans discusses people who were guilty of all the sins of which the human race has been guilty, but because they had acquired a certain religious knowledge, they felt they were better than others. Paul points out that they knew the difference between right and wrong. However, rather than making them better, their knowledge merely increased their responsibility.

Paul was writing nearly two thousand years ago, so he was addressing his remarks primarily to his own Jewish people. At that time, the Jewish people were the ones with the advantage over all other nations because they had *"the oracles of God"* (Romans 3:2). Today, it is not so much the Jews* with the spiritual knowledge, but rather the professing Christians, because we have behind us centuries of Christian tradition, knowledge of God, and familiarity with the Bible. That knowledge increases *our* responsibility.

## MEMORY VERSES: ROMANS 2:6–8

**Note:** Depending on the version you are using, you may wish to add "God" to the beginning of the verses.

[ ] Check here after memorizing the verses.

(Review verses from prior lessons daily.)

## QUESTIONS

### PRINCIPLES OF GOD'S JUDGMENT

1.  In Romans 2, Paul reveals five principles of God's judgment:

    a.  God's judgment is according to _____. (v. 2) [1 point]

b. God's judgment is according to our _____. (v. 6) [1 point]

c. God's judgment is without _____. (v. 11) [1 point]

d. God's judgment is according to the light, or revelation, we have received. Fill in the same word in each space in verse 12:

*"For as many as have sinned without _____ will also perish without _____, and as many as have sinned in the _____ will be judged by the _____."* [1 point]

e. God judges the _____ of men. (This includes our motives and intentions.) (v. 16) [1 point]

2. In James 1:23–25, to what does James compare Scripture? [1 point]

_____

3. How do we avoid God's judgment? (1 Cor. 11:31) [1 point]

_____

4. In Romans 2:7–10, four categories of judgment are revealed. Fill in the blanks below with the various judgments:

a. "_____ _____ to those who by patient continuance in doing good seek for glory, honor, and immortality." (v. 7) [1 point]

b. "To those who are self-seeking and do not obey the truth, but obey unrighteousness—_____ and _____." (v. 8) [2 points]

c. "_____ and _____, on every soul of man who does evil." (v. 9) [2 points]

d. "But _____, _____, and _____ to everyone who works what is good." (v. 10) [3 points]

5. Due to their greater knowledge, who will receive stricter judgment? (James 3:1) [1 point]

_____

6. What is it that bears witness to those who do not have God's law as to whether a choice or action is right or wrong? (Rom. 2:15) [1 point]

   _____

7. Does knowledge build us up or puff us up? (1 Cor. 8:1–3) [1 point]

   _____

8. Should we judge ourselves or others first? (Matt. 7:1–5; Luke 6:39–42) [1 point]

   _____

## CIRCUMCISION OF THE HEART

9. What is the meaning of the name *Judah*\*? Fill in the blank in Genesis 29:35 to answer the question:
   *"Now I will _____ the* LORD.*"* [1 point]

10. What was the sign of the covenant\* between God and Abraham, along with all Abraham's descendants? (Gen. 17:9–11) [1 point]

    _____

11. What does Paul say is the nature of true circumcision? Fill in the blanks:

    *"…he is a Jew who is one inwardly and circumcision is that of the _____, in the
    _____, not in the letter."* (Rom. 2:29) [2 points]

12. If *repentance* is a change of mind followed by a change in direction, and *remorse* is merely regretting, or being sorry for, having done something wrong, which one indicates a true inward change—repentance or remorse? (Matt. 27:3–5; Luke 3:7–9; Rom. 2:4) [1 point]

    _____

13. Can people's unfaithfulness affect the faithfulness of God? (Rom. 3:3–4; 2 Tim. 2:13) [1 point]

_____

14. Knowing that by forgiving our unrighteousness, God demonstrates His righteousness* and mercy, is God unjust when He judges the world? (Rom. 3:5–6) [1 point]

_____

15. Is there ever a case for doing evil so that good may come? (Rom. 3:8) [1 point]

_____

## MEMORY WORK: ROMANS 2:6–8

Write out these verses from memory: [12 points]

_____

_____

_____

_____

_____

Check your answers on pages 168–69 in the "Correct Answers with Notes" section at the back of the book.

## PRAYER RESPONSE

Thank You, Lord, for revealing the principles of Your judgment through Your Word ahead of time so that I can live my life in accordance with Your will. I choose to look into the *"perfect law of liberty,"* as it says in James 1:25, and to continue to obey what I read there so I will be blessed in all that I do.

If there is any sin I have not yet acknowledged as such, or if my heart has not been completely circumcised, I ask that You would help me to come to a place of true repentance. I don't want to live any longer with blockages in my relationship with You, and so I yield myself afresh to You today in unreserved obedience. In Jesus's name, amen.

# STAGE 3: ACCOUNTABILITY TO GOD

*Read Romans 3:9–20*

## INTRODUCTION

Whether we were born Jew or Gentile, many of us were raised to believe that admitting we have sinned is a sign of weakness. Yet that outlook only reveals the commonality of pridefulness that exists throughout the human race. Every one of us is guilty before God. All of us are corrupt. All of us have gone astray from God.

*Legalism** refers to the attempt to achieve righteousness* with God by keeping any set of rules. Additionally, it signifies adding to what God has required for righteousness. But law* (whether the law of Moses* or other law) is not the solution for sin, because the more we embrace a set of "do not's," the more these rules dominate our thinking. We cannot save ourselves but must come humbly before God and recognize our need for His Son Jesus to save us. There are, of course, good reasons for the law, and we will explore those reasons in this lesson.

As we start looking at the law of Moses, it will be helpful to understand that not only is it made up of the "Ten Commandments," but it includes all of the first five books of the Bible, and it forms part of the Hebrew Scriptures called the Torah (these five books are also often referred to as the Pentateuch). The first part of the Bible, which Christians call the "Old Testament," is referred to in Judaism as the *Tanakh*, an acronym derived from the names of the three divisions of the Hebrew Bible:

- Torah (Instruction, or Law)

- Nevi'im (Prophets)

- Ketuvim (Writings)

## MEMORY VERSES: ROMANS 3:19–20

[ ] Check here after memorizing the verses.

(Review verses from prior lessons daily.)

# QUESTIONS

## JEWS* AND GENTILES* ALL NEED GRACE

1.  Are Jews better than Gentiles? (Rom. 3:9) [1 point]

    _____

2.  According to Romans 3:10–12, how many people can be described as righteous*, having understanding, seeking after God, and doing good? [1 point]

    _____

3.  Who says that there is no God? (Ps. 14:1) [1 point]

    _____

## EVERY MOUTH CLOSED

4.  In Romans 3:13–14, what area of the body does Paul highlight as being a potential source of great evil? [1 point]

    _____

5.  Fill in the blanks to reveal the fate of those without God, as Paul describes it in Romans 3:16–18:

    a.  "_____ and _____ are in their ways." (v. 16) [2 points]

    b.  "The way of _____ they have not known." (v. 17) [1 point]

    c.  "There is no _____ of God before their eyes." (v. 18) [1 point]

## SEVEN PURPOSES OF THE LAW OF MOSES

6.  Purpose 1: To Be a Unique Revelation of God's Names and Attributes

    The names of God is a full study on its own and is beyond the scope of this course. However, to give you a taste of this topic, let's look at some of God's names as revealed in Scripture. Some of this is lost in translation, as one English word may be used to translate more than one name of God in Hebrew.

a.  Who created the heavens and the earth in the beginning? (Gen. 1:1) [1 point]

_____

b.  Who formed man from the dust of the earth and breathed into his nostrils the breath of life? (Gen. 2:7) [1 point]

_____

c.  What does God pledge never to violate? (Ps. 89:34) [1 point]

_____

d.  In Genesis 22:14, what does Abraham call the place where God substituted a ram for Isaac to be sacrificed on the altar? [1 point]

_____

e.  At the waters of Marah (meaning "bitterness"), what was God's revelation of Himself? (Exod. 15:26) [1 point]

_____

f.  Following the defeat of the Amalekites at Rephidim, what does Moses name the altar that he builds as a memorial? (Exod. 17:15) [1 point]

_____

g.  After Gideon encountered the angel of the Lord in Judges 6, he was terrified until the Lord reassured him, saying, _"Peace be with you; do not fear, you shall not die"_ (Judges 6:23). What does Gideon call the altar that he builds to commemorate that event? (Judg. 6:24) [1 point]

_____

h.  In Psalm 23, who does David reveal the Lord to be? (v. 1) [1 point]

_____

i.  Jeremiah 23:5–6 is a prophetic picture of the Messiah who was to come to Israel*. By what name was He to be called? (v. 6) [1 point]

_____

j.  The last nine chapters of Ezekiel are connected with the restoration of Israel, and they describe both the rebuilding of a city and the building of a temple. What is the name given to the city upon its completion? (Ezek. 48:35) [1 point]

_____

7. Purpose 2: To Show the Reality and Power of Sin

    a.   According to Romans 3:20, what comes by the law? [1 point]

_____

    b.   Is the law sin? (Rom. 7:7) [1 point]

_____

    c.   By what means did Paul come to know about the sin of coveting? (Rom. 7:7) [1 point]

_____

8. Purpose 3: To Demonstrate There Is No Righteousness Through Our Own Efforts

    a.   In what part of Paul's being does he say that nothing good dwells? (Rom. 7:18) [1 point]

_____

    b.   Is Paul able to do good the way he desires to? (Rom. 7:18–19) [1 point]

_____

    c.   What does Paul say lives in him? (Rom. 7:20) [1 point]

_____

    d.   Into what state does the law in our members (the parts of the body) bring us? (Rom. 7:22–23) [1 point]

_____

9. Purpose 4: To Bring Us to Christ

    a.   How does Paul describe the law in Galatians 3:24? [1 point]

_____

    b.   To whom is the law intended to bring us? (Gal. 3:24) [1 point]

_____

    c.   By what are we justified*, if not by the law? (Gal. 3:24) [1 point]

_____

10. Purpose 5: To Keep Israel as a Separate Nation

    a. According to Galatians 3:23, in the time *before faith came*, what effect did the law have for the Jews? [1 point]

    _____

    b. In Numbers 23:9, according to Balaam's prophetic vision of God's people, would the Jews assimilate with other nations when they were dispersed from their land into those nations through exile, or would they dwell alone? [1 point]

    _____

    c. Could Christ have come through a nation that was not under the laws of God? (Gal. 4:4–5) [1 point]

    _____

11. Purpose 6: To Provide Humanity with a Pattern

    a. From where did God speak when He gave Israel the ordinances called the law of Moses* on Mount Sinai? (Neh. 9:13) [1 point]

    _____

    b. What three terms did Nehemiah use to describe God's ordinances, laws, statutes, and commandments? (Neh. 9:13) [3 points]

        i. _____

        ii. _____

        iii. _____

12. Purpose 7: To Provide Content for Spiritual Meditation

    a. In Psalm 1, the person who is blessed delights in what? (v. 2) [1 point]

    _____

    b. What does this person spend their time doing (day and night)? (v. 2) [1 point]

    _____

c. What summary statement does the psalmist make about this blessed person? (v. 3) [1 point]

_____

## MEMORY WORK: ROMANS 3:19–20

Write out these verses from memory: [8 points]

_____

_____

_____

_____

_____

Check your answers on pages 170–73 in the "Correct Answers with Notes" section at the back of the book.

## PRAYER RESPONSE

Thank You, Lord, for law, whether it is the law of Moses or laws that helps to govern society. I can see more clearly the seven purposes of the law of Moses, and I understand that this law was absolutely necessary for the revelation of our Savior, who could never have been counted righteous without a law against which to be judged. I recognize that whether we are Jews or Gentiles, we are all sinners, and that law is not the answer to our need for righteousness. Thank You, Lord Jesus, for the price that You paid to redeem us from *"the curse of the law,"* as it says in Galatians 3:13. Amen.

# STAGE 4: GOD'S PROVISION OF RIGHTEOUSNESS

*Read Romans 3:21–31*

## INTRODUCTION

Romans 3:20 is a milestone that tells us how far we have come in our pilgrimage, repeating emphatically that *"by the deeds of the law no flesh will be justified in His sight, for by the law is the knowledge of sin."*

Now we begin to see God's solution. Once more, in His great wisdom, God does not offer the solution until He has exposed the problem. Paul has wonderfully, systematically, and in great detail outlined the problem and shown us that law* is not the solution. What is the solution? In the subsequent verses, Paul begins to unfold it to us: a righteousness* of God *apart from the law* is revealed, and it comes through faith in Jesus, the promised Messiah.

## MEMORY VERSES: ROMANS 3:27–28

[  ]  Check here after memorizing the verses.

(Review verses from prior lessons daily.)

## QUESTIONS

### ALL HAVE SINNED

1.  Can man be justified* in God's sight through the deeds of the law? (Rom. 3:20) [1 point]

_____

2. By what was the righteousness of God apart from law witnessed? (Rom. 3:21) [1 point]

_____

3. By faith in whom does this righteousness from God come? (Rom. 3:22) [1 point]

_____

4. Who have sinned and fallen short of the glory of God? (Rom. 3:23) [1 point]

_____

## BEING JUSTIFIED

5. According to Romans 3:24, what does God offer us by His grace? [1 point]

_____

6. According to the first part of Isaiah 61:10, in what two ways will the person who has been made righteous* respond? [2 points]

   a. _____

   b. _____

7. Fill in the blanks to complete the middle portion of Isaiah 61:10:

   a. *"For He has clothed me with the garments of _____."* [1 point]

   b. *"He has covered me with the robe of _____."* [1 point]

## A GIFT BY HIS GRACE

8. Our redemption is in Christ Jesus (see Romans 3:24), whom God set forth as a propitiation* for us. By what and through what did this wonderful atonement* come? (v. 25)

   a. *"By _____ _____."* [1 point]

   b. *"Through _____."* [1 point]

9. In what manner had God treated the sins that were previously committed under the old covenant*? (Rom. 3:25) [1 point]

_____

10. Under the new covenant*, what did Jesus accomplish by the sacrifice of Himself? (Heb. 9:26) [1 point]

_____

11. In Romans 3:26, Paul tells us that God's demonstration of His righteousness enabled Him to be both "_____ and the _____ of the one who has faith in Jesus." [2 points]

## BOASTING IS EXCLUDED

12. By what law is boasting excluded? (Rom. 3:27) [1 point]

_____

13. Just, or righteous, people live by what? (Hab. 2:4) [1 point]

_____

## PRAISED FOR THEIR FAITH

14. There are some key statements in the account from Matthew 8:5–13 where Jesus ministers to a Roman centurion. Fill in the blanks:

   a. The centurion says, "I am _____ _____ that You should come under my roof." (v. 8) [1 point]

   b. He continues, "Only _____ ____ _____, and my servant will be healed." (v. 8) [1 point]

   c. Jesus says, "Assuredly, I say to you, I have not found such great _____, not even in Israel!" (v. 10) [1 point]

   d. Jesus closes by saying to the centurion, "Go your way; and as you have _____, so let it be done for you." (v. 13) [1 point]

15. Another person who is praised for their faith is described in one of my favorite stories in the Bible: that of the Syro-Phoenician woman with the demon-possessed daughter. Read the story in Mark 7:24–30 and then answer the questions below:

   a. What did the woman do when she encountered Jesus? (v. 25) [1 point]

   _____

   b. Was a single request for Jesus to deliver her daughter sufficient? (v. 26) [2 points]

   _____

   c. In verse 27, Jesus says that the *children* should be filled first. Who are these "children"? (Matt. 15:24.) [1 point]

   _____

   d. What word picture does Jesus use to describe healing and deliverance? (v. 27) [1 point]

   _____

   e. How does Jesus describe the Syro-Phoenician woman? (v. 27) [1 point]

   _____

   f. Does the woman respond to Jesus's comment in pride and anger or in humility? And what is her reply? (v. 28) [2 points]

   _____

   g. Does the woman receive what she asked for? (vv. 29–30) [2 points]

   _____

## MEMORY WORK: ROMANS 3:27–28

Write out these verses from memory: [8 points]

_____

_____

_____

_____

Check your answers on pages 174–75 in the "Correct Answers with Notes" section at the back of the book.

## PRAYER RESPONSE

I proclaim that:

+ No flesh will be justified by law.

+ My righteousness is in Christ alone.

+ I am justified freely by God's grace through the redemption that is in Christ Jesus.

Lord Jesus, I thank You for the grace that You have shown toward me. As it says in James 1:21, please help me to receive with meekness* the implanted word, which is able to save my soul. I choose to walk in faith and to begin to move into the inheritance that You have bought for me. I set aside all boasting except that which is about You, Lord, and what You have done. You deserve all the glory for every aspect of goodness in me. I give You praise and honor, for You alone are worthy to receive it. Amen.

# STAGE 5: JUSTIFICATION BY FAITH, NOT WORKS

*Read Romans 4:1–25*

## INTRODUCTION

In the previous lesson, at the end of Romans 3, we looked at God's provisions for man's problems. Up to that point, Paul has simply been unfolding these problems, which have intensified. In the latter part of Romans 3, however, beginning with verse 21, he reveals God's final, total, all-sufficient provision, which is through faith in the atoning* death and shed blood of the Lord Jesus Christ.

In this lesson, we will examine Romans 4, where Paul looks to two of the great fathers of Israel*—Abraham and David—and proves from Scripture that each of them was justified* not by works but by faith. He focuses mainly on Abraham, the father of all who believe, but he also quotes from a psalm of David.

## MEMORY VERSES: ROMANS 4:20–21

[ ] Check here after memorizing the verses.

(Review verses from prior lessons daily.)

## QUESTIONS

### ABRAHAM'S FAITH COUNTED AS RIGHTEOUSNESS*

1. What does Paul tell us Abraham did that was accounted to him for righteousness? (Rom. 4:3) [1 point]

_____

2. How much work must we do to be accounted righteous*? (Rom. 4:5) [1 point]

_____

3. In Romans 4:5, in what way does Paul describe God? [1 point]

_____

## GOD'S VIEW OF ABRAHAM'S SIN

4. We have learned that Abraham's faith was counted to him as righteousness. Does that mean that Abraham never made any mistakes after that? (See chapters 16 and 20 of Genesis if you need some direction.) [1 point]

_____

5. Did Jesus take His own initiative while He was on the earth? (John 5:19) [1 point]

_____

## THAT YOUR FAITH MAY NOT FAIL

6. In the account of the Last Supper told in Luke 22, who, according to Jesus's statement to Peter, has asked to sift the apostles like wheat? (v. 31) [1 point]

_____

7. What did Jesus pray for Peter? (v. 32) [1 point]

_____

## DAVID'S TESTIMONY

8. Fill in the blank: _"David also describes the blessedness of the man to whom God imputes righteousness apart from _____."_ (Rom. 4:6) [1 point]

9. List the four features of the life of the blessed person described in Psalm 32:1–2: [4 points]

   a. _____

   b. _____

   c. _____

   d. _____

## DOES CIRCUMCISION BRING RIGHTEOUSNESS?

10. Are the blessings mentioned in question 9 only for the circumcised (Israel), or are they for the uncircumcised (Gentiles*) as well? (Ps. 32:1–2; Rom. 4:9–12) [1 point]

   _____

11. Was Abraham's faith reckoned to him as righteousness before or after he was circumcised? (Rom. 4:10–11) [1 point]

   _____

12. Why did Abraham receive the sign of circumcision at the point when God gave it? (Rom. 4:11) [1 point]

   _____

## ABRAHAM'S STEPS OF FAITH

13. If faith was required for Abraham to be reckoned as righteous, what steps do we need to walk in to be reckoned righteous and to be considered his "children"? (Rom. 4:12) [1 point]

   _____

14. Is it sufficient to be *of the circumcision* to have Abraham as your father? (Rom. 4:12) [1 point]

   _____

## LAW* DOES NOT BRING US CLOSER TO GOD

15. Through what was the promise made to Abraham that he would be *the heir of the world*? (Rom. 4:13) [1 point]

_____

16. What does the law bring about? (Rom. 4:15) [1 point]

_____

17. If the law is *"the strength of sin"* (1 Corinthians 15:56), or *"the power of sin"* (NIV, NASB), can law ultimately bring us closer to God? (See also Isaiah 59:1–2.) [1 point]

_____

## BY GRACE, THROUGH FAITH

18. Romans 4:16 tells us that the promise of righteousness is *"of faith that it might be according to grace."*

    a. Why did God make the promise of righteousness by faith? (Rom. 4:16) [1 point]

    _____

    _____

    b. What is God guarding against by requiring faith rather than works? (Eph. 2:8–9) [1 point]

    _____

## CALLING INTO EXISTENCE

19. Romans 4:17 gives two descriptions of God:

    a. One who *"gives _____ to the dead."* [1 point]

    b. One who *"_____ those things which do not exist as though they did."* [1 point]

20. Based on the state of Abraham's body and the deadness of Sarah's womb mentioned in Romans 4:19, was there any natural reason for hope that God's promise to Abraham of many descendants would be fulfilled? [1 point]

_____

21. Is it right to be realistic in our faith? [Thought question; no points. See Derek's note for number 21 under "Lesson 6 Answers."]

_____

22. Is it possible for you and me to receive revitalization in our bodies? (Rom. 4:20–21; 8:11) [1 point]

_____

## UNWAVERING FAITH

23. In Romans 4:20, we read that Abraham *"did not waver at the promise of God through unbelief."* What does James say we will receive if we doubt? (James 1:6–8) [1 point]

_____

24. Who received the glory when God fulfilled His promise of a son to Abraham? (Rom. 4:20) [1 point]

_____

## RIGHTEOUSNESS TO THOSE WHO BELIEVE

25. Romans 4:23 tells us that the words *"it was accounted to him for righteousness"* in verse 22 were written for Abraham's sake. For whom else were they written? (vv. 23–24) [1 point]

_____

26. Who was buried with Christ in baptism and also raised with Him through faith? (Col. 2:12) [1 point]

_____

## MEMORY WORK: ROMANS 4:20–21

Write out these verses from memory: [8 points]

_____

_____

_____

_____

_____

Check your answers on pages 176–79 in the "Correct Answers with Notes" section at the back of the book.

## PRAYER RESPONSE

Thank You, Lord, for the faith of Abraham and for the wonderful example that he is to all those who believe. I see that righteousness is a gateway to receiving the marvelous promises contained in Your Word, and that the latch to open that gateway is faith.

As I hear Your Word, please help me to grow in my faith and to receive and believe what I hear. At times when I struggle to believe, I pray, along with the father in Mark 9:24 who brought his son to Jesus for deliverance, *"Lord, I believe; help my unbelief!"* Thank You, Lord Jesus, that as my Advocate on high, You continue to pray for me that my faith would not fail during times of testing. In Your name I pray, amen.

# STAGE 6: FIVE EXPERIENTIAL RESULTS OF BEING JUSTIFIED BY FAITH

*Read Romans 5:1–11*

## INTRODUCTION

Now we move on to stage 6 in our pilgrimage through Romans. Earlier, I pointed out that the gospel is not just an abstract set of theories; it is anchored in *history* and *human experience*. It is tied to history because it is based on the historical facts that Jesus died, was buried, and rose again on the third day. If those facts are not true, then the gospel is not true. The gospel is also anchored in human experience because when we believe the gospel and act on it, it produces results in our lives that could not be produced in any other way.

So, next, we will look at the results in experience of being justified* by faith. What happens in us when we meet the conditions to have righteousness* reckoned to us by faith? Once again, let's remember the alternative renderings of *justified*: "acquitted," "not guilty," "reckoned righteous*," and "made 'just-as-if-I'd' never sinned."

## MEMORY VERSES: ROMANS 5:3–4

[ ] Check here after memorizing the verses.

(Review verses from prior lessons daily.)

## QUESTIONS

1. How are we justified? (Rom. 5:1) [1 point]

_____

## FIRST RESULT OF BEING JUSTIFIED

2.  Answer the following:

    a.  We have _____ with God. (Rom. 5:1) [1 point]

    b.  Through whom is this result made possible? (Rom. 5:1) [1 point]

    _____

    c.  Part of this experience is having peace with creation. In Job 5:23, what is Job said to make a covenant* with? [1 point]

    _____

    d.  Who is said to be at peace with Job? (v. 23) [1 point]

    _____

## SECOND RESULT OF BEING JUSTIFIED

3.  Answer the following:

    a.  Scripture tells us that through our Lord Jesus, where once we were excluded due to our sin, we now have _____ by faith. (Rom. 5:2) [1 point]

    b.  In what does Paul tell us that we are now standing? (Rom. 5:2) [1 point]

    _____

    c.  Peter gives four descriptions of those of us who have been called out of darkness and into God's marvelous light. List those descriptions: (1 Pet. 2:9) [4 points]

    i.  _____

    ii.  _____

    iii.  _____

    iv.  _____

    d.  When God looks at us with favor, we become beautiful. What do we receive in the light of the King's face? (Prov. 16:15) [1 point]

    _____

e. To what does Solomon liken God's favor? (Prov. 16:15) [1 point]

_____

f. What does David say will surround the righteous like a shield? (Ps. 5:12) [1 point]

_____

g. Does God enjoy His people? (Ps. 149:4) [1 point]

_____

## THIRD RESULT OF BEING JUSTIFIED

4. Answer the following:

   a. Fill in the blanks to show the third result: *"And _____ in _____ of the glory of God."* (Rom. 5:2) [2 points]

   b. How does Paul describe Christ in us? (Col. 1:27) [1 point]

   _____

   c. How is hope described in 1 Thessalonians 5:8? [1 point]

   _____

## FOURTH RESULT OF BEING JUSTIFIED

5. Answer the following:

   a. The fourth result is that we *"glory in _____."* (Rom. 5:3) [1 point]

   b. What does James tell us to do when we fall into various trials? (James 1:2) [1 point]

   _____

   c. As expressed by the apostles Paul and James, what is the first thing produced in us by trials or the testing of our faith?

   _____ (Rom. 5:3) [1 point]

   _____ (James 1:3) [1 point]

   d. List three results of allowing patience to have its perfect work in us. (James 1:4)

   That we may be:

   _____ [1 point]

---

44

_____ [1 point]

_____ _____ [1 point]

e. Paul shows us that if we glory in tribulations, it produces a series of three blessings. Earlier, we noted the first result. Below, list that blessing and the two that follow it: (Rom. 5:3–4)

_____ (vv. 3–4) [1 point]

_____ (v. 4) [1 point]

_____ (v. 4) [1 point]

f. What has been poured out in our hearts by the Holy Spirit who was given to us? (Rom. 5:5) [1 point]

_____

## GOD'S UNCONDITIONAL LOVE

In questions 6–12, we will look in more depth at the love of God because it is so vital to our lives and Christian character. Paul says, *"The goal of our instruction is love"* (1 Timothy 1:5 NASB). The ultimate purpose of these lessons is to enable you to encounter the Lord through His Word and His Spirit so that you may experience more of His love and, in turn, love Him and love others.

6. To what does Solomon compare love's strength? (Song 8:6) [1 point]

_____

7. What is the ultimate source of both endurance and hope? (1 Cor. 13:4–7) [1 point]

_____

8. In Romans 5:6–10, Paul uses four phrases to describe what we were like at the time Jesus died for us:

a. *"When we were still _____ _____...."* (v. 6) [1 point]

b. *"Christ died for the _____."* (v. 6) [1 point]

c. *"While we were still _____...."* (v. 8) [1 point]

d. *"When we were _____...."* (v. 10) [1 point]

9. How does the apostle John describe God in 1 John 4:8, 16? [1 point]

_____

10. Romans 5:5 tells us that *"the love of God has been poured out in our hearts by the Holy Spirit."* Is there a limit to the Spirit (and thus the love) that is poured into us? (John 3:34) [1 point]

_____

## FIFTH RESULT OF BEING JUSTIFIED

11. According to Romans 5:11, in *whom* do we rejoice? [1 point]

_____

12. In Psalm 43:2, David asks himself, *"Why do I go mourning because of the oppression of the enemy?"* His remedy comes in verses 3–4. Read Psalm 43 and then answer these questions:

    a. In verse 3, which two things does David ask God to send out? [2 points]

  i. _____

  ii. _____

    b. In verse 4, how does David describe God? [1 point]

_____

# MEMORY WORK: ROMANS 5:3–4

Write out these verses from memory: [8 points]

_____

_____

_____

_____

_____

Check your answers on pages 180–83 in the "Correct Answers with Notes" section at the back of the book.

# PRAYER RESPONSE

Prayer is not just one form of communication with God but rather many different forms. To me, it is like a whole orchestra that includes different "instruments" of thanksgiving, praise, worship, supplication, intercession, and so forth. One thing that the Lord has shown me is that proclamation, based on Scripture, forms a very important part of prayer and spiritual warfare.

To practice and apply Scripture-based proclamation, I recommend that you read Romans 5:1–11 again, but this time personalize it by changing the pronouns because you and I are the subject of the discussion. (If you are proclaiming the passage with someone else, the wording does not need to be changed, and you can read the passage directly from the Bible.)

*Therefore, having been justified by faith, [I] have peace with God through our Lord Jesus Christ, through whom also [I] have access by faith into this grace in which [I] stand, and rejoice in hope of the glory of God. And not only that, but [I] also glory in tribulations, knowing that tribulation produces perseverance; and perseverance, character; and character, hope. Now hope does not disappoint, because the love of God has been poured out in [my heart] by the Holy Spirit who was given to [me].*

*For when [I was] still without strength, in due time Christ died for the ungodly. For scarcely for a righteous man will one die; yet perhaps for a good man someone would even dare to die. But God demonstrates His own love toward [me], in that while [I was] still [a sinner], Christ died for me. Much more then, having now been justified by His blood, [I] shall be saved from wrath through Him. For if when [I was an enemy, I was] reconciled to God through the death of His Son, much more, having been reconciled, [I] shall be saved by His life. And not only that, but [I] also rejoice in God through [my] Lord Jesus Christ, through whom [I] have now received the reconciliation.*

# STAGE 7: COMPARISON BETWEEN ADAM AND JESUS

*Read Romans 5:12–21*

## INTRODUCTION

We have now worked through the first half of Romans 5, which was stage 6 of our pilgrimage. The five experiential results of being justified* by faith are as follows:

1.  Peace with God

2.  Access to grace that upholds us

3.  Rejoicing in hope of God's glory

4.  Rejoicing in tribulation because of what tribulation does for us

5.  The climax: rejoicing in God Himself

Now we move to the second half of Romans 5, in which Paul compares death in Adam to life in Jesus. Here we find Paul at his most Talmudic*—with perhaps the most intense and concentrated piece of reasoning we will find anywhere in the Bible. Working through this material is not easy, but, like Joshua, we will be strong and courageous and go in to possess the land.

## MEMORY VERSES: ROMANS 5:20–21

[ ] Check here after memorizing the verses.

(Review verses from prior lessons daily.)

# QUESTIONS

## TWO TIME PERIODS

1. In Romans 5:12–14, Paul contrasts two time periods. Circle the correct response of "Y" for "Yes" and "N" for "No" for the elements that apply to each time period in sections "a." through "f." [6 points]

| TIME PERIOD | Sin? | Law? | Sin Imputed? |
|---|---|---|---|
| Adam to Moses | a. Y/N | b. Y/N | c. Y/N |
| Moses to Christ | d. Y/N | e. Y/N | f. Y/N |

2. Fill in the blanks to complete the verse:

   *"For the law was given through* _____*, but grace and truth came through* _____ _____*."* (John 1:17) [2 points]

## LAST ADAM, SECOND MAN

Paul says that Jesus was the fulfillment of a pattern given initially in Adam. Adam received one commandment; and, in a garden, Eden, with everything his heart could desire, he disobeyed that commandment. (See Genesis 2:17; 3:6.)

Jesus received the commandment from the Father to lay down His life for the world; and, in a garden, Gethsemane, He accepted that commandment and obeyed it. (See John 10:15–18; Luke 22:41–43.)

In 1 Corinthians 15:45–47, Paul makes some brief but very important comparisons between Adam and Christ:

| | Adam | Jesus |
|---|---|---|
| 3. Where do they originate? (v. 47) [2 points] | a. | b. |
| 4. First or last Adam? (v. 45) [2 points] | a. | b. |
| 5. First or second man? (v. 47) [2 points] | a. | b. |
| 6. What did they become? (v. 45) [2 points] | a. | b. |

7. To what has God begotten us again through the resurrection of Jesus Christ from the dead? (1 Pet. 1:3) [1 point]

   _____

8. In Colossians 1:15–17, Paul makes five statements about Jesus's eternal nature:

   a. *"He is the* _____ *of the invisible God."* (v. 15) [1 point]

b. *"He is...the firstborn over all* _____*."* (v. 15) [1 point]

c. *"By Him all things were* _____*.... All things were* _____
*through Him and for Him."* (same word) (v. 16) [1 point]

d. *"He is* _____ *all things."* (v. 17) [1 point]

e. *"In* _____ *all things consist."* (v. 17) [1 point]

9. Paul continues in Colossians 1:18 with two statements about Christ's redemptive work:

a. *"He is the* _____ *of the body."* [1 point]

b. *"He is the...* _____*from the dead."* [1 point]

In Romans 5:15–19, Paul's comparison between Adam and Jesus has two aspects. In some points, Jesus was like Adam, and in other points, Jesus was unlike Adam. Paul puts the points in which Jesus was unlike Adam first; then he gives the points in which Jesus was like Adam. I have chosen to reverse the order because it will be easier to identify the likenesses before we look at the differences.

## SIMILARITIES BETWEEN ADAM AND JESUS

10. Fill in the blanks:

a. *"Through one man's [Adam's]* _____*judgment came to all men, resulting in*
_____*."* (Rom. 5:18) [2 points]

b. *"Through one Man's [Jesus's]* _____ _____ *the free gift came to*
*all men, resulting in* _____ *of life."* (v. 18) [2 points]

11. Fill in the blanks:

a. *"By one man's [Adam's]* _____ *many were made*
_____*."* (Rom. 5:19) [2 points]

b. *"By one Man's [Jesus's]* _____ *many will be made*
_____*."* (v. 19) [2 points]

## DIFFERENCES BETWEEN ADAM AND JESUS

12. Was the grace of God only just sufficient to pay for the offense that came through Adam? Why?
(Rom. 5:15) [2 points]

_____

13. Answer the following questions regarding mankind's offenses:

    a.  How many offenses resulted in condemnation? (Rom. 5:16) [1 point]

_____

    b.  How many offenses were covered by the free gift? (v. 16) [1 point]

_____

14. Answer the following questions regarding two contrasting reigns:

    a.  What reigned on the earth through Adam's offense? (Rom. 5:17) [1 point]

_____

    b.  In what will we reign through Christ Jesus? (v. 17) [1 point]

_____

15. Answer the following questions regarding two different forms of "abounding":

    a.  What entered that the offense might abound? (Rom. 5:20) [1 point]

_____

    b.  In contrast, what *abounded much more* and now reigns through righteousness* to eternal life through Jesus? (vv. 20–21) [1 point]

_____

## MEMORY WORK: ROMANS 5:20–21

Write out these verses from memory: [8 points]

_____

_____

_____

_____

_____

Check your answers on pages 184–86 in the "Correct Answers with Notes" section at the back of the book.

## PRAYER RESPONSE

Blessed be You, the God and Father of our Lord Jesus Christ, who, according to Your abundant mercy, have begotten us again to a living hope through the resurrection of Jesus Christ from the dead, to an inheritance incorruptible and undefiled and that does not fade away, reserved in heaven for us, who are kept by the power of God through faith for salvation ready to be revealed in the last time. [Based on 1 Peter 1:3–5.]

I thank You that before time began, You foresaw Adam and Eve's sin and already had a plan to restore human beings to the place of sonship through the sacrifice of Jesus. I acknowledge that my sins were added to Adam's sin and to all the other sins of mankind, but that Jesus's sacrifice was unique: there is nothing I can add to it; it is complete and perfect. I receive Your invitation to reign with Christ through His life, and I ask that You would teach me as I offer my life for Your eternal purposes. Amen.

# STAGE 8: GOD'S SOLUTION FOR THE OLD MAN: EXECUTION

*Read Romans 6:1–11*

## INTRODUCTION

We now commence stage 8 of our pilgrimage: the first eleven verses of Romans 6—one of my favorite chapters in the Bible. It is simpler than Romans 5 but very drastic. It lays out God's solution for the *"old man"*—the Adamic nature. God's solution is execution. He has no "plan B" for our old man. He does not send him to church or Sunday school. He does not teach him to memorize Scripture. He has sentenced him to death, and there is no reprieve.

It is one thing to have your past sins forgiven. That is tremendous, but it is not all that is required, because inside every one of us descendants of Adam, without exception, there dwells a rebel. Even if our past sins have been forgiven, that rebel inside us will go on committing the same sins—unless he is dealt with.

It is significant that Adam never fathered any children until he was a rebel. Every descendant of Adam, then—every one of us—is born out of rebellion and is, as such, a rebel. Sometimes that rebel is conspicuous; he can be seen in our attitudes and actions. And sometimes he is concealed; he can be very religious, very polite, very nice. But he is still, at heart, a rebel. And, again, God will make no peace with that rebel; He has sentenced him to death.

The good news is that, in the mercy of God, the execution took place twenty centuries ago, when Jesus died on the cross, taking our place. That is God's solution.

## MEMORY VERSES: ROMANS 6:8—9

[ ] Check here after memorizing the verses.

(Review verses from prior lessons daily.)

## QUESTIONS:

### DEALING WITH THE BODY OF SIN

1. In Romans 6:6, does the term *"body of sin"* refer to our physical bodies or to our carnal nature? [1 point]

   _____

2. In Romans 8:10, when Paul says, *"The body is dead…,"* is he referring to our dying physically? [1 point]

   _____

3. In lesson 3, we dealt with the need for "circumcision of the flesh" and "circumcision of the heart" due to our carnal nature. In Colossians 2:11, does the phrase *"putting off the body of the sins of the flesh"* indicate physical death or circumcision of the heart? [1 point]

   _____

### SHALL WE CONTINUE TO SIN?

In Romans 5:20, we read, *"Where sin abounded, grace abounded much more."* In Romans 6:1, Paul seems to have a Jewish objector in mind, whose question he anticipates, saying, *"Shall we continue in sin that grace may abound?"*

4. Does Paul entertain this suggestion that we might take advantage of grace and continue in sin? (Rom. 6:2) [1 point]

   _____

5. Is it possible to be living in willful sin within the grace of God? (Rom. 6:2) [1 point]

   _____

### THE SIGNIFICANCE OF BAPTISM

6. When Paul uses the phrase *"as many of us"* in reference to baptism, does he mean "all of us"? (Rom. 6:3) [1 point]

   _____

7. According to Mark 16:16, what are the two requirements for salvation? [2 points]

    a. _____

    b. _____

8. Acts 16:25–34 describes the conversion experience of a Philippian jailer. How many days did the Philippian jailer wait after coming to salvation before being baptized? (v. 33) [1 point]

    _____

9. The word *baptize* means "to dip" or "to immerse." With each kind of baptism mentioned in the Bible, people are baptized *in* something and *into* something. When we come to faith, we are baptized *in* water. What are we baptized *into*? (Rom. 6:3) [1 point]

    _____

10. Fill in the blanks to complete Romans 6:4:

    a. *"Therefore we were buried with Him through baptism into* _____...*"* [1 point]

    b. *"...that just as Christ was raised from the dead by the glory of the Father, even so we also should walk in newness of* _____.*"* [1 point]

## IDENTIFYING WITH HIS DEATH

11. In Romans 6:5, Paul says that we are invited to be *"united together"* with Christ in two ways, but the second way is dependent on the first. We will certainly be united *"in the likeness of His* _____*"* (second way) *if*, and only if, we are first united *"in the likeness of His* _____.*"* (first way) [2 points]

12. Answer the following questions about our death and resurrection in Christ:

    a. Who was crucified with Jesus on the cross? (Rom. 6:6) [1 point]

    _____

    b. How are we identified with Jesus to go through death, burial, and resurrection? (Rom. 6:4) [1 point]

    _____

13. Isaiah 1:5–6 describes how God deals with Israel's root problem of rebellion. For these verses, I prefer the translation in the *New International Version*, so I have put two key words from that rendering in brackets below. This is a vivid picture of Jesus as He hung on the cross:

    a. *"The whole _____ is sick ["injured" NIV]." (v. 5)* [1 point]

    b. *"And the whole _____ faints ["is…afflicted" NIV]." (v. 5)* [1 point]

    c. *"From the sole of the _____ even to the _____, there is no soundness in it." (v. 6)* [2 points]

14. Was Jesus recognizable as He hung on the cross? (Isa. 52:14) [1 point]

    _____

15. What was laid on Jesus on the cross? (Isa. 53:6) [1 point]

    _____

16. As a result of Jesus's sinless obedience on our behalf, God vindicated Jesus by raising Him from the dead. Fill in the word that completes both verses to show the result of our Lord's humility:

    a. *"Behold, My Servant shall deal prudently; He shall be _____ and extolled and be very high." (Isa. 52:13)* [1 point]

    b. *"God also has highly _____ Him." (Phil. 2:9)* [1 point]

Here is the exchange: all the evil due to our rebellion came upon Jesus so that all the good due to His perfect obedience might be offered to us.

17. Answer the following questions regarding our relationship to sin:

    a. What was our relationship to sin before we identified with Jesus in baptism? (Rom. 6:6) [1 point]

    _____

    b. What is our relationship to sin once we have identified with Jesus in baptism? (Rom. 6:7) [1 point]

    _____

18. Romans 6:8 contains another conditional statement with an "*if*":

    a. "*If we* _____ *with Christ….*" [1 point]

    b. "*…we believe that we shall also* _____ *with Him.*" [1 point]

19. Romans 6:11 tells us that we should "*reckon* ["*consider*" NASB] [*ourselves*] *to be dead indeed to*

    _____, *but alive to* _____ *in Christ Jesus our Lord.*" [2 points]

## MEMORY WORK: ROMANS 6:8–9

Write out these verses from memory: [8 points]

_____

_____

_____

_____

_____

Check your answers on pages 187–89 in the "Correct Answers with Notes" section at the back of the book.

## PRAYER RESPONSE

In this lesson, we have discussed in some depth God's dealings with our old man through our identification* with Christ in His death through baptism. As you meditate on these truths, I want to suggest that you settle this matter once and for all. If you have never been baptized by full immersion, then ask the Lord what person can baptize you. Scripture is clear that the way to follow Jesus into life is to follow Him through His death by way of baptism. As an exchange at the cross, I put it this way: Jesus died our death so that we might share His life. The way into that new life is through baptism.

I should add that this point in the book of Romans is a watershed*. If you don't follow through on baptism, there is no point carrying on because what follows is dependent on our being separated from sin through identification with Christ in His death, burial, and resurrection.

**If you have not yet been baptized**, will you join me in praying this prayer?

Heavenly Father, I thank You for the clarity of Your Word, which shows the tremendous importance of baptism as the means of being cut off from the body of sin. I recognize my need for this severance from my past life of sin and ask that You would show me who the right person is to baptize me right away. Prepare their heart and open the way to seal my translation out of the kingdom of darkness into Your marvelous light.

Lord Jesus, thank You for coming to earth to redeem me from the curse of sin and death. I choose to follow You through death, burial, and resurrection by dying to myself and being buried with You through baptism so that I, too, may live a new life to the Father's glory, empowered by Your Spirit. Amen.

**If (or once) you have been baptized,** let's pray a little differently:

Heavenly Father, I thank You for the practical way in which You have allowed me to make a public confession of my faith in Jesus's atoning* sacrifice through baptism. I recognize that in so doing, I have made my decision clear to die to myself and to live for You. I pray that You would empower me by Your Spirit to stand up to all the attacks of the enemy.

I proclaim that:

+ I am no longer a slave to sin. (Rom. 6:6)

+ When I identified with Christ in His death through baptism, I was freed from sin. (vv. 3–7)

+ Death no longer has dominion over me. (vv. 8–9)

+ I reckon myself to be dead to sin but alive to God in Christ Jesus my Lord. (v. 11)

In His name I pray, amen.

# STAGE 9: HOW TO APPLY GOD'S SOLUTION FOR THE OLD MAN IN OUR LIVES

*Read Romans 6:12–23*

## INTRODUCTION

Stage 8 of our pilgrimage discussed God's solution for the "old man," which can be summed up in one word: *execution*. God has no other program for the old man. But, because of His mercy, the execution took place when Jesus died on the cross. Our old man was crucified with Him, and we are given the privilege through baptism of identifying ourselves with Christ in His death, burial, resurrection, and everything that follows.

In stage 8, Paul also answered the objection, "If we want more grace, let's go on living in sin, and sin all the more." Paul pointed out that such a response is impossible because, to be in the grace of God, we have to be dead to sin. Sinning all the more is a misunderstanding of how God's grace operates.

Up to this point in Romans 6, Paul has given the doctrinal basis for God's solution to the problem of the old man, which is death. Now we go on to stage 9 in the second part of Romans 6, which is a very practical discussion of how we apply God's solution in our lives.

## MEMORY VERSE: ROMANS 6:23

[ ] Check here after memorizing the verse.

(Review verses from prior lessons daily.)

## QUESTIONS

The Bible's definition of sin is given in Romans 3:23: "*All have sinned and **fall short of the glory of God.**" The essence of sin is something we *don't* do rather than something we do. To sin is not necessarily to commit some terrible crime. It is to fail to give God His rightful place in our lives; it is to lead lives that withhold from God the glory that all His creatures owe Him.

Once we understand the human condition in this way, we must acknowledge that what Paul says is true: we have all sinned, and we all fall short of the glory of God.

## DO NOT LET SIN REIGN

1. Verses 12 and 13 of Romans 6 each contain *"do not"* statements:

    a. *"Do not let sin _____ in your mortal body, that you should obey its lusts."* (v. 12) [1 point]

    b. *"Do not present your members as instruments of _____ to sin."* (v. 13) [1 point]

2. Verse 13 shows us the positive alternatives:

    a. *"Present yourselves to _____ as being alive from the dead."* [1 point]

    b. *"Present...your members as instruments of _____ to God."* [1 point]

3. In our newfound position of grace, what ceases to have dominion over us? (v. 14) [1 point]

    _____

## YIELD YOUR MEMBERS

4. Each time we pray the Lord's Prayer, after we ask God to bring His kingdom to earth, in what area do we defer to Him? (Matt. 6:10) [1 point]

    _____

5. Once we have arisen with Christ in baptism, what are we invited to present to God as being alive from the dead? (Rom. 6:13) [1 point]

    _____

6. After Paul has finished laying out his theology in the first eleven chapters of Romans, what does he ask us to present as a living sacrifice to God? (Rom. 12:1) [1 point]

    _____

## NOT UNDER LAW* BUT GRACE

7.   How do we escape the dominion of sin in our lives? (Rom. 6:14) [1 point]

_____

8.   We are not under law if we are led by the _____. (Gal. 5:18) [1 point]

9.   What is the outworking of our love for Jesus? (John 14:23) [1 point]

_____

## SLAVE TO THE ONE YOU OBEY

10.   Shall we sin because we are not under law but under grace? (Rom. 6:15) [1 point]

_____

11.   What determines whose slaves we are? (Rom. 6:16) [1 point]

_____

12.   In the closing chapter of the book of Joshua, how does Joshua express the decision that is required of the Israelites? (Josh. 24:15) [1 point]

_____

13.   What does Paul commend the Roman believers for doing in response to *that form of doctrine to which* [they] *were delivered*"? (Rom. 6:17) [1 point]

_____

## SLAVES OF RIGHTEOUSNESS*

14.   What did we become when we were set free from sin? (Rom. 6:18) [1 point]

_____

15. Did lawlessness remain at the same level when we were slaves to it? (Rom. 6:19) [1 point]

   _____

16. What is the goal of presenting ourselves to the Lord for the purpose of righteousness? (Rom. 6:19) [1 point]

   _____

17. Was there any good fruit from our lives when we were slaves of sin? (Rom. 6:20–21) [1 point]

   _____

## HOLINESS AND ETERNAL LIFE

18. In Romans 6:22, Paul tells us two primary benefits of our having been set free from sin and having become slaves of God:

   a. *"You have your fruit to _____."* [1 point]

   b. *"You have…the end, _____ _____."* [1 point]

19. In the last verse of Romans 6 (v. 23), Paul sums up the choice with characteristic clarity:

   a. *"For the _____ of sin is death."* [1 point]

   b. *"But the _____ of God is eternal life in Christ Jesus our Lord."* [1 point]

## MEMORY WORK: ROMANS 6:23

   Write out this verse from memory: [4 points]

   _____

   _____

   _____

   Check your answers on pages 190–92 in the "Correct Answers with Notes" section at the back of the book.

## PRAYER RESPONSE

Let's continue using Scripture to proclaim the positive statements Paul makes in this second part of Romans 6:

- ✦ I present myself to God as being alive from the dead. (v. 13)

- ✦ I present the members of my body as instruments of righteousness to God. (v. 13)

- ✦ I am not under law but under grace. (v. 14)

- ✦ I have been set free from sin and have become a slave of righteousness for holiness. (vv. 18–19)

- ✦ Because I have willingly become a slave to God, my fruit is to holiness and, ultimately, everlasting life. (v. 22)

- ✦ The gift of God is eternal life in Christ Jesus my Lord. (v. 23)

Thank You, Lord, for the wonderful invitations and promises that You have given to me through the Word of God. Help me to take full advantage of these gifts that You have offered and to have faith that, as I believe what You say about me in the Bible, I will begin to see myself as You see me. Amen.

# STAGE 10: THE BELIEVER'S RELATIONSHIP TO LAW

*Read Romans 7:1–25*

## INTRODUCTION

We have seen God's solution for the "old man": execution. And we have discussed how to apply that solution in our own lives. It consists of two actions: first, being *willing* to do what is right; and, second, *yielding* ourselves and our members to God continuously as instruments or weapons of righteousness*. Now we come to the final stage before we reach the climax of this pilgrimage—Romans 8—and before we explore its effects in the broad spectrum of life. Romans 7 might be the hardest stage to go through.

You may think Paul is discussing this subject of the believer's relationship to law* in the wrong place since it deals with law, and, after we are converted, we should think nothing more about law. Yet we know by both observation and experience that this is not true. After we have been saved and have experienced deliverance from the old man, we come face-to-face with a tremendously difficult issue: what is the place of law in our lives now? How do we relate to it? Are we bound to live by rules and regulations? Or are we released from law and free to live another way?

These questions attracted me from the moment I was converted and began to read the New Testament. My training in philosophy showed me that this problem—living under law or living free from law—must be resolved for the Christian life to work.

However, the majority of Christians today are not even aware of the problem, let alone what the solution is. They may wonder how to live for God, or they may sense that their Christian life is falling short. But they are not aware of the source of the problem or that they are wrongly related to law. So, by God's grace, we are going to explore Paul's teaching in Romans 7, which covers this issue of the believer's relationship to law.

## MEMORY VERSES: ROMANS 7:24–25

[ ] Check here after memorizing the verses.

(Review verses from prior lessons daily.)

# QUESTIONS

## COVENANT* COMMITMENT

1. According to Romans 7:1, when does the law no longer have dominion over a man? [1 point]

   _____

2. As discussed by Paul in Romans 7:2–6:

   a. Under the law of Moses*, was a woman free to marry another man while her husband remained alive? (v. 2) [1 point]

   _____

   b. If her husband died, was a woman free to marry again without becoming an adulteress? (v. 3) [1 point]

   _____

3. Which is the only nation that ever came under the law of Moses? (Exod. 19:3–6) [1 point]

   _____

## ONE SPIRIT WITH HIM

4. Genesis 2:24 is the first mention of an indelible truth found throughout the Bible: *"A man shall…be joined to his wife, and they* [or *"the two"* (see, for example, Matthew 19:5)] *shall become one flesh."* What happens when a man is joined to a *"harlot"* (prostitute)? (1 Cor. 6:16) [1 point]

   _____

5. In contrast, how does Paul describe the person who is joined to the Lord? (1 Cor. 6:17) [1 point]

   _____

6.  What kind of works are described in Galatians 5:19–21? Note that *those who practice such things will not inherit the kingdom of God"* (v. 21). [1 point]

_____

7.  If a person abides in Jesus, what will he bear, or produce? (John 15:5) [1 point]

_____

8.  Is any law needed when we are living according to the fruit of the Spirit? (Gal. 5:23) [1 point]

_____

## NOT EFFORT BUT UNION

9.  In the well-known parable of the vine in John 15, three persons are mentioned directly; another is implicit:

    a.  Jesus is the true _____. (vv. 1, 5) [1 point]

    b.  The Father is the _____. (v. 1) [1 point]

    c.  We are the _____. (v. 5) [1 point]

    d.  (Bonus Question): Grapes are produced on vines by the sap that rises through the vine. In this parable, who do you think would be represented by the sap? [1 point]

_____

10.  Is the Father pruning us due to our lack of fruitfulness or for a different reason? (John 15:2) [1 point]

_____

11.  Can branches bear fruit without being part of the vine? (John 15:4) [1 point]

_____

12. When we abide in Jesus, and He in us, what do we bring forth? (John 15:5) [1 point]

_____

## THE LAW BRINGS SIN TO LIFE

13. In lesson 4, one of our discussions was about the "Seven Purposes of the Law of Moses." According to Romans 3:20, what comes by the law? [1 point]

_____

14. When we were in the flesh, what were aroused by the law? (Rom. 7:5) [1 point]

_____

15. Having been delivered from the law, in what are we called to serve? (Rom. 7:6) [1 point]

_____

16. Which commandment does Paul reference in Romans 7:7–12? (See also Exodus 20:17.) [1 point]

_____

17. What was produced in Paul through this commandment? (Rom. 7:8) [1 point]

_____

## LAW, SIN, AND DEATH

18. What two effects of sin are mentioned in Romans 7:11?

    a. *"Sin, taking occasion by the commandment,* _____ *me."* [1 point]

    b. *"…and by it* _____ *me."* [1 point]

19. What three words does Paul use to describe the commandment not to covet? Fill in the blanks:

    *"The commandment [is]* _____ *and* _____ *and* _____*."* (Rom. 7:12)
    [3 points]

20. In Romans 7:14, how does Paul describe the law? [1 point]

_____

21. Is Paul able to do what is good while still living under the law? (Rom. 7:19) [1 point]

_____

## THE CURSE OF LEGALISM*

22. Legalism is the theme of Paul's letter to the Galatians.

    a. In his first statement of the letter, in Galatians 3:1, what adjective does Paul use to describe the Galatian church? [1 point]

    _____

    b. What had happened to the church? (Gal. 3:1) [1 point]

    _____

    c. How were the Galatians seeking to be made perfect? (Gal. 3:3) [1 point]

    _____

    d. What happens when we come back under law? (Gal. 3:10) [1 point]

    _____

## THE WAY OUT

23. In Romans 7:24, how does Paul describe himself? [1 point]

_____

24. From what does Paul seek deliverance? (Rom. 7:24) [1 point]

_____

25. Who provides the only way out of the conflict Paul describes in verses 21–23? (Rom. 7:25) [1 point]

_____

26. What qualifies us to cease from sin? (1 Pet. 4:1) [1 point]

_____

27. When we have ceased from sin, what do we live for? (1 Pet. 4:2) [1 point]

_____

28. What three things are required of you if you wish to be Jesus's disciple? (Matt. 16:24)

    a. _____ yourself. [1 point]

    b. Take up your _____. [1 point]

    c. _____ Jesus. [1 point]

## MEMORY WORK: ROMANS 7:24–25

Write out these verses from memory: [8 points]

_____

_____

_____

_____

Check your answers on pages 193–96 in the "Correct Answers with Notes" section at the back of the book.

## PRAYER RESPONSE

Dear Lord, the more I learn, the more I can see the significance of baptism and how identifying with Jesus in His death releases me from an ungodly relationship to law. Having been released from my Adamic nature, I am free to be *"one spirit"* with You, as it says in 1 Corinthians 6:17.

Thank You for making me part of Jesus, the true Vine, for the purpose of bringing forth much fruit. Father, I trust You to prune me to bring forth more fruit; and, Holy Spirit, I welcome Your sap rising through Jesus and through me so that, together, we can produce fruit that will last.

Please protect me from legalism and the temptation to go back to a set of rules to try to produce righteousness. I recognize the witchcraft behind that, and I want no part of it. I desire only the righteousness that comes through my Savior, Jesus.

Each day, please help me to deny myself, take up my cross, and follow Jesus, in whose name I pray. Amen.

# THE DESTINATION: THE SPIRIT-FILLED LIFE, PART 1

*Read Romans 8*

## INTRODUCTION

Following the prelude to the letter of Romans (1:1–1:17), we have progressed through the ten stages of the Roman pilgrimage to bring us to the climax of our journey: the Spirit-filled life. Let's review those stages:

1.  Romans 1:18–32: God's Self-Revelation: Man's Rejection and Its Consequences

2.  Romans 2:1–3:8: Moral Knowledge and Personal Responsibility

3.  Romans 3:9–20: Accountability to God (sums up stages 1 and 2)

4.  Romans 3:21–31: God's Provision of Righteousness*

5.  Romans 4:1–25: Justification* by Faith, Not Works

6.  Romans 5:1–11: Five Experiential Results of Being Justified* by Faith

7.  Romans 5:12–21: Comparison Between Adam and Jesus

8.  Romans 6:1–11: God's Solution for the Old Man: Execution

9.  Romans 6:12–23: How to Apply God's Solution for the Old Man in Our Lives

10. Romans 7:1–25: The Believer's Relationship to Law*

Having completed the ten stages of our Roman pilgrimage, we now stand at the entrance to our destination—Romans 8. This chapter beautifully unfolds the nature of the Spirit-controlled, Spirit-filled, supernatural life of the Christian who has met God's preconditions.

The next four lessons of this study are devoted to Romans 8. After that, we will go on to explore the destiny* of Israel* and the church in Romans 9–11, and then we will examine how to live out our faith under pressure in chapters 12–16. In this lesson, we will focus on the first four verses of Romans 8.

## MEMORY VERSES: ROMANS 8:1–2

[ ] Check here after memorizing the verses.
(Review verses from prior lessons daily.)

## QUESTIONS

### NO CONDEMNATION

As noted in the introduction, Romans 8 is the destination to which our pilgrimage through chapters 1–7 has been leading. Paul indicates this in his use of the word *"therefore"* in Romans 8:1: *"There is therefore now…."* Answer the following questions about our new life in the Spirit:

1.  Do those who are in Christ Jesus stand under condemnation? (Rom. 8:1) [1 point]

    _____

2.  In the chart below, circle the correct answer or fill in the blanks to indicate what God has accomplished for us through Jesus's death on the cross: (Col. 2:13–14) [6 points]

|            | Dead/Alive                  | Trespasses                          | Law                                              |
|------------|-----------------------------|-------------------------------------|--------------------------------------------------|
| Pre-Cross  | a. We were:<br>Dead/Alive   | c. We were _____ in trespasses. | e. We were under it./It has been Wiped Out.      |
| Post-Cross | b. We are:<br>Dead/Alive    | d. We are _____ all trespasses. | f. We are under it./It has been wiped out.       |

3.  What three things did Jesus do to the evil principalities and powers? (Col. 2:15)

    a.  He _____ them. [1 point]

    b.  He made a _____ _____ of them. [1 point]

    c.  He _____ over them in the cross. [1 point]

4.  In our newfound righteousness, whom should we allow to judge us regarding food, drink, festivals, new moons, or sabbaths? (Col. 2:16) [1 point]

    _____

5. According to Romans 8:2, there are two laws at work.

    a. Which law only operates in Jesus and always blesses us? [1 point]

    _____

    b. Which law inevitably condemns us? [1 point]

    _____

6. What is the problem with the law? (Rom. 8:3) [1 point]

_____

7. Whom did God send in the likeness of sinful flesh? (Rom. 8:3) [1 point]

_____

8. What has Jesus done to sin by the sacrifice of Himself? (Heb. 9:26) [1 point]

_____

9. Did the sacrifices of the law take away sin? (Heb. 10:1–4) [1 point]

_____

## WHAT IS REQUIRED?

10. For those of us *"who do not walk according to the flesh but according to the Spirit,"* it is not the law that must be fulfilled in us but the _____ _____ of the law. (Rom. 8:4) [1 point]

11. The following two commandments are the most important, according to Jesus. Fill in the blanks to indicate the heart of these commandments: (Matt. 22:35–40)

    a. *"You shall _____ the LORD your God with all your heart, with all your soul, and with all your mind."* (v. 37) [1 point]

b.  "You shall _____ your neighbor as yourself." (v. 39) [1 point]

12.  What is the only thing we are to owe anyone? (Rom. 13:8) [1 point]

_____

13.  What have we done when we love others? (Rom. 13:8) [1 point]

_____

14.  What proportion of the law is fulfilled when we love our neighbors as we love ourselves? (Gal. 5:14)
[1 point]

_____

15.  What are the three requirements for love? (1 Tim. 1:5)

a.  A pure _____ [1 point]

b.  A good _____ [1 point]

c.  Sincere _____ [1 point]

16.  How will the world know that we are Jesus's disciples? (John 13:35) [1 point]

_____

## THE NATURE OF LOVE

Having learned that the righteous* requirement of the law is love, let's get a biblical perspective on what love truly is.

17.  What is the ultimate source of love? (1 John 4:8, 16) [1 point]

_____

18.  What is the transformation that makes it possible for us to love one another fervently with a pure heart?
(1 Pet. 1:22–23) [1 point]

_____

19. Who pours out the love of God in our hearts? (Rom. 5:5) [1 point]

_____

20. List two attributes of everyone who loves: (1 John 4:7)

    a. Everyone who loves is _____ of God. [1 point]

    b. Everyone who loves _____ God. [1 point]

21. Fill in the blanks to complete John 14:21:

"He who _____ My commandments and _____ them, it is he who loves Me." [2 points]

22. What is the evidence that we love Jesus? (John 14:15, 23) [1 point]

_____

23. Is godly obedience motivated by fear? (Rom. 8:15) [1 point]

_____

24. Can our love increase, or do we receive a particular measure of love when we are born again and no more? (Phil. 1:9–11) [1 point]

_____

25. What happens in us as we keep God's word? (1 John 2:5) [1 point]

_____

## MEMORY WORK: ROMANS 8:1–2

Write out these verses from memory: [8 points]

_____

_____

_____

Check your answers on pages 197–99 in the "Correct Answers with Notes" section at the back of the book.

## PRAYER RESPONSE

As we begin to consider the Spirit-filled life unfolded in Romans 8, I am aware that not all of my readers will have received the baptism in the Holy Spirit. I have taught extensively on this topic elsewhere, but I will summarize what Scripture tells us about how to undergo this glorious experience:

+ Ask for the Holy Spirit. (Luke 11:13)

+ Be thirsty to receive. (John 7:37–39)

+ Come to Jesus as the Baptizer in the Holy Spirit. (John 7:37)

+ Drink (John 7:37): we can open our mouths and begin to "drink" or "breathe in" the invisible Holy Spirit.

+ Release the outflow: the *inflow* is supernatural and through your mouth, so the *outflow* will also be supernatural and through your mouth. The Bible tells us, *"Out of the abundance of the heart [the] mouth speaks"* (Luke 6:45).

With this understanding, let's pray:

Lord Jesus Christ, I believe that You are the Son of God and that, on the cross, You died for my sins and then rose again from the dead. I trust You for forgiveness and for cleansing. I believe You have received me as a child of God. And because You have received me, I receive myself as a child of God.

If there is any resentment or any unforgiveness in my heart against anyone, I lay it down. I forgive every other person as I would have God forgive me. If I've ever been involved in the occult, I acknowledge that as a sin. I ask for Your forgiveness, and I loose myself now from every contact with Satan and with occult power, in the name of Jesus.

And now, Lord Jesus, I come to You as my Baptizer in the Holy Spirit. I present to You my body to be a temple of Your Spirit. I yield to You my tongue to be an instrument of righteousness, to worship You in a new language. By faith, I receive this gift now, and I thank You for it in the name of Jesus. Amen.

Begin to breathe in the Holy Spirit, and, as you are filled, allow Him to overflow through Your mouth as You speak with a new language from heaven that you have never known before.

For **those who have already received the baptism in the Holy Spirit**, let's start by proclaiming our memory verses:

*There is therefore now no condemnation to those who are in Christ Jesus, who do not walk according to the flesh, but according to the Spirit. For the law of the Spirit of life in Christ Jesus has made me free from the law of sin and death.*

(Romans 8:1–2)

Heavenly Father, help me to fulfill the righteous requirement of the law, which is love. As it says in 1 John 4:8 and 16, You are love, and I want to receive and be transformed by that love day by day. I marvel to think, as Paul expresses in Romans 5:5, that the love of God has been poured out into my heart by the Holy Spirit who was given to us. I want to share that love with those around me, and I need Your help to do it most effectively.

Thank You, Lord, for Your Holy Spirit, who empowers me to live for You. Amen.

# THE DESTINATION: THE SPIRIT-FILLED LIFE, PART 2

*Read Romans 8*

## INTRODUCTION

In Romans 8:5–17, Paul focuses on the opposition between the flesh and the Spirit of God. Once again, "the flesh" in this context does not mean our physical bodies but the nature we received by inheritance from Adam. Its essence is summed up in one word: *rebel*. Remember that God, for His part, dealt with the rebel within us. (See Romans 6.) As far as God is concerned, the rebel has been executed.

In your experience, you may not feel as if the rebel within you is entirely dead, but we are discussing your legal inheritance in Christ. You may have heard people say, "I got it all when I was born again." If they got it all, we might ask them, "Where is it all? Let us see it." In a certain sense, though, what they say is true. Legally, they did get it all. They—and we—are entitled to every spiritual benefit and blessing. But there is a vast difference between having these benefits and blessings legally and having them experientially. This is the nature of the Christian life: moving from the legal to the experiential.

## MEMORY VERSES: ROMANS 8:14–15

[ ] Check here after memorizing the verses.

(Review verses from prior lessons daily.)

## QUESTIONS

### ENTERING OUR INHERITANCE

1. Verb tenses are very important in Scripture because they help to both uncover truth and tell us *when* that truth has relevance. Note the contrast in what God says to Joshua about the promised land:

   a. *"Now therefore, arise, go over this Jordan, you and all this people, to the land which I _____ _____ to them—the children of Israel."* (Josh.1:2) [1 point]

   b. *"Every place that the sole of your foot will tread upon I _____ _____ you, as I said to Moses."* (Josh. 1:3) [1 point]

2. The Israelites received the promised land as an inheritance. Inheritance is a pivotal theme in the New Testament too. We will consider just one Scripture passage to illustrate this, as well as to reaffirm the importance of verb tense. For each verse from 1 Peter 1, circle the correct answer to indicate whether it is speaking about the past, the present, or the future:

   a. *"Blessed be the God and Father of our Lord Jesus Christ, who according to His abundant mercy **has begotten us** again to a living hope through the resurrection of Jesus Christ from the dead...."* (v. 3) [1 point]    Past/Present/Future

   b. *"To an inheritance incorruptible* [or imperishable] *and undefiled and that does not fade away, **reserved in heaven** for you...."* (v. 4) [1 point]    Past/Present/Future

   c. *"Who **are kept** by the power of God through faith for salvation ready to be revealed in the last time."* (v. 5) [1 point]    Past/Present/Future

### THINKING LIKE THE SPIRIT OR THE FLESH?

3. In Romans 8:5, Paul distinguishes between the two alternative ways of living:

   a. *"Those who live according to the _____."* [1 point]

   b. *"Those who live according to the _____."* [1 point]

4. Verse 6 continues the comparison:

   a. *"To be carnally minded is _____."* [1 point]

   b. *"To be spiritually minded is _____ and _____."* [2 points]

5. Is your natural, un-regenerated mind at peace with God or at enmity with Him? (Rom. 8:7) [1 point]

_____

6. Is it possible for the carnal mind to be subject to the law* of God? (Rom. 8:7) [1 point]

_____

7. Can those who are in the flesh please God? (Rom. 8:8) [1 point]

_____

8. What kind of children were we in our old nature? (Eph. 2:3) [1 point]

_____

9. In Colossians 1:21, Paul says that before we were reconciled to God, we were *"alienated and enemies"* in our _____. [1 point]

10. What is the alternative to being conformed to this world? (Rom. 12:2) [1 point]

_____

## FROM FLESH TO SPIRIT

11. What is the test that we are not in the flesh but in the Spirit? (Rom. 8:9) [1 point]

_____

12. Romans 8:10 tells us two results of Christ living in us:

    a. *"The _____ is dead because of sin."* [1 point]

    b. *"The _____ is life because of righteousness."* [1 point]

13. How are we taught to cease walking *"as the rest of the Gentiles walk"* (Ephesians 4:17)?

    a. *"Put off…the _____ _____."* (Eph. 4:22) [1 point]

    b. *"Be renewed in the spirit of your _____."* (v. 23) [1 point]

c. *"Put on the _____ _____."* (v. 24) [1 point]

14. What is the only solution to corruption—a solution that is possible only in Christ? (2 Cor. 5:17)
[1 point]

_____

15. What do we receive through Christ's Spirit who dwells in us? (Rom. 8:11) [1 point]

_____

16. In Romans 8:13, what are we called to do *"by the Spirit"*? [1 point]

_____

## LED BY THE SPIRIT

17. What is the key characteristic of the *"sons of God"*? (Rom. 8:14) [1 point]

_____

18. What two opposite spirits are mentioned in Romans 8:15? [2 points]

a. _____

b. _____

## CHILDREN OF GOD

19. What right or authority does God give to those who receive Jesus and believe in His name? (John 1:12)
[1 point]

_____

20. Who bears witness with our spirits that we are children of God? (Rom. 8:16) [1 point]

_____

21. If we are truly children of God, what is the implication regarding inheritance? (Rom. 8:17) [1 point]

_____

22. What is the condition on which we may also be glorified with Christ? (Rom. 8:17) [1 point]

_____

## MEMORY WORK: ROMANS 8:14–15

Write out these verses from memory: [8 points]

_____

_____

_____

Check your answers on pages 200–202 in the "Correct Answers with Notes" section at the back of the book.

### PRAYER RESPONSE

Thank You, Lord Jesus, for Your Holy Spirit, who enables me to move into my inheritance in You. Please continue helping me to move from a legal position to an experiential position where I am living in the fullness of the promises. I will not conform to the pattern of this world. I ask You to transform me by the renewing of my mind so that I am changed from the inside out. I want to be spiritually minded and full of life and peace—both for my own sake and so that I may share Your life and peace with those around me.

I ask that You would help me to grow in spiritual maturity as I continually choose to be led by the Holy Spirit. I acknowledge Him as the Spirit of Truth, Teacher, Provider, Comforter, Guide, Counselor, and Administrator of our eternal inheritance.

Lord, when suffering comes, please strengthen and encourage me so that I may also be glorified together with You. Amen.

# THE DESTINATION: THE SPIRIT-FILLED LIFE, PART 3

*Read Romans 8*

## INTRODUCTION

We ended the last lesson with the realization that to be glorified with Christ, we must be willing to suffer with Him. That may not be a welcome thought, so I would now like to consider the nature and purpose of suffering, since it is something that every one of us experiences to some degree.

In this lesson, we will focus on Romans 8:18–25, a passage that contains a marvelous revelation of God's purpose for creation. As believers in Jesus who have received the Holy Spirit, we are not to be preoccupied solely with our own concerns or with the affairs of this age or even with the total destiny* of the church. God wants us to be so enlarged in our understanding of, and responses to, His will that we can identify with and long for His total program for creation.

Here is one reason for this: we humans are responsible for all the trouble that has come upon creation. God made the first man steward over the creation, but unfaithful Adam failed in his stewardship, which brought disaster not only on him and his descendants but also on the creation over which he was steward. The whole earth is in a mess because of our rejection of righteousness* and because evil took the place of righteousness.

In His limitless wisdom, God has ordained that the redemption of creation be closely tied in with the redemption of the Adamic race. Creation will not be redeemed until our own redemption is complete. Because our sin brought corruption and disaster upon creation, it will be our moment of complete redemption that will redeem creation.

Thus, Paul speaks about our "groaning"—not just for our own petty concerns but in longing for that wonderful, glorious day of redemption, sharing the longing of creation for the return of righteousness to the earth. (See Romans 8:22–23.)

## MEMORY VERSES: ROMANS 8:22–23

[ ] Check here after memorizing the verses.

(Review verses from prior lessons daily.)

# QUESTIONS

## THE NATURE AND PURPOSE OF SUFFERING

1. Are the sufferings of this present time worthy to be compared with the glory that shall be revealed in us? (Rom. 8:18) [1 point]

   _____

2. Hebrews 2:10 calls Jesus *"the captain of* [our] *salvation."* How does that verse tell us that He was made perfect? [1 point]

   _____

3. Jesus was the Son of God, and yet He still had to learn obedience. How did that learning occur? (Heb. 5:8) [1 point]

   _____

4. The writer to the Hebrews speaks of a time when *"you endured a great struggle with sufferings."* What brought about that struggle? (Heb. 10:32) [1 point]

   _____

5. Is all suffering to our credit? (1 Pet. 2:19–20) [1 point]

   _____

6. What is the end result of our suffering? (2 Cor. 4:17) [1 point]

   _____

7. When we experience affliction, where are we to look? (2 Cor. 4:18) [1 point]

   _____

8. Our revelation as the sons of God is earnestly expected by what? (Rom. 8:19) [1 point]

_____

9. Complete the statements below from Psalm 96:11–13:

  a. "Let the _____ rejoice." (v. 11) [1 point]

  b. "Let the _____ be glad." (v. 11) [1 point]

  c. "Let the _____ roar, and all its fullness." (v. 11) [1 point]

  d. "Let the _____ be joyful, and all that is in it." (v. 12) [1 point]

  e. "Then all the _____ of the _____ will rejoice before the LORD. For He is coming…." (vv. 12–13) [2 points]

10. Psalm 98:7–9 contains a similar theme:

  a. "Let the _____ roar, and all its fullness." (v. 7) [1 point]

  b. "Let the _____ clap their hands." (v. 8) [1 point]

  c. "Let the _____ be joyful together before the LORD, for He is coming…." (vv. 8–9) [1 point]

## EMPATHIZING WITH CREATION

11. What was creation subjected to as a result of man's sin? (Rom. 8:20) [1 point]

_____

12. Into what will creation be delivered from the bondage of corruption and decay? (Rom. 8:21) [1 point]

_____

13. Adam and Eve were given stewardship of the earth. However, due to their disobedience, what pronouncement did God make about the "ground" in Genesis 3:17? [1 point]

_____

14. What two types of plants are a visible mark of the curse? (Gen. 3:18) [2 points]

    a. _____

    b. _____

## ALL CREATION GROANING

15. Along with groaning, what has the whole of creation been experiencing together up to the present day? (Rom. 8:22) [1 point]

    _____

16. Who else is groaning for redemption? (Rom. 8:23) [1 point]

    _____

17. What is the culmination of our adoption as God's children, for which we should so eagerly wait? (Rom. 8:23) [1 point]

    _____

## THE AIM OF THE CHRISTIAN LIFE

18. In Philippians 3:10–11, Paul expresses his own aim in life. Fill in the blanks to complete the phrases:

    a. *"That I may _____ Him [Christ]."* (v. 10) [1 point]

    b. *"And the power of His _____."* (v. 10) [1 point]

    c. *"And the fellowship of His _____."* (v. 10) [1 point]

    d. *"Being conformed to His _____."* (v. 10) [1 point]

    e. *"If, by any means, I may attain to the _____ from the*
       *_____."* (v. 11) [2 points]

19. What is Paul referring to when he says, *"But I press on, that I may lay hold of that for which Christ Jesus has also laid hold of me"* (Philippians 3:12)? (v. 11) [1 point]

    _____

20. Read Philippians 3:20–21 as a summary of our current theme and then answer the questions below:

    a.   Where is our citizenship? (v. 20) [1 point]

_____

    b.   Whom are we eagerly awaiting? (v. 20) [1 point]

_____

    c.   What will happen to our bodies? (v. 21) [1 point]

_____

21. Whom will we resemble when Jesus Christ appears? (1 John 2:28–3:2) [1 point]

_____

## THE REGENERATION OF ALL CREATION

22. In Matthew 24, Jesus is talking about the signs that will mark the close of the age. How does He describe them in verse 8? [1 point]

_____

23. Referring to these same end-time events, why does Jesus tell us in Luke 21:28 to *"look up and lift up your heads"*? [1 point]

_____

24. Is hope for the present day, or is it future-focused? (Rom. 8:24) [1 point]

_____

25. What does hope produce in us as we eagerly wait for the redemption of our bodies? (Rom. 8:25) [1 point]

_____

26. In Colossians 1:24–27, Paul talks about a *"mystery which has been hidden from ages and from generations, but now has been revealed to His [God's] saints"* (v. 26). What is this mystery that has now been revealed? (v. 27) [1 point]

_____

### HOLY SPIRIT INTERCESSION

27. What is the human weakness that Paul speaks about in Romans 8:26? [1 point]

_____

28. How does the Holy Spirit help us? (Rom. 8:26) [1 point]

_____

29. According to what does the Holy Spirit make intercession? (Rom. 8:27) [1 point]

_____

## MEMORY WORK: ROMANS 8:22–23

Write out these verses from memory: [8 points]

_____

_____

_____

_____

_____

Check your answers on pages 203–06 in the "Correct Answers with Notes" section at the back of the book.

## PRAYER RESPONSE

Father, I thank You for this reminder of the purposes and outcome of suffering. By Your perfect love, I ask that You would drive out all fear from my heart and mind concerning trials and tribulations, and prepare me for all that lies ahead.

Thank You, too, for the reminder of creation's anticipation of the revelation of the sons of God. Help me to empathize with creation and to participate in its longing for the revelation of the Son of God, Jesus Christ, and the fullness of my adoption, the redemption of my body. Holy Spirit, I am grateful that You help me in my weaknesses, and I invite You to make intercession through me.

I proclaim that:

+ All things work together for my good because I love God, and I am called according to His purpose. (Rom. 8:28)

+ God foreknew me and predestined me to be conformed to the image of Jesus. (v. 29)

+ God has also called me, justified* me, and glorified me. (v. 30)

Amen.

# THE DESTINATION: THE SPIRIT-FILLED LIFE, PART 4

*Read Romans 8*

## INTRODUCTION

This is the last of the four lessons based on Romans 8. We started lesson 12 by learning that *"there is therefore now no condemnation to those who are in Christ Jesus"* (verse 1) and how we are freed from *"the law of sin and death"* (verse 2). The wonderful alternative we find ourselves under is *"the law of the Spirit of life in Christ Jesus"* (verse 2). We also considered the *"righteous requirement of the law"* (verse 4) and the nature of love.

In lesson 13, we began looking at our inheritance in Christ and learned about being led by the Spirit as mature children of God.

In lesson 14, we dealt with the nature and purpose of suffering; we also focused on creation and how it groans in anticipation of the revelation of the sons of God, which we are. We were reminded of our call to empathize with creation and that, ultimately, there will be a regeneration of all creation with the help of the Holy Spirit's intercession.

In lesson 15, we will work through the remainder of Romans 8 and learn more of God's plan for us, which began in eternity, continues throughout time, and goes back into eternity.

## MEMORY VERSES: ROMANS 8:29–30

[ ] Check here after memorizing the verses.

(Review verses from prior lessons daily.)

## QUESTIONS

### SECURITY IN GOD'S CHOICE

1. Did we choose God or did God choose us in the first place? (John 15:16) [1 point]

2. James 1:18 tells us that God *"brought us forth [caused us to be born again] by the word of truth, that we might be a kind of firstfruits of His creatures."* What was the impetus for our becoming new creations in Christ? [1 point]

_____

## ALL THINGS...FOR GOOD

3. In Romans 8:28, Paul sets out two conditions for having *"all things work together for good"*:

   a. *"To those who _____ God."* [1 point]

   b. *"To those who are the _____ according to His purpose."* [1 point]

4. In Hosea 2:6, we catch a glimpse of how God dealt with Israel* when she was going the wrong way. What did God say about His plans to stop Israel from finding her own paths?

   a. *"I will _____ up your way with thorns."* [1 point]

   b. *"I will..._____ her in."* [1 point]

## GOD'S PLAN: FROM ETERNITY TO ETERNITY

The tremendous statements in Romans 8:29–30 explain why we know everything is working together for good. They tell us God's total plan for us from eternity to eternity. If we grasp that plan, believe it, and align ourselves with it, we will have total security.

In the table below, you need to read all the Scriptures related to each stage in God's program and come up with the common thread between those verses. The first one is completed as an example.

| Question | Stage | What did God do? | Scripture references |
|---|---|---|---|
| | **IN ETERNITY** | | |
| 5. | 1 | He __foreknew__ us. | Rom. 8:29; 1 Pet. 1:2 [sample; no points] |
| 6. | 2 | He _____ us. | Eph. 1:4; 1 Pet. 1:2 [1 point] |
| 7. | 3 | He _____ us. | Rom. 8:29–30; Eph. 1:5, 11; 2:10 [1 point] |
| | **IN TIME, CONTINUING ON INTO ETERNITY** | | |
| 8. | 4 | He _____ us. | Rom. 8:28, 30; 11:29; 2 Thess. 2:14 [1 point] |
| 9. | 5 | He _____ us. | 2 Tim.1:9; Titus 3:5 [1 point] |
| 10. | 6 | He _____ us. | Rom. 3:24; 5:1; 8:30; 1 Cor. 6:11 [1 point] |
| 11. | 7 | He _____ us. | Rom. 8:30; 1 Cor. 2:7; Heb. 2:10; see also Eph. 2:4–6 [1 point] |

12. In Romans 8:31, is Paul implying that we will not have opposition if God is for us? (See also vv. 35–36.) [1 point]

_____

13. Our confidence in God's lifetime commitment to us is based solely on the price that He paid to redeem us. Fill in these two words from Romans 8:32:

*"He who did not spare His* _____ _____*."* [1 point]

## INTERCESSOR AND ADVOCATE

14. Does anyone have the right to condemn us? (Rom. 8:33–34) [1 point]

_____

15. Who makes intercession for us at the right hand of God? (Rom. 8:34) [1 point]

_____

16. Hebrews 3:1 calls Jesus *"the Apostle and High Priest of our confession."* In Hebrews 7:25, what more does the writer tell us about our High Priest's ongoing ministry? [1 point]

_____

17. What role does Jesus fulfill when interceding with the Father for us if we sin? (1 John 2:1) [1 point]

_____

18. Who is told to condemn every tongue that rises against us in judgment? (Isa. 54:17) [1 point]

_____

19. In Romans 8:35, Paul asks a rhetorical question. Does he expect us to answer yes or no? [1 point]

_____

20. List the seven challenges Paul anticipates Christians might face: (Rom. 8:35) [7 points]

a. _____

b. _____

c. _____

d. _____

e. _____

f. _____

g. _____

21. What happens to us for the sake of Christ? (Rom. 8:36) [1 point]

_____

## OVERWHELMING CONQUERORS

22. Following a negative list of possible trials that we will have to face, what word does Paul use to shift our attention at the beginning of Romans 8:37? [1 point]

_____

23. Verse 37 goes on to say that *"we are _____ than _____ through Him who loved us."* [2 points]

24. In Romans 8:38–39, Paul comes to a glorious conclusion. Complete the list of things that will *not "be able to separate us from the love of God which is in Christ Jesus our Lord"*:

a. *"Neither _____ nor _____...."* (v. 38) [2 points]

b. "Nor _____ nor principalities nor _____...." (v. 38) [2 points]

c. "Nor things _____ nor things to _____...." (v. 38) [2 points]

d. "Nor _____ nor _____...." (v. 39) [2 points]

e. "Nor any other _____ thing." (v. 39) [1 point]

25. When our old man is dead, where is our new man positioned? (Col. 3:3) [1 point]

_____

26. What will happen when Christ appears? (Col. 3:4) [1 point]

_____

27. Which single word completes this phrase from Colossians 3:11?

"Christ is _____ and in _____." [1 point]

## MEMORY WORK: ROMANS 8:29–30

Write out these verses from memory: [8 points]

_____

_____

_____

_____

Check your answers on pages 207–10 in the "Correct Answers with Notes" section at the back of the book.

## PRAYER RESPONSE

Thank You, Father, that my life and my future are secure in Your choice to save me and that the value You place on me is indicated by the price You paid—Your own Son, Jesus. I marvel as I am reminded that Your plan of redemption began in eternity and will continue throughout all time and back into eternity.

I proclaim that I am foreknown, chosen, predestined to conform to the image of Jesus; I am called, saved, and justified.

I praise You that I am more than a conqueror through Jesus who loved me and that nothing will separate me from the love of God that is in Christ. Hallelujah*!

# THE DESTINY OF ISRAEL AND THE CHURCH, PART 1: GOD'S SOVEREIGNTY OR HUMANISM?

*Read Romans 9*

## INTRODUCTION

We will now work systematically through Romans 9–11. These three chapters could best be described as "the destiny* of Israel* and the church." Their central theme is God's sovereignty and grace operating through His own choice.

Today, there is a wide gap in Christians' understanding of the Bible. According to my observation, very few contemporary Christians have laid hold of the great central truths of the New Testament. Much of the church is like astronomy before Copernicus, when people still believed that the sun revolved around the earth (a geocentric model). Mankind's view of the universe was earth-centered, so that many other areas of the cosmos could not be accurately measured or understood. It took an intellectual and religious revolution before the truth could be established that the earth and the other planets in our solar system revolve around the sun (a heliocentric model).

In the same way, many Christians today have a view of God that is human-centered. They view Jesus Christ as revolving around us, present to meet our needs and answer our prayers and do what we want. That is a distorted picture of God. Thank God, Jesus *is* there, and He does answer our prayers, take care of us, love us, and provide for us. But we are not the center; Jesus Christ is the center. He is the sun, and our little earths revolve around Him. When we put Him in the center of the picture, many other things fall into place that we cannot accurately understand when we view everything from a self-centered perspective.

The word *sovereignty* is little used among contemporary Christians, who think that God needs their permission to do things in their lives. My simple, down-to-earth definition of God's sovereignty is that "God does what He wants, when He wants, in the way He wants—and He asks no one's permission." That is sovereignty. There is a contrary philosophy called *humanism* that is a kind of religion and is very prevalent in our society today. Humanism says that human beings are at the center of all things. If any of those who embrace humanism even acknowledge God's existence, they usually have the attitude that if God does anything, He should first get their approval. If they do not approve of something, God ought not to do it.

When I began to study this subject from a biblical perspective, I decided to look up the dictionary definition of *humanism*. I had always thought about humanism, if I thought about it at all, as a rather neutral influence that just expected man to work out his own problems and solve his own destiny. However, when I read one of the definitions of humanism in the *Collins English Dictionary*, it shocked me:

> Humanism: the denial of any power or moral value superior to that of humanity; the rejection of religion in favour of a belief in the advancement of humanity by its own efforts.

The two words that impacted me in this definition were *denial* and *rejection*. I suddenly realized that humanism is a very strong negative force.

Even more, humanism is an extremely powerful evil force—in fact, it is the main force that is preparing the way for the Antichrist. As Christians, we need to understand its nature and how it works. Due to my background, I feel it would be helpful to give a historical overview of humanism. My particular field of study at Cambridge University was Greek philosophy. I haven't studied it for more than fifty years, and there are a lot of facts I have forgotten, but I do have hold of certain basic facts. First of all, there were three main elements in Greek culture:

+ Rationalism*

+ Athletics

+ Homosexuality

You can observe that all of these elements are being reproduced in our culture today.

Let me also give you a little background on philosophy (translated literally as "the love of wisdom"). The first known Greek philosopher was called Heraclitus, and he "flourished," as they say, around the first half of the fifth century BC. So, we are talking about something that goes back about 2,500 years.

Two statements from Heraclitus are very significant in this context:

The first one is "Everything flows."

The second one is, in essence, "You can never step twice into the same river."

A third statement, by Protagoras, a student of Democritus, is generally quoted as, "Man is the measure of all things."

When you put those three statements together, you get a perfect summation of *humanism*; it could not be more accurately stated:

+ Everything flows: there are no absolutes; everything is relative.

+ You can never step twice into the same river: what was true yesterday isn't necessarily true today.

+ Man is the measure of all things: man has the last word on everything.

In this lesson, we will look at the roots and consequences of humanism, as well as God's answer to it.


# MEMORY VERSE: PSALM 14:1

[ ] Check here after memorizing the verse.

(Review verses from prior lessons daily.)

# QUESTIONS

## THE ROOTS OF HUMANISM

1.  In Ezekiel 28:11–19, we read of an *"anointed cherub"* (verse 14) who is described as *"perfect…till iniquity was found in you"* (verse 15). According to verse 17, what was the first sin in the universe (even before creation): murder, adultery, or pride? [1 point]

    _____

2.  We read the result of Lucifer's (Satan's) pride in Isaiah 14:12–15. Complete the statements below from the text:

    *"For you have said in your heart…*

    a.  *'I will ascend into _____.'"* (v.13) [1 point]

    b.  *'I will exalt my _____ above the stars of God.'"* (v. 13) [1 point]

    c.  *'I will also sit on the mount of the _____.'"* (v. 13) [1 point]

    d.  *'I will ascend above the heights of the _____.'"* (v. 14) [1 point]

    e.  *'I will be like the _____ _____.'"* (v. 14) [1 point]

3.  In Zechariah 9:12–13, two types of sons are mentioned. Fill in the blanks to tell where they came from:

    a.  Sons of _____ (v. 13) [1 point]

    b.  Sons of _____ (v. 13) [1 point]

4.  In the second chapter of Daniel, Nebuchadnezzar has a dream about an image that portrays the future course of Gentile empires. Historically, we know that the order of succeeding empires was the following: Babylon, Medo-Persia, Greece, and Rome (which incidentally split into two and had capitals in both Rome and Constantinople). By putting Daniel's prophecy together with history, we can say that which empire is represented by the *"belly and thighs of bronze"*? (Dan. 2:31–33) [1 point]

    _____

5. What does God pronounce on *"those who call evil good, and good evil; who put darkness for light, and light for darkness; who put bitter for sweet, and sweet for bitter"*? (Isa. 5:20) [1 point]

   _____

6. What does God pronounce on *"those who are wise in their own eyes, and prudent in their own sight"* (Isa. 5:21)? [1 point]

   _____

7. What kind of throne is described in Psalm 94:20? [1 point]

   _____

8. When I look at the society in which we live (particularly in Western nations), created by humanism, I am reminded of a scenario in Isaiah 59:14. Note the four statements made about this scenario:

   a. " _____ *is turned back."* [1 point]

   b. *"And* _____ *stands afar off."* [1 point]

   c. *"For* _____ *is fallen in the street."* [1 point]

   d. *"And* _____ *cannot enter."* [1 point]

9. In the next verse (Isaiah 59:15), we see that due to this failure of truth, even those who do not follow this departure from God are under threat. What happens to the one who departs from evil under such circumstances? [1 point]

   _____

## GOD'S ANSWER TO HUMANISM

Chapters 9–11 of Romans provide eight truths of a biblical worldview, which is God's answer to humanism. Answer the following questions to discover these eight truths:

10. First truth: Whose purpose will ultimately stand? (Rom. 9:11) [1 point]

    _____

11. Second truth: What does God's choice depend on? (Rom. 9:16) [1 point]

_____

12. Third truth: Who is *"the end of the law for righteousness to everyone who believes"*? (Rom. 10:4) [1 point]

_____

13. Fourth truth: What are the two things Paul tells us we need to do to be saved? (Rom. 10:9)

    a.  "_____ *with your mouth the Lord Jesus.*" [1 point]

    b.  "_____ *in your heart that God has raised Him from the dead.*" [1 point]

14. Fifth truth: According to what does Paul say there is a remnant of believers *"at this present time"*? (Rom. 11:5) [1 point]

_____

15. Sixth truth: Which aspect of God's nature will people experience, depending on whether they do, or do not, continue in His goodness? (Rom. 11:22)

    Either _____ or _____ [2 points]

16. Seventh truth: Does God withdraw the gifts and calling He gives to each of us? (Rom. 11:29) [1 point]

_____

17. Eighth truth: Of whom, through whom, and to whom are all things? (Rom. 11:33–36) [1 point]

_____

# MEMORY WORK: PSALM 14:1

Write out this verse from memory: [4 points]

_____

_____

_____

Check your answers on pages 211–13 in the "Correct Answers with Notes" section at the back of the book.

## PRAYER RESPONSE

Lord Jesus, when I look at the world around me, I see much evidence of humanism—a denial of Your existence and a rejection of Your ways. Forgive me for any way in which I have been seduced into thinking along the same lines and for the times when I have looked to earthly solutions for humanity.

I recognize the destructive power of pride, and I ask You to deliver me completely from every root of it in my life, along with its consequences. I choose Your way of truth and humility, acknowledging Your sovereignty and unique ability to deal with man's sin.

Help me never to bow to humanistic thought and never to feel inferior to man's cleverness, because *"the foolishness of God* [Christ's death on the cross] *is wiser than men, and the weakness of God is stronger than men"* (1 Corinthians 1:25). Thank You, Lord, for the cross and its infinite power of redemption and transformation. Amen.

## CLOSING THOUGHT

Often, people who are highly rational* seek to undermine Christianity—in particular, its supernatural elements. However, I have never had a theological or an intellectual problem with believing that the Bible is the Word of God, ever since I got to know its Author, the Holy Spirit. As a matter of fact, with my intellectual background, I personally do not feel in any way intellectually inferior to people who don't believe the Bible.

I was a professional logician. I excelled in that particular field, and I would have to say, on the basis of my own examination, that the Bible is the most intellectually sound and logical book that I have ever read. And, for me, it is a meaningful book. It is the Word of God. It is a personal God speaking to me with a living voice, as a Person.

# THE DESTINY OF ISRAEL AND THE CHURCH, PART 2: CHILDREN OF PROMISE

*Read Romans 10*

## INTRODUCTION

Many theologians and preachers refer to Romans 9–11 as a digression or a set of parentheses by Paul—as if discussing Israel* is a side issue of little importance. Nothing whatever in these chapters supports this view. Furthermore, in the middle of chapter 10, we find God's answer to the most important question in human life: "How can I be saved?" How ridiculous to call that chapter, or the chapters around it, a digression or a set of parentheses! I have to say that, although I am not Jewish, classifying these chapters like that is an expression of Gentile prejudice.

God's dealings with Israel—which is the main theme but by no means the exclusive theme of chapters 9 through 11—provide a historical demonstration of many essential spiritual principles that apply equally to Christians. These principles have been worked out in the history of Israel; they are part of recorded history; and they are there for our benefit because God has not changed His principles. The principles Paul outlines are at work in our own lives. We need to know them because they vitally concern us.

While this subject of God's plan for Israel and the church straddles three chapters in our Bibles, it is important to remember that chapter divisions did not appear in Paul's original letter to the Romans. As in the rest of the English New Testament, they were inserted during the thirteenth and fourteenth centuries. Also, in the original text, there are no capital letters, periods, or paragraph breaks. These elements are all helpful for modern readers, but they are subjective and not necessarily correct; they are just the best that the translators could do.

For an overview of the beginnings of Israel's history, review the following diagram, which shows the lineage from Abraham to the twelve tribes. After the reigns of David and Solomon, the twelve tribes split into the southern kingdom, called "Judah*," and the northern kingdom, also called "Israel." It's important to understand that, depending on the context, the name *Israel* may variously refer to (1) the land God gave to Abraham and his descendants; (2) Abraham's grandson Jacob, whom God renamed Israel (see Genesis 32:28); (3) all twelve tribes, descended from Jacob's sons, until the end of King Solomon's reign; (4) the northern kingdom in contrast to the southern kingdom after Israel divided in the days of King Rehoboam; (5) the Jews* after the return from exile in Babylon (such as those depicted in the New Testament); and (6) the modern state of Israel in the Middle East.

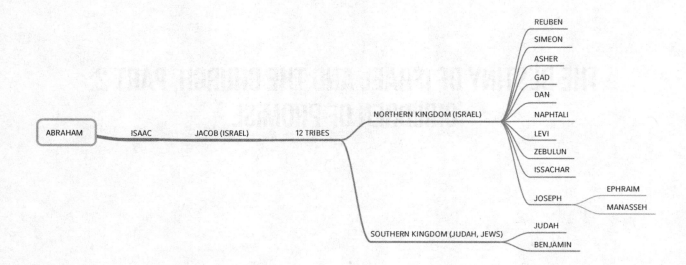

## MEMORY VERSE: ROMANS 9:8

[ ] Check here after memorizing the verse.

(Review verses from prior lessons daily.)

## QUESTIONS

### PAUL AND HIS FELLOW ISRAELITES

1. Romans 8 ends with Paul saying, *"I am persuaded that* [nothing] *shall be able to separate us from the love of God which is in Christ Jesus our Lord"* (verses 38–39). And yet, Paul then says this (fill in the blank):

   *"For I could wish that I myself were accursed from Christ for* [the sake of] *my _____, my countrymen according to the flesh."* (Rom. 9:3) [1 point]

2. When Paul is defending himself in Jerusalem before the Jews, we see the turning point in their attitude toward him. (Acts 22:21–22)

   a. To whom did God say He was sending Paul? (v. 21) [1 point]

   _____

   b. What do the Jews demand should happen to Paul? (v. 22) [1 point]

   _____

# ISRAEL'S DISTINCT PRIVILEGES

3.  In Romans 9:4–5, Paul describes what makes Israel a special people. In particular, he identifies eight distinctive privileges that Israel enjoys. Fill in the blanks as these privileges appear sequentially:

    a.  *"To whom pertain the _____."* (v. 4) [1 point]

    b.  *"To whom pertain…the _____."* (v. 4) [1 point]

    c.  *"To whom pertain…the _____."* (v. 4) [1 point]

    d.  *"To whom pertain…the giving of the _____."* (v. 4) [1 point]

    e.  *"To whom pertain…the _____ of God."* (v. 4) [1 point]

    f.  *"And the _____."* (v. 4) [1 point]

    g.  *"Of whom are the _____."* (v. 5) [1 point]

    h.  *"And from whom, according to the flesh, _____ came."* (v. 5) [1 point]

# GOD'S CHOICE: CHILDREN OF PROMISE

4.  In Romans 9:6–13, Paul starts by addressing the concern that despite Israel's privileges, they did not all believe in Jesus as the Messiah. Does Paul agree that the word of God has taken no effect? [1 point]

    _____

5.  Are all the people who are Israelites by natural birth accepted as Israel by God? (Rom. 9:6–8) [1 point]

    _____

6.  Paul uses the story of the patriarchs to demonstrate how God limits those who are His people by His sovereign choice. Abram (Abraham) is our starting point. After answering questions *a* through *m*, fill in the key words in the blanks on the diagram below corresponding to the applicable letters.

    a.  To whom does the Lord promise to give the land of Canaan? (Gen. 12:5–7) [1 point]

    _____

    b.  What is the name of the servant by which Abram had a child? (Gen. 16:3) [1 point]

    _____

c. What is the name of the child born to Abram when he was eighty-six years old? (Gen. 16:15–16) [1 point]

_____

d. What does God make between Abraham and Himself? (Gen. 17:2, 7, 9–10, 13–14) [1 point]

_____

e. What does God promise to Abraham's wife, Sarah? (Gen. 17:19) [1 point]

_____

f. What does God promise to their child? (Gen. 17:19, 21) [1 point]

_____

g. Why does Isaac plead with the Lord for his wife Rebekah? (Gen. 25:21) [1 point]

_____

h. When Rebekah inquires of the Lord regarding why her twin babies struggled with each other in her womb, which child does the Lord tell her will be served? (Gen. 25:23) [1 point]

_____

i. What does God rename Jacob? (Gen. 35:10) [1 point]

_____

j. Whom does Jacob beget? (Acts 7:8) [1 point]

_____

k. What term is used to describe the families of the twelve sons of Jacob? (Gen. 49:28) [1 point]

_____

l. What is the qualifying feature of the true sons of Abraham? (Gal. 3:7) [1 point]

_____

m. To whom must you belong to be considered Abraham's seed and an heir according to the promise? (Gal. 3:29) [1 point]

_____

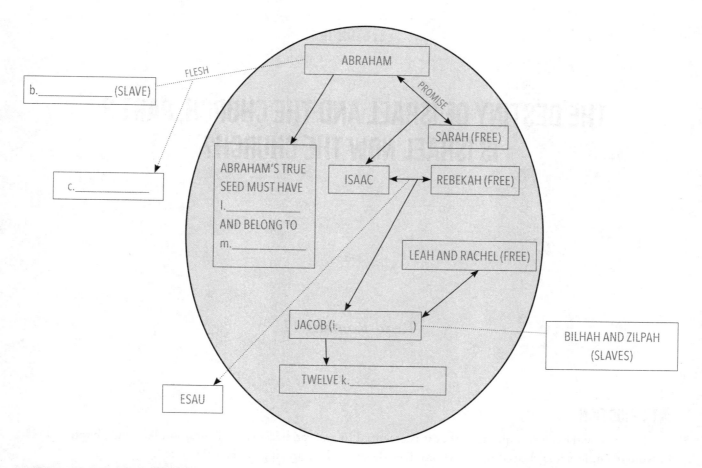

## MEMORY WORK: ROMANS 9:8

Write out this verse from memory: [4 points]

_____

_____

_____

Check your answers on pages 214–16 in the "Correct Answers with Notes" section at the back of the book.

## PRAYER RESPONSE

Heavenly Father, I recognize Your sovereign choice of Israel as a distinct and special nation. I also acknowledge the uniqueness of the Jewish people, as expressed in Romans 9:4–5: *"To whom pertain the adoption, the glory, the covenants, the giving of the law, the service of God, and the promises; of whom are the fathers and from whom, according to the flesh, Christ came, who is over all, the eternally blessed God."*

Tracing children of promise throughout Scripture, I thank You that, through Your sovereign choice, I, too, am Your child. I share in the blessings of Abraham, whom You blessed in all things, according to Genesis 24:1. I pray all this in the name of the One who made it all possible, Jesus Christ, my Lord. Amen.

# THE DESTINY OF ISRAEL AND THE CHURCH, PART 3: IS ISRAEL NOW THE CHURCH?

*Read Romans 11*

## INTRODUCTION

Now we will explore a question that it is essential to answer, because we cannot understand chapters 9–11 of Romans unless it is cleared up: to whom does the New Testament give the title *Israel*\*?

For some sixteen centuries, there has been a teaching in the church that, because the Israelites were so rebellious and disobedient, and because they were responsible, in a measure, for the crucifixion of the Lord Jesus, God has set aside Israel and replaced Israel with the church. This theory is called "supersessionism" or, more commonly, "replacement theology." Many proponents say, in essence, that God has finally and forever rejected Israel as a people, that all His commitments and promises to Israel are no longer valid, and that He has chosen the church in Israel's place.

After much study of the Bible and much prayer, I want to say categorically that I cannot personally accept this theory, and I do not believe the term *Israel* is ever used in the New Testament as a title for the church. As we examine this teaching, let's agree that the New Testament is the last authoritative word of God. Much theology and many church traditions and opinions have been held over the centuries, but the ultimate, final, authoritative, deciding factor is this: what does the New Testament say? Church traditions can be helpful, but if they are contrary to Scripture, we must reject them.

One or the other of these words, *Israel* or *Israelite(s)*, is used seventy-nine times in the New Testament in the *New King James Version*, and, in seventy-five of the instances, to the best of my understanding, there is no possibility the term can be applied to the church. Nine instances are direct quotations from the Old Testament; in every one of them, the name *Israel* has precisely the same meaning in the New Testament as it has in the Old. And many of these seventy-five passages are applied in a sense that actually distinguishes Israel from the church. (Please see the appendix at the back of this book that lists the seventy-nine occurrences of the words *Israel* and *Israelite(s)* in the New Testament.)

Just four passages out of the seventy-nine, or about 5 percent, could possibly be applied to the church. I say "possibly" because I do not believe any of them should be. And in any case of translating or interpreting, if a certain usage is as small as 5 percent, there must be strong external, objective reasons for accepting that usage.

We will start by examining the four passages of Scripture in which the label *Israel* could (but I do not believe should) be interpreted as referring to the church. We will not examine the open-and-shut cases, where there is no possibility of any other interpretation, but the more difficult passages.

## MEMORY VERSES: ROMANS 11:11–12

[ ] Check here after memorizing the verses.

(Review verses from prior lessons daily.)

## QUESTIONS

### VERSES WHERE "ISRAEL" MIGHT MEAN "THE CHURCH"

#### FIRST TWO INSTANCES

1.  **First instance:** We start with a verse that we have already considered. Fill in the same word in both blanks to complete the phrase: *"For they are not all _____ who are of _____."* (Rom. 9:6) [1 point]

2.  **Second instance:** In Galatians 6:15–16, how is Israel described? [1 point]

    _____

### CONTINUATION OR COMPLETELY NEW RELATIONSHIP?

3.  The Gentiles* are like an unplowed field; they need a completely new relationship with God, because He has never related to them like He has related to Israel. By contrast, the Israelites, the plowed field, only had to be completed by acknowledging the Messiah. What does God declare was His work on *"this people,"* Israel? (Isa. 43:21) [1 point]

    _____

4.  According to Paul, what role does Jesus fulfill toward Israel *"to confirm the promises made to the fathers"*? (Rom. 15:8) [1 point]

    _____

5. Who is to glorify God for His mercy? (Rom. 15:9) [1 point]

_____

## THIRD AND FOURTH INSTANCES

6. Romans 2:28–29 defines what it means to be a true Jew. Complete the phrase:

   "...*but he is a Jew who is one* _____." (v. 29) [1 point]

7. **Third instance:** Of whom did Jesus say, *"Behold, an Israelite indeed, in whom is no deceit!"*? (John 1:47) [1 point]

_____

8. **Fourth instance:** Whom are we told to observe in 1 Corinthians 10:18? [1 point]

_____

## REASONS WHY THE CHURCH HAS NOT REPLACED ISRAEL

In the New Testament, *Israel* is never a synonym for *the church*, and Israel is certainly not replaced by the church. Israel is Israel, and the church is the church. At the same time, throughout the Bible, Israel is a type of the church. Much of what has happened to Israel, as Paul says in 1 Corinthians 10:11, is *"written for our admonition, upon whom the ends of the ages have come,"* so that we may not make the same mistakes. What has happened to Israel contains important lessons for us as Christians today.

Now, following our discussion of to whom the New Testament gives the title *Israel*, I will offer three reasons why I reject the teaching that the church has replaced Israel.

### #1: IT DISCREDITS SCRIPTURE

The Bible contains many clear, specific statements of what God says He will do—promises that will never be fulfilled if He has finally and forever set aside Israel. In other words, the Bible would no longer be a reliable book. Accepting such an idea would be an appalling reason for supporting any particular theology or theory. Answer the following questions regarding the promises of God to Israel:

9. What does God promise to do to *"the outcasts of Israel"*? (Isa. 11:12; see also v. 11) [1 point]

_____

10. Where will God cause His people Israel and Judah* to return to out of their captivity? (Jer. 30:3) [1 point]

_____

11. Jeremiah 31:10 states that it was God who scattered Israel. What further two things does God promise to do for Israel in this verse? [2 points]

   a. _____

   b. _____

12. Read Jeremiah 31:35–37 and then answer this question: have these ordinances of the sun, moon, stars, and sea ceased to exist, meaning that Israel has ceased to be a nation before God forever? [1 point]

_____

13. Jeremiah 32:37–41 speaks of what God has done and will do regarding Israel. In the last verse of this passage, what two things does God promise to do for Israel with all His heart and with all His soul?

   a. "I will _____ over them to do them good." [1 point]

   b. "I will assuredly _____ them in this land." [1 point]

14. The last example I will give of Israel's return and of God's response is from Ezekiel 20:40–44. What does God say will be a witness *"before the Gentiles"*? (v. 41) [1 point]

_____

If you want to study this topic further, read Ezekiel 36:22–28; Amos 9:14; and Zechariah 14:2–5, 8–11. As you do, ask yourself whether you believe that God has fulfilled these promises to Israel. If He hasn't yet done so, then we must believe that His faithfulness will continue to bring them all to completion.

### #2: IT DISCREDITS GOD'S FAITHFULNESS

15. Read Jeremiah 33:24–26 and then answer the following questions by either filling in the blanks or answering yes/no:

   a. In verse 24, God says, "They have _____ *My people, as if they should no more be a* _____ *before them.*" [2 points]

b.  Has God cast away the descendants of Jacob and David His servant? (vv. 25–26) [1 point]

_____

### #3: IT UNDERMINES THE SECURITY OF THE CHURCH

If God could replace Israel despite all the covenants and commitments He has made, then what guarantee is there that He would not replace the church as well?

If I believed that God was replacing Israel, then I would be looking over my shoulder all the time to see who was going to replace us! Because, if you had to consider which group has been less faithful, Israel or the church, it would be very hard to pick.

16.  Read Revelation 3:1–3 and then answer the questions below:

a.  Was John told to write to Israel or to people in the church (via an *angel,* or messenger)? (v. 1) [1 point]

_____

b.  Were these people spiritually alive or dead? (v. 1) [1 point]

_____

c.  What five things were they told to do? (vv. 2–3) [5 points]

i.  _____

ii.  _____

iii.  _____

iv.  _____

v.  _____

d.  What would happen if they did not watch for Jesus's return? (v. 3) [1 point]

_____

17.  The following questions are based on Revelation 3:14–16, which is Jesus's message to the last of the seven churches in Revelation:

a.  List the three names Jesus uses for Himself in verse 14: [3 points]

i.  _____

ii.  _____

iii.  _____

b. What was Jesus's description of the church of the Laodiceans? (v. 16) [1 point]

_____

## MEMORY WORK: ROMANS 11:11–12

Write out these verses from memory: [8 points]

_____

_____

_____

_____

_____

Check your answers on pages 217–19 in the "Correct Answers with Notes" section at the back of the book.

## PRAYER RESPONSE

Lord Jesus, as I read through all the questions and answers of this study, I am so grateful to You for Your faithfulness. Thank You for Your faithfulness to Israel, not just to Judah, who returned from the exile in Babylon, but also to the ten "lost tribes" who were exiled to Assyria, most of whom have not yet returned. Along with Jeremiah, I proclaim that *"He who scattered Israel will gather him, and keep him as a shepherd does his flock."*

I thank You, too, that Your ongoing faithfulness to Israel gives me confidence that You will fulfill all the promises to Your believing people. Amen.

# THE DESTINY OF ISRAEL AND THE CHURCH, PART 4: GOD'S MERCY

*Read Romans 9:14–33*

## INTRODUCTION

All of us, whether we are of Israel* or "the nations," need God's mercy. And yet none of us is able to earn that mercy; rather, we must receive it by faith. God is sovereign in granting His mercy, but, at the same time, He is uncompromising in His justice.

In lesson 5, we considered the passage in Romans 3 that tells us we were *"justified freely by [God's] grace through the redemption that is in Christ Jesus,…to demonstrate at the present time His righteousness, that He might be just and the justifier of the one who has faith in Jesus"* (Romans 3:24, 26). Christ's sacrifice on the cross was the price required to pay for our redemption, and, in that sacrifice, God made a way for all to enter into His mercy, His grace, and the kingdom of God.

All people serve God's purposes. We may think that only righteous* people are able to uphold God's purposes, but Scripture is clear that both the righteous and the wicked serve His purposes. God molds each person as a vessel according to His plans. As His vessels of mercy, we are designed to bring glory to the Lord.

## MEMORY VERSES: ROMANS 9:30–31

[ ] Check here after memorizing the verses.

(Review verses from prior lessons daily.)

## QUESTIONS

In the context of God's sovereignty, His choice, and the "children of promise" that we have explored in Romans 9:1–13, we will continue in chapter 9 of Romans, starting at verse 14.

### NO ONE CAN EARN GOD'S MERCY

1. Paul poses another of his anticipated objections from his readers regarding God's election. Is God unfair in His choice of some people over others? (Rom. 9:14–15) [1 point]

   _____

2. Can people do anything to force God to show them mercy? (Rom. 9:16) [1 point]

   _____

3. Based on your growing understanding of living under law* and the invitation to live under God's grace, would you want to be judged against the law? [Thought question; no points. See Derek's note for number 3 under "Lesson 19 Answers."]

   _____

4. What are our wages for sin? (Rom. 6:23) [1 point]

   _____

### GOD USES THE WICKED

5. What has the Lord made for the day of doom? (Prov. 16:4) [1 point]

   _____

6. God raises up opposition to Himself for His own purposes. Whom does Paul identify as an example of this? (Rom. 9:17) [1 point]

   _____

7. What two objectives did God have when He raised up this famous ruler against Himself and His people, Israel? (Rom. 9:17) [2 points]

    a. _____

    b. _____

8. In Genesis 15:7, God promised Abraham that He would give him the land of Canaan. But He explained in verse 16 that it would not be until the fourth generation. What reason did God give for the delay? [1 point]

    _____

9. What two couplets (the same in both instances) complete Romans 9:18?

    "Therefore He has mercy on whom _____ _____, and whom _____ _____ He hardens." [1 point]

## GOD MOLDS EACH VESSEL

10. What did God do with the dust of the ground before imparting the breath of life into man? (Gen. 2:7) [1 point]

    _____

11. Who has power over the clay? (Rom. 9:21) [1 point]

    _____

12. What are two reasons why God patiently endures wickedness? (Rom. 9:22) [2 points]

    a. _____

    b. _____

13. In Romans 9:22–23, Paul reveals two kinds of vessels that have been prepared for two different purposes:

    a. "Vessels of _____ prepared for _____." (v. 22) [2 points]

b. *"Vessels of* _____*,…prepared beforehand for* _____*."* (v. 23) [2 points]

## MERCY FOR BOTH JEWS* AND GENTILES*

Romans 9:23–26 says that God extends mercy not to Jews alone, and not to Gentiles alone, but to both Jews and Gentiles.

14. In Romans 9:25–26, Paul references the prophet Hosea. Answer the questions below to gain a fuller understanding of Paul's meaning:

   a. What was the name of Hosea and Gomer's son? (Hos. 1:4) [1 point]

   _____

   b. What was the name of their daughter? (Hos. 1:6) [1 point]

   _____

   c. What was the name of their second son? (Hos. 1:9) [1 point]

   _____

   d. What was Hosea to declare to his brethren? (Hos. 2:1) [1 point]

   _____

   e. What was Hosea to declare to his sisters? (Hos. 2:1) [1 point]

   _____

   List the three steps of Israel's restoration that God will bring to pass: (Hos. 2:23)

   a. *"Then I will* _____ *her for Myself in the earth."* [1 point]

   b. *"And I will have* _____ *on her who had not obtained mercy."* [1 point]

   c. *"Then I will say to those who were not My people, 'You are* _____ _____*!'"* [1 point]

15. According to Paul's quote from Isaiah, what will be saved? (Rom. 9:27) [1 point]

   _____

16. In Romans 9:30–33, Paul analyzes the differences between the Gentiles and the people of Israel. Circle the correct answer for the following options: [6 points]

|  | The Gentiles | Israel |
| --- | --- | --- |
| Pursued righteousness*? | a. Yes/No | b. Yes/No |
| Attained righteousness? | c. Yes/No | d. Yes/No |
| Means of righteousness: | e. Faith/law | f. Faith/law |

17. Why did the Israelites fail to attain righteousness? (Rom. 9:32) [1 point]

_____

18. In Romans 9:33, when Paul talks about the *"stumbling stone,"* he is quoting from Isaiah 8:14, as well as Isaiah 28:16, and he is referring to the Messiah. In Isaiah, people are given two options regarding Jesus's relationship to them, depending on whether they live by faith or by law:

   a. *"He will be as a _____."* (Isa. 8:14) [1 point]

   b. *"But a stone of stumbling and a rock of _____ to both the houses of Israel."* (Isa. 8:14) [1 point]

19. In 1 Corinthians 1:23, Paul says that he and his fellow workers preach Christ crucified, and that there are two consequences for those who do not believe: [2 points]

   a. To the Jews:

_____

   b. To the Greeks:

_____

## MEMORY WORK: ROMANS 9:30–31

Write out these verses from memory: [8 points]

_____

_____

_____

_____

_____

Check your answers on pages 220–22 in the "Correct Answers with Notes" section at the back of the book.

## PRAYER RESPONSE

Heavenly Father, we all need Your mercy, whether we are Jew or Gentile. I marvel as I meditate on Your Word in Romans 9:23–24, which tells us why You endured with such patience the vessels of wrath: "*that* [You] *might make known the riches of* [Your] *glory on the vessels of mercy, which* [You] *had prepared beforehand for glory, even us whom* [You] *called.*" Help me to begin to understand and appreciate that calling, and to live a life worthy of it, all for Your glory.

Thank You, Lord, for Your mercy. It is very clear to me that I do not deserve it and that I could never earn it, but I am so grateful for it. Mold me according to Your pleasure and purposes so that I may glorify You as a vessel of honor and mercy. Amen.

# THE DESTINY OF ISRAEL AND THE CHURCH, PART 5: SALVATION THROUGH MESSIAH

*Read Romans 10*

## INTRODUCTION

The theme of the tenth chapter of Romans follows naturally on the theme Paul has already been discussing: righteousness* based on faith versus righteousness based on law*.

Paul begins with a plea for Israel's salvation. Although what is going on in the land of Israel* today is exciting, with many prophecies being fulfilled, we must bear in mind that the sole provision that can meet the need of the people of Israel is salvation through their Messiah, Jesus Christ.

## MEMORY VERSES: ROMANS 10:12–13

[ ] Check here after memorizing the verses.

(Review verses from prior lessons daily.)

## QUESTIONS

### RIGHTEOUSNESS BY FAITH OR BY LAW?

1. What is the most important prayer we can pray on behalf of the people of Israel? (Rom. 10:1) [1 point]

_____

2. Paul stands witness that the people of Israel are zealous for God, but what do they lack? (Rom. 10:2) [1 point]

_____

3. In their ignorance and self-righteousness, what have they failed to do? (Rom. 10:3) [1 point]

_____

4. When Messiah came, did He come to remove, or to destroy, the Law of Moses* completely? (Matt. 5:17) [1 point]

_____

5. To what aspect of law did Jesus bring an end for everyone who believes? (Rom. 10:4) [1 point]

_____

   I suggest that you go back and review stage 3, "Accountability to God," of the "Seven Purposes of the Law of Moses" found in lesson 4, because when we are confronted with the fact that Jesus has fulfilled the law, we may be tempted to put the law aside completely. However, the law has very specific purposes, all of which have relevance to our understanding and appreciation of God's plan of redemption for Israel and the church.

## TWO WAYS TO RIGHTEOUSNESS

6. How much of the law does one have to keep in order to be made righteous*? (Rom. 10:5; James 2:10) [1 point]

_____

7. What is the only alternative to what Paul calls *"the righteousness which is of the law"* (Romans 10:5)? (v. 6) [1 point]

_____

8.  Which two parts of the body are mentioned three times each in Romans 10:8–10? [2 points]

    a. _____

    b. _____

9.  What does Paul say that he and others preach? (Rom. 10:8) [1 point]

    _____

10. If you believe the Bible and receive and accept its message, then the way to get it into your heart is by way of your mouth. Complete the phrases below that explain the conditions of your salvation: (Rom. 10:9)

    *"That **if you**...*

    a.  _____ *with your* _____ *the Lord Jesus* [or Jesus as Lord]... [2 points]

    b.  *and* _____ *in your* _____ *that God has raised Him from the dead, you will be saved."* [2 points]

11. Read Romans 10:10 once more and then complete the statements below:

    a.  Belief (or faith) is the path to _____. [1 point]

    b.  Confession is the path to _____. [1 point]

## WHOEVER BELIEVES

12. Is God's plan of salvation restricted to Jews*? (Rom. 10:11–13) [1 point]

    _____

13. To whom is the Lord rich? (Rom. 10:12) [1 point]

    _____

14. Fill in the blanks below to see how God describes the gospel and those who take it to the unreached:

    *"How _____ are the feet of those who preach the gospel of*

    *_____, who bring _____ tidings of _____ things!"* (Rom. 10:15)
    [4 points]

15. Does everyone receive the gospel and obey it? (Rom. 10:16) [1 point]

    _____

16. Has everyone had a witness to God's eternal power and divine nature? (Rom. 1:18–20; 10:18) [1 point]

    _____

## PROVOKING JEALOUSY

17. In Romans 10:19, Paul quotes Moses once more, this time from Deuteronomy 32:21. Read both verses and then answer the questions below:

    a. Who was provoked first, God or Israel? (Deut. 32:21) [1 point]

    _____

    b. What practice of the Israelites started the provocation? (Deut. 32:21) [1 point]

    _____

    c. To what did God provoke Israel? (Deut. 32:21; Rom. 10:19) [1 point]

    _____

    d. By what did God move Israel to anger? (Deut. 32:21; Rom. 10:19) [1 point]

    _____

18. In response to the Israelites' widespread disbelief in their Messiah, Paul quotes a prophecy from Isaiah written about seven hundred years before Jesus. Fill in the blanks:

    a. *"Isaiah is very bold and says [of the Gentiles]: 'I was _____ by those who did not seek Me; I was made _____ to those who did not ask for Me.'"* (Rom. 10:20; see also Isaiah 65:1) [2 points]

b. *"But to Israel he* [Isaiah, speaking on God's behalf] *says: 'All day long I have stretched out My hands to a* _____ *and* _____ *people.'"* (Rom. 10:21; see also Isaiah 65:2) [2 points]

## MEMORY WORK: ROMANS 10:12–13

Write out these verses from memory: [8 points]

_____

_____

_____

_____

Check your answers on pages 223–25 in the "Correct Answers with Notes" section at the back of the book.

## PRAYER RESPONSE

Heavenly Father, as it says to do in Romans 10:9, I confess with my mouth the Lord Jesus and believe in my heart that God has raised Him from the dead, so I will be saved. *"For with the heart one believes unto righteousness, and with the mouth confession is made unto salvation"* (Romans 10:10).

Thank You, Lord, for the righteousness that has been revealed apart from law. I join Paul in his heart's desire and prayer to God for Israel, that they may be saved. As a coheir with Christ, I ask of You, Father, as Psalm 2:8 expresses, that You will give us the nations as an inheritance and the ends of the earth for our possession. Empower me by Your Holy Spirit and give me the courage to be a witness, as You call me to be in Acts 1:8, to the mercy and righteousness that I have received so that others may enjoy freedom in Christ. In His name, I pray. Amen.

# THE DESTINY OF ISRAEL AND THE CHURCH, PART 6: ALL ISRAEL WILL BE SAVED

*Read Romans 11*

## INTRODUCTION

Romans 10 ends on a low point where Paul reminds his readers of the following portion of Isaiah's prophecy: *"But to Israel he says: 'All day long I have stretched out My hands to a disobedient and contrary people'"* (verse 21). As we turn to Romans 11, the outlook begins to brighten, and Paul encourages us that Israel's rejection of the Messiah was neither total nor final. God has reserved a remnant, whom He has foreknown, by His sovereignty and grace.

Paul goes on to give a beautiful picture of Israel* as a cultivated olive tree that has had some of its natural (Israelite) branches broken off so that Gentile branches could be grafted in to become *"a partaker of the root and fatness of the olive tree"* (Romans 11:17).

In the New Testament, a "mystery" is something that has been kept secret by God but is now revealed. So, the mysteries Paul unfolds in his teaching are no longer mysterious but rather those secrets that God has seen fit to reveal to us in the church age. In Romans 11:25–26, Paul reveals a mystery that *"blindness in part has happened to Israel until the fullness of the Gentiles has come in. And so all Israel will be saved."*

Paul ends the chapter and this section of Romans with the only fitting response to God's unfathomable wisdom: worship.

## MEMORY VERSES: ROMANS 11:25–27

[ ] Check here after memorizing the verses.

(Review verses from prior lessons daily.)

## HAS GOD REJECTED ISRAEL?

1. Paul begins Romans 11 with an important question in the light of chapters 9 and 10: *"Has God cast away His people* [Israel]*?"* Read Romans 11:1 and then circle the correct answer to this question: Yes/No [1 point]

   _____

2. Whom does Paul use as an example that God has not cast away His people? (Rom. 11:1) [1 point]

   _____

3. Which of His people has God not cast away? (Rom. 11:2) [1 point]

   _____

4. Which of the prophets does Paul mention as having made intercession *against* Israel? (Rom. 11:2) [1 point]

   _____

5. Was the prophet correct when he said, as we read in 1 Kings 19:10, 14 and Romans 11:3, *"I alone am left"*? (1 Kings 19:18; Rom. 11:4) [1 point]

   _____

6. As in the story from 1 Kings 19, what remains at the present time? (Rom. 11:5) [1 point]

   _____

7. Do you think that the phrase *"at this present time"* in Romans 11:5, which was written nearly two thousand years ago, is still relevant today? [Thought question; no points. See Derek's note for number 7 under "Lesson 21 Answers."]

   _____

8.  Is it possible to earn grace through works? (Rom. 11:6) [1 point]

    _____

9.  May we boast about grace? (Eph. 2:8–9) [1 point]

    _____

10. In Hebrews 4:16, God's throne is described as being the throne of what? [1 point]

    _____

11. What was the starting place of God's relationship with Abraham? Fill in the blank to complete the phrase:

    *"For I have* _____ *him…."* (Gen. 18:19) [1 point]

## A REJECTION OF GOD'S TRUTH

12. In Romans 11:7–9, Paul states numerous negative results of Israel's unfaithfulness. What is the common condition mentioned in all three verses? [1 point]

    _____

13. After Saul, the first king of Israel, rejected God's revealed purpose and turned against it, an exchange took place, as recorded in 1 Samuel 16:14. Fill in the blanks to complete these phrases:

    a. *"The* _____ *of the* _____ *departed from Saul."* [2 points]
    b. *"A distressing* _____ *from the* _____ *troubled him."* [2 points]

14. Second Thessalonians 2:9–10 describes the coming of the *"lawless one"* (the Antichrist). What ultimately opens the way for his coming? (v. 10) [1 point]

    _____

15. What will God send to those who do not believe the truth but take pleasure in unrighteousness? (2 Thess. 2:11–12) [1 point]

_____

## SALVATION FOR THE GENTILES*

16. In Romans 11:11, Paul asks this question regarding Israel:

    _"Have they _____ that they should _____?"_ [2 points]

17. What result of Israel's fall has God used to provoke the Jewish people to jealousy? (Rom. 11:11) [1 point]

_____

18. Before Jesus's death, burial, and resurrection, to whom did Jesus send His twelve disciples? (Matt. 10:5–6) [1 point]

_____

19. After His resurrection, of whom did Jesus commission His disciples to go and make disciples? (Matt. 28:18–19) [1 point]

_____

20. In the parable of the wicked vinedressers in Matthew 21:33–46, Jesus tells His Jewish listeners that the kingdom of God will be removed from them. Whom does He say will receive this kingdom? (v. 43) [1 point]

_____

## RESTORING THE KINGDOM TO ISRAEL

21. What was the last question the disciples asked Jesus before His ascension? (Acts 1:6) [1 point]

_____

22. In Acts 1:7–8, Jesus makes three important statements in His response to the disciples' question. Fill in the blanks to complete these statements:

    a. *"It is not for you to know _____ or _____ which the Father has put in His own authority."* (v. 7) [2 points]

    b. *"But you shall receive _____ when the Holy Spirit has come upon you."* (v. 8) [1 point]

    c. *"And you shall be _____ to Me in Jerusalem…, and to the end of the earth."* (v. 8) [1 point]

23. Jesus says in Matthew 24:14, *"This gospel of the kingdom will be preached in all the world as a witness to all the nations…."* What will happen then? [1 point]

    _____

24. Will Israel's restoration have a good effect on the world and the Gentiles? (Rom. 11:12) [1 point]

    _____

25. For what reason did Paul magnify his ministry and try to provoke jealousy in his fellow Israelites? (Rom. 11:13–14) [1 point]

    _____

26. If Israel's being cast away enabled the world to be reconciled to God, what will their reconciliation bring about? (Rom. 11:15) [1 point]

    _____

## GENTILES GRAFTED IN

27. In Romans 11:16, Paul compares Israel to both a ceremony from the law of Moses* and an olive tree. Fill in the blanks to complete these phrases:

    a. *"If the _____ is holy, the _____ is also holy."* [2 points]

    b. *"And if the _____ is holy, so are the _____."* [2 points]

28. What term does Paul use to describe the Gentiles who were grafted in where branches of Israel were broken off? (Rom. 11:17) [1 point]

_____

29. Are Gentiles free to boast that they were grafted in at the expense of some of the branches of Israel? (Rom. 11:17–18) [1 point]

_____

30. Despite their having been grafted in by faith, what might happen to the "wild olive branches," as happened to the "natural branches," if they cease standing in faith? (Rom. 11:19–21) [1 point]

_____

31. Romans 11:22 reminds us of two sides to God: [2 points]

a. _____

b. _____

## ISRAEL GRAFTED IN AGAIN

32. What will happen to the natural branches of Israel who were formerly broken off if they come to faith? (Rom. 11:23) [1 point]

_____

33. What phrase does Paul use to describe the method by which wild olive branches are grafted into a cultivated olive tree? (Rom. 11:24) [1 point]

_____

34. In Romans 11:25, Paul implies that knowing and understanding the mystery of Israel's partial blindness will keep us from being wise in our own opinions. This blindness will last until what happens? [1 point]

_____

35. When the fullness of the Gentiles has come in, what proportion of Israel will be saved? (Rom. 11:26) [1 point]

_____

36. Paul quotes from Isaiah 59:20–21 when he says, *"The Deliverer will come out of Zion, and He will turn away ungodliness from Jacob"* (Romans 11:26). On what basis does the Deliverer come and take away Israel's sins? (Rom. 11:27) [1 point]

_____

37. What word does Paul use to describe the gifts and calling of God? (Rom. 11:29) [1 point]

_____

38. What blessing does God seek to bring to Israel through the mercy that He has shown to the Gentiles? (Rom. 11:30–31) [1 point]

_____

39. Who committed both the Gentiles and Israel to disobedience, *"that He might have mercy on all"*? (Rom. 11:32) [1 point]

_____

## OF HIM, THROUGH HIM, AND TO HIM

40. How does Paul describe God's judgments? (Rom. 11:33) [1 point]

_____

41. Paul closes the eleventh chapter of Romans with this glorious statement about the Lord: *"For of Him and through Him and to Him are all things"* (Romans 11:36). What belongs to the Lord forever? (v. 36) [1 point]

_____

## MEMORY WORK: ROMANS 11:25-27

Write out these verses from memory: [12 points]

_____

_____

_____

_____

_____

_____

_____

Check your answers on pages 226–30 in the "Correct Answers with Notes" section at the back of the book.

## PRAYER RESPONSE

Thank You, Father, that You have not rejected Israel forever. I have come to see the outworking of Your plans more clearly:

+   The Messiah came to Israel, but many of the Jewish people did not believe.

+   The elect received Him, but the rest were blinded.

+   Through Israel's fall, and to provoke the Israelites to jealousy, salvation came to the Gentiles.

+   Israel's being "cast away" meant the reconciliation of the world (nations).

+   Israel's blindness (in part) will continue until the fullness of the Gentiles has been brought in.

+   Israel's acceptance and regrafting into the olive tree will be *"life from the dead"* (Romans 11:15)!

Lord, when I consider the outworking of Your plans, I respond as Paul did—in worship:

*Oh, the depth of the riches both of the wisdom and knowledge of God! How unsearchable are His judgments and His ways past finding out! "For who has known the mind of the LORD? Or who has become His counselor?" "Or who has first given to Him and it shall be repaid to him?" For of Him and through Him and to Him are all things, to whom be glory forever. Amen.* (Romans 11:33–36)

# LIVING OUT YOUR FAITH UNDER PRESSURE, PART 1

*Read Romans 12*

## INTRODUCTION

Most of us who are trying to put our Christian faith into action would agree that, today, we are under all sorts of pressure—social pressure, mental pressure, emotional pressure, and spiritual pressure. Putting our faith into practice is where our faith is tested. We can say amen to the glorious theology of the first eleven chapters of Romans, but, again, living it out is where our faith will be proved or disproved. Will it stand the test?

This is true of our application of all the Scriptures. We cannot find abstract, intellectual theology anywhere in the Bible. God is not interested in it. He is interested in life and in the way we live. The Word of God presents truth, and then, with assistance from our Helper, the Holy Spirit, we are shown how it relates to the way we live. All the truths of the Bible are designed to help us live godly, victorious, fruitful lives. If we have a lot of knowledge, even some higher education, but are not living godly, fruitful lives, then we are frustrating God's purposes.

## MEMORY VERSES: ROMANS 12:1–2

[ ] Check here after memorizing the verses.

(Review verses from prior lessons daily.)

## QUESTIONS

### A LIVING SACRIFICE

1.  Why does Paul use the word *"therefore"* near the beginning of Romans 12:1? [Thought question and review from lesson 12; no points. See Derek's note for number 1 under "Lesson 22 Answers."]

2. What part of ourselves are we to present to God as our act of reasonable service toward Him? (Rom. 12:1) [1 point]

_____

3. In Old Testament times, animal sacrifices were slain, and then their bodies were placed on the altar. What kind of sacrifice is God now asking of *us?* (Rom. 12:1) [1 point]

_____

4. What has the Lord done to those who are godly? (Ps. 4:3) [1 point]

_____

5. In Romans 12:2, Paul presents three related statements:

   a. *"Do not be _____ to this world* [age]." [1 point]

   b. *"But be _____ by the renewing of your mind."* [1 point]

   c. *"That you may prove what is that _____ and _____ and _____ will of God."* [3 points]

## SERVING GOD APPROPRIATELY

6. In Romans 12:2, we saw that God wants our thinking transformed. In verse 3, Paul contrasts two kinds of thinking:

   a. We are not to think more _____ of ourselves than we ought to think. [1 point]

   b. Rather, we should think _____. [1 point]

   c. Why? Because God has dealt to each of us a measure of _____. [1 point]

7. In Romans 12:4–5, we are introduced to the concept of ourselves as believers who have been set apart to God (a concept we also saw in Psalm 4:3) and who are part of something bigger than ourselves.

   a. What do the *"many members"* come together to form? (v. 4) [1 point]

_____

b. Do all members have the same function? (v. 4) [1 point]

_____

c. Although there are many believers, in whom are we brought together as one organism? (v. 5) [1 point]

_____

8. What do we have according to the grace that is given to us? (Rom. 12:6) [1 point]

_____

9. In Romans 12:6–8, Paul talks about seven "grace" gifts, or *charismata*. The list of charismata in Romans 12 is not comprehensive. We find other gifts listed in 1 Corinthians 12 and Ephesians 4. I count twenty-two different gifts in all that I call charismata.[1] Below, list the gifts from Romans 12 in the order in which they appear:

a. _____ (v. 6) [1 point]

b. _____ (v. 7) [1 point]

c. _____ (v. 7) [1 point]

d. _____ (v. 8) [1 point]

e. _____ (v. 8) [1 point]

f. _____ (v. 8) [1 point]

g. _____ _____ (two words) (v. 8) [1 point]

10. As we discussed, in other writings, Paul mentions additional types of charismata, while also including some gifts previously mentioned. Below, list only the *additional* charismata in the order in which they appear (check the above list from Romans to avoid repetition):

a. The/a word of _____ (1 Cor. 12:8) [1 point]

b. The/a word of _____ (1 Cor. 12:8) [1 point]

c. _____ (1 Cor.12:9) [1 point]

d. Gifts of _____ (1 Cor. 12:9; 28) [1 point]

e. The working(s) of _____ (1 Cor. 12:10; see also v. 28) [1 point]

1. For further teaching on spiritual gifts, please see Derek Prince, *The Gifts of the Spirit* (New Kensington, PA: Whitaker House, 2007).

f. Discerning of _____ (1 Cor. 12:10) [1 point]

g. Different kinds/varieties of _____ (1 Cor. 12:10; 28) [1 point]

h. The _____ of tongues (1 Cor. 12:10) [1 point]

i. _____ (ministry role) (1 Cor. 12:28; Eph. 4:11) [1 point]

j. _____ (ministry role) (1 Cor. 12:28; Eph. 4:11) [1 point]

k. _____ (ministry role) (1 Cor. 12:28) [1 point]

l. _____ (1 Cor. 12:28) [1 point]

m. _____ (1 Cor.12:28) [1 point]

n. _____ (ministry role) (Eph. 4:11) [1 point]

o. _____ (ministry role) (Eph. 4:11) [1 point]

## FRUITS THAT GROW FROM THE ROOT OF LOVE

In lesson 7, we considered the theme of God's unconditional love, and, in lesson 12, we studied the nature of love. In this lesson, we return to the subject of love because it is so very important to all that we do as Christians.

11. What must we do without hypocrisy? (Rom. 12:9) [1 point]

_____

12. I love the translation of 1 Timothy 1:5 in the *New American Standard Bible* (NASB). It begins, *"But the goal of our instruction is love."* List the three sources of love mentioned in this verse (the NKJV and NASB are almost identical in this portion):

a. From a pure _____ [1 point]

b. From a good _____ [1 point]

c. From sincere _____ [1 point]

Paul says that love must be *"without hypocrisy"* (Romans 12:9), or *"sincere"* (NIV). And everything else in this chapter flows out of love. This is not a set of rules that you have to follow; it is guidance for how to direct the love God has put in your heart. Can you see the difference?

Suppose you are trying to water a big garden using only a watering can, and you have to keep going back to a faucet to refill it. You are walking back and forth and getting hot, sweaty, and tired. You are not making good progress. But then somebody says to you, "Why don't you try a hose? Attach it to the faucet, and then all you have to carry is the hose." When you have the hose, you simply need to know where to direct the water.

That is what Paul is teaching in Romans 12—how to direct the love that God has put into your heart. In the verses that follow, Paul gives twelve suggestions for how to direct God's love—as well as the different "crops" you can water—when you have the hose. If you have no hose, you have nothing to direct. In that case, the first thing you need to do is to get a hose and attach it to the faucet. In other words, do not try to lead the Christian life as a set of wearisome religious rules but from love.

13. First direction: *"Let love be without hypocrisy. Abhor what is _____. Cling to what is _____."* (Rom. 12:9) [2 points]

14. Second direction: *"Be kindly affectionate to one another with brotherly _____, in honor giving _____ to one another."* (Rom. 12:10) [2 points]

15. Third direction: Which two phrases in Romans 12:11 are another way of saying, "Don't be lazy"? [2 points]

    a. _____

    b. _____

16. Whom are we called to serve with a fervent spirit? (Rom. 12:11) [1 point]

    _____

17. Fourth direction: *"Rejoicing in _____, _____ in tribulation, continuing steadfastly in _____."* (Rom. 12:12) [3 points]

18. Fifth direction: *"Distributing to the needs of the _____, given to _____."* (Rom. 12:13) [2 points]

19. Sixth direction: *"Bless those who _____ you; bless and do not _____."* (Rom. 12:14) [2 points]

20. Seventh direction: *"Rejoice with those who _____, and weep with those who _____."* (Rom. 12:15) [2 points]

21. Eighth direction: *"Be of the same mind toward one another. Do not set your _____ on high things, but associate with the _____. Do not be _____ in your own opinion."* (Rom. 12:16) [3 points]

22. Ninth direction: *"Repay no one _____ for _____."* (same word) (Rom. 12:17) [1 point]

23. Tenth direction: *"If it is _____, as much as depends on you, live _____ with all men."* (Rom. 12:18) [2 points]

24. Eleventh direction: *"Beloved, do not avenge yourselves, but rather give place to _____; for it is written, '_____ is Mine, I will repay,' says the Lord."* (Rom. 12:19) [2 points]

25. Twelfth direction: *"Do not be overcome by _____, but overcome evil with _____."* (Rom. 12:21) [2 points]

## MEMORY WORK: ROMANS 12:1–2

Write out these verses from memory: [8 points]

_____

_____

_____

_____

_____

Check your answers on pages 231–36 in the "Correct Answers with Notes" section at the back of the book.

## PRAYER RESPONSE

For the prayers in this lesson, I would like to teach you one way of studying the Bible and applying it to your life. Ask the Holy Spirit to highlight the instructions in Romans 12 so you can personalize them into proclamations. For example, you may read the first two verses and come up with the following:

+ By God's mercy, I present my body as a living sacrifice, holy, acceptable to God, which is my reasonable service.

+ I will not be conformed to this world, but I will be transformed by the renewing of my mind so that I may prove what is the good and acceptable and perfect will of God.

There are many possible statements to write out, and some of them may trigger a negative response in you. If that happens, it is the Holy Spirit working and saying, "Here is something we need to work on together." Perhaps you write out from verse 14, "I will bless those who persecute me," but you feel an inward tremor because you have been, or are currently, undergoing painful persecution.

Ask the Lord to show you what is going on in your heart and to reveal His higher way (see Isaiah 55:9) in the situation. He wants to take away the evil and give you a good gift in its place. In the matter of persecution, He may highlight that your desire is for vengeance but that He wants to give you love for your enemies.

Each of us is unique, so this is an exercise in listening to the voice of the Holy Spirit and being transformed by the renewing of our minds as we offer our bodies as living sacrifices. Now it is your turn to write out the statements from Romans 12 with the help of the Holy Spirit.

# LIVING OUT YOUR FAITH UNDER PRESSURE, PART 2

*Read Romans 13*

## INTRODUCTION

This lesson is the second part of "Living Out Your Faith Under Pressure." We continue to look at how we should live in the light of the invitation of grace we have accepted through the gospel. The first part of Romans 13, which includes verses 1–7, discusses how to relate to secular governmental authority—an important but delicate subject. There are many divergent views among Christians regarding this topic. I will do my best to bring out what the Scripture says and leave it to the Holy Spirit to apply it to our hearts.

In the second part of Romans 13, which is verses 8–10, Paul provides directions for releasing the love of God, which He has placed in our hearts. If you do not have God's love in your heart, you will not be able to release it. It all starts with love. I hope you agree that it will be refreshing and beautiful in this section to come back to the theme of love.

Then, in verses 11–14, we move on to Paul's reminder to live in eager anticipation of Christ's return. Personally, I get excited when I think about the Lord's return. That is what motivates me to live the Christian life. We are going to see Jesus in His glory. We are going to see His kingdom established on earth. That is the only solution to humanity's innumerable problems.

Remember, our motivation for holy living is not a set of rules but the fact that we are going to meet Jesus, whom we love—and we need to be ready. As Christians, we will all stand before His judgment seat to have our service for Jesus in this life assessed. This judgment is for those whose names are in the Lamb's Book of Life and is not for condemnation.

## MEMORY VERSES: ROMANS 13:8, 10

[ ] Check here after memorizing the verses.

(Review verses from prior lessons daily.)

# QUESTIONS

## RELATING TO GOVERNMENTAL AUTHORITY

1. Read 1 Peter 2:13–17 and then answer the following questions:

   a. What should our position be toward every ordinance of man? (v. 13) [1 point]

   _____

   b. For whose sake should we take that position? (v. 13) [1 point]

   _____

   c. What does Peter say we should do, according to God's will, to silence the ignorance of foolish men? (v. 15) [1 point]

   _____

   d. In 1 Peter 2:16, what is the negative opportunity that Peter warns us against? [1 point]

   _____

   e. Fill in the blanks to complete the conclusion Peter comes to in verse 17: "_____ all people. _____ the brotherhood. _____ God. _____ the king." [4 points]

2. Paul's commentary on our attitude toward governing authorities is much the same as Peter's. In Romans 13:1, what does Paul tell us...

   a. ...that every soul should be toward the governing authorities? [1 point]

   _____

   b. ...about the source of all authority? [1 point]

   _____

   c. ...concerning who appoints those in authority? [1 point]

   _____

3. Who has all authority in heaven and on earth? (Matt. 28:18) [1 point]

   _____

4.  In Colossians 2:9, we read, *"In [Jesus] dwells all the fullness of the Godhead bodily."* The next verse goes on to say that we *"are complete in Him, who is the* _____ *of all principality and power."* (v. 10) [1 point]

5.  Since God is the source of all authority, what will those who resist that authority bring on themselves? (Rom. 13:2) [1 point]

    _____

6.  What are we to do to receive praise from rulers? (Rom. 13:3) [1 point]

    _____

7.  In Romans 13:4, what two-word phrase does Paul use twice to describe the authority God has appointed—either for our good or to execute wrath? [1 point]

    _____

8.  In verse 5, Paul gives us two reasons why we must be subject to God-ordained authority:

    *"Not only because of* _____ *but also for* _____ *' sake."* [2 points]

9.  Considering what government does for us, what does Paul say is the obvious requirement? (v. 6) [1 point]

    _____

10. Verse 7 concludes that we should *"render"* (give) to all what is due to them. List the four things Paul mentions as being due: [4 points]

    a. _____

    b. _____

    c. _____

    d. _____

# PRAYING FOR THE GOVERNMENT

11. What order of importance does Paul give to making supplications, praying, interceding, and giving thanks for *"kings and all who are in authority"*? (1 Tim. 2:1–2) [1 point]

_____

12. Paul goes on to give the primary reason why we want good government:

*"That we may lead a* _____ *and* _____ *life in all*

_____ *and* _____*."* (1 Tim. 2:2) [4 points]

13. What does God desire, which good government can help enable? (1 Tim. 2:3–4) [1 point]

_____

# UNGODLY GOVERNMENT

We will now explore what happens when an ungodly or wicked leader or even a persecutor is occupying the position of authority. In dealing with ungodly government, Jesus is our pattern. He faced Pontius Pilate, who questioned Him about His claim to be a king.

14. How did Christ say His servants would respond to threats if His kingdom were of this world? (John 18:36) [1 point]

_____

15. Will God's kingdom be established by earthly might or power? (Zech. 4:6) [1 point]

_____

16. In John 19:10, who says that he has power (or authority) to crucify Jesus? [1 point]

_____

17. In His response, where does Jesus say that this ruler's authority emanates from? (John 19:11) [1 point]

_____

18. In Acts 5:17–42, we read the story of how the apostles were imprisoned by the high priest *"and all who were with him* [the Sadducees]" (v. 17).

    a. Who opened the prison doors and brought the apostles out? (v. 19) [1 point]

       _____

    b. Where did he tell them to go in order to *"speak to the people all the words of this life"?* (v. 20) [1 point]

       _____

    c. When they were brought back before the council and accused of disobedience, how did Peter and the other apostles answer? Fill in the blank: [1 point]

       *"We ought to* _____ *God rather than men."* (v. 29)

    d. The apostles were following the instruction of the angel, but also a specific command from Jesus. What was that command? (Mark 16:15) [1 point]

       _____

    e. What did the Jewish leaders do to the apostles before commanding them not to speak in the name of Jesus and releasing them? (Acts 5:40) [1 point]

       _____

    f. Why did the apostles rejoice? (Acts 5:41) [1 point]

       _____

    g. Did they cease teaching and preaching Jesus as the Christ following their treatment by ungodly authority? (Acts 5:42) [1 point]

       _____

19. By what three ways do we overcome the accuser of the brethren and cause him to be cast down from the heavenlies? (Rev. 12:11; see also vv. 7–10) [3 points]

    a. _____

    b. _____

    c. _____

## THE RIGHTEOUS* REQUIREMENT OF THE LAW*

20.  What is the one debt that is acceptable? (Rom. 13:8) [1 point]

_____

21.  What do we fulfill when we love others? (Rom. 13:8) [1 point]

_____

22.  According to Romans 13:9–10, what does Paul state is the fulfillment of the law? [1 point]

_____

23.  How are we required to love one another? (John 13:34) [1 point]

_____

## THE LAW OF LIBERTY

24.  What *"perfect law"* does James mention in James 1:25? [1 point]

_____

25.  In James 2:8, what name does James give to the law *"You shall love your neighbor as yourself"*? [1 point]

_____

## KNOWING THE TIME

26.  Who is the son who causes shame? (Prov. 10:5) [1 point]

_____

27.  What did the sons of Issachar have an understanding of? (1 Chron. 12:32) [1 point]

_____

28. Paul assumes that we know the times we are living in. What does he tell us to do in response? (Rom. 13:11) [1 point]

_____

29. In the closing verses of Romans 13, Paul again says, *"Therefore…."* (v. 12), so we must ask, "What is it there for?" He tells us it is there because *"the night is far spent, the day is at hand"* (v. 12), and he also gives us some instructions. Fill in the blanks to complete these instructions:

   a. *"Let us cast off the works of _____."* (v. 12) [1 point]

   b. *"Let us put on the armor of _____."* (v. 12) [1 point]

   c. *"Let us _____ properly, as in the day, not in revelry and drunkenness, not in lewdness and lust, not in strife and envy."* (v. 13) [1 point]

   d. *"Put on the _____ _____ _____, and make no provision for the flesh, to fulfill its lusts."* (v. 14) [3 points]

30. In his letter to Titus, Paul reveals in chapter 2, verses 11–14, that grace instructs us to *"live soberly, righteously, and godly in the present age."* What should we be looking for that motivates us to holiness? Fill in the blanks:

   *"Looking for the blessed _____ and glorious _____ of our great God and Savior Jesus Christ."* (v. 13) [2 points]

31. Colossians 3:5 begins, *"Therefore put to death your members which are on the earth…."* Again, I will ask, "What is the *therefore* there for?" Fill in the blanks to complete the reason:

   *"For you _____, and your _____ is hidden with Christ in God. When Christ who is our _____ appears, then _____ also will appear with Him in glory."* (Col. 3:3–4) [4 points]

## MEMORY WORK: ROMANS 13:8, 10

Write out these verses from memory: [8 points]

_____

_____

_____

_____

_____

Check your answers on pages 237–41 in the "Correct Answers with Notes" section at the back of the book.

## PRAYER RESPONSE

In this lesson, we are again challenged to make very practical application of the Word of God to our lives, beginning with our calling to have a correct attitude toward government and our need to submit to governing authorities, to pay taxes, and, most important, to pray for our leaders. I have often said that if Christians would exchange the time they spend criticizing their governments with the time that they pray for them, they would have remarkably different governments.

Read through the questions and answers for lesson 23 again and ask the Holy Spirit to show you two or three areas in which He wants you to renew your mind, and then spend time praying about those areas. Building a relationship with the Holy Spirit is critical in our path of maturing as God's children, and no time that we dedicate to doing this will ever be wasted.

# LIVING OUT YOUR FAITH UNDER PRESSURE, PART 3

*Read Romans 14*

## INTRODUCTION

In Romans 14, we come to a very important point: a warning against judging our fellow believers. This warning is needed as much today as when it was originally written. Many Christians suffer all sorts of problems in their lives because they sin by judging their fellow believers. There is only one Judge: God.

The examples Paul considers in Romans 14 concern religious rules about Jewish diets and holidays. These are still thorny issues today, especially in Jerusalem, as more and more Jews* are coming to believe in Jesus as their Messiah and identifying with Him and His people. Even some believers from a non-Jewish background are concerned about issues of diet and the observance of holy days—for instance, whether to observe the Sabbath on Saturday or on Sunday. (The Jewish Sabbath begins on Friday evening at sunset and ends on Saturday evening at sunset.) So, such questions arise not only from the remote past or from the early days of the church but also today.

The main focus of Romans 14 is receiving others, or accepting them. *"Receive ["accept"* NIV, NASB] *one who is weak in the faith,"* Paul entreats in verse 1. Later in Romans, he writes, *"Receive ["accept"* NIV, NASB] *one another"* (Romans 15:7). Do not criticize others, tear apart their opinions, or point out to them how incomplete their understanding is. Such observations may prove how clever you are, but they do not show the love that Paul says we owe one another. (See Romans 13:8.) And they do not build up the body of Christ. Thus, Paul's themes in Romans 14 are *acceptance* and *harmony*. God is more concerned with harmony in the body of Christ than He is with the exact observance of certain set rules.

## MEMORY VERSE: ROMANS 14:17

[ ] Check here after memorizing the verse.

(Review verses from prior lessons daily.)

# QUESTIONS

## RELIGIOUS RULES

1. How should we respond to people who are weak in faith? (Rom. 14:1) [1 point]

   _____

2. Fill in the blanks to indicate the difference between the way the two people in Paul's example view what is allowable for them to eat:

   *"For one believes he may eat* _____ _____, *but he who is weak eats*

   _____ _____*."* (Rom. 14:2) [2 points]

3. Romans 14:3 speaks of believers despising and judging each other for feeling free to eat or for not eating. How has God responded to both types of people? [1 point]

   _____

4. To whom does a servant stand or fall? (Rom. 14:4) [1 point]

   _____

5. In Romans 14:5–6, Paul goes on to talk about some people who consider certain "days" to be more or less important than others, and other people who consider all days to be the same. He is referring particularly to the distinct ways in which people observe the Sabbath. How are we told to resolve this potential conflict in belief? (v. 5) [1 point]

   _____

6. Read Colossians 2:13–17 and then answer the following questions:

   a. What phrase does Paul use to describe the law*, which was against us, but which has now been wiped out or erased? (v. 14) [1 point]

      _____

   b. In what manner did Jesus *take the law out of the way*? (v. 14) [1 point]

      _____

c. Fill in the blanks to identify three things that Jesus did to the enemy through the cross: (v. 15)

"Having _____ principalities and powers, He made a public _____ of them, _____ over them in it [meaning in, or through, the cross]." [3 points]

d. What are we told *not* to let others do to us regarding food, drink, festivals, new moons, or sabbaths? (v. 16) [1 point]

_____

## CULTIVATING INTIMACY WITH THE LORD

7. To whom do we live and die? (Rom. 14:8) [1 point]

_____

8. To what end did Christ die, rise, and live again? (Rom. 14:9) [1 point]

_____

## PREPARING FOR JUDGMENT

We have seen that we should not judge others or allow others to judge us with respect to food and drink, festivals, new moons, or sabbaths, but there is another side to judging. In certain areas, we do have to exercise judgment. For example, a father has to exercise judgment with respect to his family, and a pastor has to exercise judgment with respect to his congregation. But let me give you this simple principle: Where you have responsibility, you have authority to judge. Where you do not have responsibility, you do not have authority to judge. You are not responsible for your fellow believer's life, so do not judge them.

9. Where shall we all ultimately stand? (Rom. 14:10) [1 point]

_____

10. In Romans 14:11, Paul quotes from Isaiah 45:23. What two things does that quoted passage tell us will happen at the judgment seat of God? (Rom. 14:11) [2 points]

a. _____

b. _____

11. About whom will we give an account to God? (v. 12) [1 point]

_____

12. Read 2 Corinthians 5:6–10 and then answer the following questions:

   a. When Paul speaks about the motivation of his own life and ministry, what does he make his aim? (v. 9) [1 point]

   _____

   b. Where does Paul again say that we must all appear? (v. 10) [1 point]

   _____

   c. According to what will we be judged? (v. 10) [1 point]

   _____

13. In view of the fact that we will have to give an account of ourselves, what does Paul instruct us *not* to do? (Rom. 14:12–13) [1 point]

_____

## BE GUIDED BY LOVE

As we have previously discussed, in chapters 12–14 of Romans, the guiding principle is love. From time to time, Paul returns to this theme and points out that love is what leads us to do the right thing.

14. If our fellow believer is grieved by the food we eat, what does that say about us? (Rom. 14:15) [1 point]

_____

15. Are certain foods unclean in and of themselves? (v. 14) [1 point]

_____

16. In Mark 7:14–15, Jesus teaches on the issue of what we eat. Is it the things that enter us from the outside or the things that come out of us that defile us? (v. 15) [1 point]

_____

17. In Jesus's further explanation to His disciples in Mark 7:18–21, He says that food does not defile us because it goes into the stomach and is eliminated. But Jesus does indicate an area of our being that can be a source of defilement. What is that area? (vv. 20–21) [1 point]

_____

18. In 1 Timothy 4:1–5, Paul talks about certain errors that will creep into the church, including those prohibiting the eating of certain foods. Through what two means does he say that our food will be sanctified (made holy)? (v. 5) [2 points]

    a. _____

    b. _____

19. What does Paul say we might do to someone for whom Christ died when we eat in an insensitive manner? (Rom. 14:15) [1 point]

_____

20. Since Christ died for you and me, what must we guard against? (Rom. 14:16) [1 point]

_____

## THE PREREQUISITE FOR PEACE

There is much talk in the world today about the need for peace. But, in these last days, the cry for peace will become a means of deception by Satan's manipulations. The world will seek peace and maybe even claim that it has achieved peace—without righteousness*. That is a deception. There is no true or permanent peace without righteousness in Christ.

21. Following his discussion about food and drink, or eating and drinking, Paul comes to an important conclusion in Romans 14:17. If the kingdom of God is not about eating and drinking, what three things *is* it about, which can only occur *"in the Holy Spirit"*? [3 points]

    a. _____

    b. _____

    c. _____

22. What does Jesus say will happen to those who hunger and thirst for righteousness? (Matt. 5:6) [1 point]

_____

23. How much peace is possible without righteousness? (Isa. 48:22; 57:21) [1 point]

_____

24. What two things are said of those who serve Christ in righteousness, peace, and joy in the Holy Spirit? (Rom. 14:17–18) [2 points]

    a. _____

    b. _____

## UPHOLDING THE WORK OF GOD

25. In Romans 14:20, Paul continues his theme of pursuing harmony with our fellow believers. Again, what common element of life has the potential to tear down the work of God when it is consumed with insensitivity and lack of consideration? [1 point]

_____

26. In Romans 14:21, Paul goes on to clarify the potential danger:

    _"It is good neither to eat meat nor drink wine nor do anything by which your brother_

    _____ _or is_ _____ _or is_ _____

    _____." [3 points]

27. How does Paul classify all activities that do not come from faith? (Rom. 14:23) [1 point]

_____

## MEMORY WORK: ROMANS 14:17

Write out this verse from memory: [4 points]

_____

_____

_____

Check your answers on pages 242–46 in the "Correct Answers with Notes" section at the back of the book.

## PRAYER RESPONSE

I proclaim, according to Romans 14:8, that if I live, I live to the Lord; and if I die, I die to the Lord. Therefore, whether I live or die, I am the Lord's.

Father, thank You again for the reminders that come through Your Word—reminders not to judge other people but to walk in love toward them. Forgive me for the times when I have judged others or imposed my personal expectations or standards on them. I ask You to release me and them from the negative effects of my words. If there are those who have judged me or spoken against me, I forgive them, and I bless them in Your name.

Please help me to serve effectively in Your kingdom in all righteousness, peace, and joy in the Holy Spirit. I choose to pursue the things that make for peace and the things that edify others. In Jesus's name, amen.

# LIVING OUT YOUR FAITH UNDER PRESSURE, PART 4

*Read Romans 15 and 16*

## INTRODUCTION

We are coming to the end of our study of the book of Romans, and it has been quite a journey! It has taken much prayer and perseverance to get to this point, but it has been worth every effort. I trust that you have come to understand the unique importance of righteousness* and how it forms a gateway to peace and joy in the Holy Spirit through the work of the cross.

For those of us who do not walk according to the flesh but according to the Spirit, it is not the law* that must be fulfilled in us but the righteous* requirement of the law, which is love. And God has invited us to share Christ's inheritance—not just a tiny portion of it, but a joint inheritance of *all* of it.

We have also considered the distinctness of Israel* and how God deals with both the Israelites and the Gentiles*, calling them together through the righteousness of faith into one body—the body of Christ.

In the previous three lessons, we have explored practical applications of the Spirit-filled life and how we are called to work this new life out in our individual and corporate experiences. Now we come to the last lesson, which covers Romans 15 and 16. Paul continues to teach us how to put our faith into action, even when life is difficult, and he highlights the particular importance of our personal relationships.

## MEMORY VERSES: ROMANS 15:1–2

[ ] Check here after memorizing the verses.

(Review verses from prior lessons daily.)

## THE MEASURE OF STRENGTH

1.  What kind of people does Paul encourage to bear with the weaknesses of those who are without strength? (Rom. 15:1) [1 point]

    _____

2.  In the revelation the apostle John received from God, we read about the glorious city of the New Jerusalem.

    a.  According to Revelation 21:14, what did the wall of the city have? [1 point]

    _____

    b.  What was written on them? (v. 14) [1 point]

    _____

3.  Why is each of us called on to please our neighbors for their good? (Rom. 15:2) [1 point]

    _____

4.  Who is our example in putting others ahead of ourselves? (Rom. 15:3) [1 point]

    _____

5.  In John 8:21–30, when Jesus predicts His departure through His death on the cross, His resurrection, and His ascension to heaven, which things does He say that He *always* does? (John 8:29) [1 point]

    _____

6.  For what purpose were *"whatever things were written before"*? (Rom. 15:4) [1 point]

    _____

7. Fill in the blanks to complete Romans 15:4:

"That we through the _____ and _____ of the Scriptures might have _____." [3 points]

8. What did Abraham need to do before he could obtain his promised son, Isaac? (Heb. 6:15) [1 point]

_____

9. What does the writer of Hebrews remind us that we have need of "*so that after* [we] *have done the will of God,* [we] *may receive the promise*"? (Heb.10:36) [1 point]

_____

## BUILDING UP A UNIFIED BODY

10. What gift does Paul pray that "*the God of patience and comfort*" would grant to us as His believing people? (Rom. 15:5) [1 point]

_____

11. As Paul's prayer is answered, what will the result be? Fill in the blanks:

"That you may with one _____ and one _____ glorify the God and Father of our Lord Jesus Christ." (Rom. 15:6) [2 points]

12. In Romans 15:7, we are again encouraged to follow Christ's example. What does Paul exhort us to do to bring glory to God? [1 point]

_____

## THE SAME GOSPEL

13. In Romans 15:8–9, Paul speaks of Jesus's ministry to both the Jews* and the Gentiles.

    a. Using a metaphor for the Jewish people, to what does Paul say that Jesus Christ has become a servant? (v. 8) [1 point]

_____

b. To whom were given the promises that Christ came to confirm? (v. 8) [1 point]

_____

c. Christ came for the Gentiles as well. How are they expected to respond? (v. 9) [1 point]

_____

14. In Romans 15:9–12, Paul again points his readers to the Scriptures to prove that the Gentiles can come into God's promises. Look for a progression that emerges in the answers below:

   a. First, in Romans 15:9, Paul quotes the psalmist David. Going back to the original source, we see that after his triumphant deliverance from all his enemies, David says he will do two things: *"I will give _____ to You, O LORD, among the Gentiles, and _____ praises to Your name."* (Ps. 18:49) [2 points]

   b. Then, in Romans 15:10, Paul quotes Moses. Looking at the original source in Deuteronomy, what does Moses instruct Gentiles to do along with Israel? (Deut. 32:43) [1 point]

   _____

   c. Next, in Romans 15:11, Paul quotes Psalm 117. What are the Gentiles exhorted to do, which the psalmist expresses using two different words? (Ps. 117:1) [1 point]

   _____

   d. In Romans 15:12, Paul's final quote is a combination of two verses from Isaiah (11:10; 42:4). What will be the Gentiles' response toward Jesus, the *"root of Jesse,"* who will rise to reign over them? (Rom. 15:12) [1 point]

   _____

15. Fill in the blanks to complete Romans 15:13:

*"Now may the God of _____ fill you with all _____ and _____ in believing, that you may abound in _____ by the _____ of the Holy Spirit."*
[5 points]

# SANCTIFYING THE OFFERING

16. In Romans 15:14, after nearly fifteen chapters of teaching, Paul exchanges an attitude of forthrightness for one of tact. In seeking to build up his readers, what does he say are the two things they are filled with? [2 points]

    a. _____

    b. _____

17. To whom is Paul specifically called as a *"minister,"* or servant, of Jesus Christ? (Rom. 15:16) [1 point]

    _____

18. In Romans 15:16, Paul uses the language of a priest who is making an offering. What is the offering that Paul is trusting will be acceptable to God? [1 point]

    _____

19. By whom will this offering be sanctified (or made holy)? (v. 16) [1 point]

    _____

# BOASTING IN CHRIST

20. Paul does not encourage his readers to boast about themselves, but what kind of boasting (or *"glorying"*) does he indicate is legitimate? (Rom. 15:17) [1 point]

    _____

21. Similarly, what is the one exception Paul gives in the book of Galatians to his attitude of never boasting? Fill in the blank below: (Gal. 6:14) [1 point]

    *"God forbid that I should boast except in the _____ of our Lord Jesus Christ."*

22. What response does Paul seek in the Gentiles as a result of what Christ has accomplished through him? (Rom. 15:18) [1 point]

    _____

23. Paul regards which characteristics as essential to a ministry that fully preaches the gospel of Christ? Fill in the blanks: (Rom. 15:18–19)

    a. "In _____ and _____." (v. 18) [2 points]

    b. "In mighty _____ and _____." (v. 19) [2 points]

    c. "By the power of the _____ of God." (v. 19) [1 point]

24. In 1 Corinthians 2:1–5, we have a parallel Scripture indicating the necessity of the demonstration of the Holy Spirit in the preaching of the gospel.

    a. Paul says that when he went to the Corinthians, he determined to know nothing among them except Jesus Christ. What aspect about Christ does he focus on in particular? (v. 2) [1 point]

    _____

    b. Paul's speech and preaching *"were not with persuasive words of human wisdom, but in demonstration of the* _____ *and of* _____." (v. 4) [1 point]

    c. Where should our faith rest? (v. 5) [1 point]

    _____

## A TRUE APOSTLE

25. Was it Paul's aim to preach the gospel among those who had already heard it or to those who were as yet unreached? (Rom. 15:20–21) [1 point]

_____

26. Scholars have determined that Paul most likely wrote the epistle* to the Romans while staying in Corinth. Does Paul indicate that he has more work to do in that area? (Rom. 15:23) [1 point]

_____

27. Acts 27–28 relates Paul's specific journey to Rome, which was fraught with his being imprisoned, chained, shipwrecked, and bitten by a venomous snake. And yet, from a kingdom perspective, how does Paul say he will come to the believers in Rome? (Rom. 15:29) [1 point]

_____

28. What words does Paul use to show that he recognizes a serious need for the believers in Rome to *"strive together"* with him in prayer? (Rom. 15:30) [1 point]

_____

29. Considering that, in the story of Paul's entire journey to Rome (told in Acts 21–28), there were three attempts to kill him; he was subjected to mob violence; and he was beaten, arrested, chained, and imprisoned, was the intercession Paul sought necessary to his success in reaching Rome? [Thought question; no points. See Derek's note for number 29 under "Lesson 25 Answers."]

_____

_____

_____

30. With what particular attribute of God does Paul bless his readers as he closes chapter 15 and the main body of his teaching? (v. 33) [1 point]

_____

## RIGHT RELATIONSHIPS

Chapter 16 of Paul's letter to the Romans is mainly a section of personal greetings. Some people question whether it really needs to be a part of Romans. It *does* need to be there, because Paul does not just give lectures and then add a postscript to say that personal relationships are important. Rather, he *demonstrates* that truth. After all this wonderful theology, Paul spends his final chapter greeting people by name—a more vivid way of showing that personal relationships are valuable. His teaching is not all in the theoretical realm of doctrine*; it is lived out in personal relationships.

31. In Romans 16, Paul mentions thirty-seven different people—those who have been associated with him in ministry—all but two of them by name. Let's consider some of the most salient individuals:

   a. Who carried the letter to the Romans and had served God in such a way that the believers should *"receive her in the Lord"* and *"assist her"* (Romans 16:2)? (v. 1) [1 point]

_____

b.  List the names of the couple who risked their lives for Paul. (v. 3) [2 points]

i. _____

ii. _____

c.  Which of Paul's countrymen were imprisoned with him? (v. 7) [2 points]

i. _____

ii. _____

d.  List the four women Paul recognizes for their hard work. (vv. 6, 12) [4 points]

i. _____

ii. _____

iii. _____

iv. _____

e.  Whom does Paul describe as his *"fellow worker"* in Corinth? (v. 21) [1 point]

_____

f.  What is the name of the scribe of the epistle (the one who wrote down Paul's words)? (v. 22) [1 point]

_____

g.  Who hosted Paul while he was ministering in Corinth? (v. 23) [1 point]

_____

32.  Whom does Paul urge the believers to avoid? (v. 17) [1 point]

_____

33.  In Romans 16:19, what does Paul encourage his readers to be?

a.  *"Wise in what is _____."* [1 point]

b.  *"Simple concerning _____."* [1 point]

34.  Where will the God of peace soon crush Satan? (v. 20) [1 point]

_____

## MEMORY WORK: ROMANS 15:1–2

Write out these verses from memory: [8 points]

_____

_____

_____

_____

_____

Check your answers on pages 247–52 in the "Correct Answers with Notes" section at the back of the book.

## PRAYER RESPONSE

As this is our final study, I would encourage you to set aside an hour or two to wait on the Lord. Waiting on God has tremendous blessing attributed to it in Scripture and should become a regular part of your lifestyle. To begin, you might like to sing or shout to the Lord, play an instrument or dance before Him, or pray in the Spirit. Yet no matter how you feel led to begin, remember to give thanks to the Lord for His goodness, praise Him for His greatness, and worship Him for His holiness.

As you wait on the Lord, do so with the expectation that He will speak to you. Ask Him to highlight specific truths that He wants you to remember from all the lessons you have worked through. To be challenged in this request, don't just ask for one or two truths but ten or more. For each truth, ask Him how He wants you to respond. He may want you to ask for, receive, or extend forgiveness. He may want you to regularly proclaim that truth until it becomes a part of you. Or perhaps He may show you that you need to press in to one of your memory verses until you have sown the seed of that word in your heart. There are innumerable ways in which the Lord may lead you, but this is your "new normal"—not being driven to and fro by the winds of doctrine (see Ephesians 4:14) but instead being led by the Holy Spirit into deeper intimacy with God and maturity in Christ.

Let's conclude our study of this wonderful book of Romans by personalizing Paul's benediction (a word that literally means "good word" or "blessing"):

_Now to Him who is able to establish [me] according to [this] gospel and the preaching of Jesus Christ, according to the revelation of the mystery kept secret since the world began but now made manifest, and by the prophetic Scriptures made known to all nations, according to the commandment of the everlasting God, for obedience to the faith—to God, alone wise, be glory through Jesus Christ forever. Amen._

(Romans 16:25–27)

# CONCLUSION: THE DEPTH OF GOD'S REVELATION

Congratulations on completing the *Self-Study Bible Course on Romans: Revealing the Righteousness of God*! With the amount of content and the depth of revelation that Paul gives in the epistle to the Romans, I would expect that many students have taken six months or more to complete this course. And no matter your total score, remember that the end purpose of Bible study is not just knowledge but practical application in your life for spiritual transformation. With the Lord's help, I am trusting that the profound effect that Paul's letter had on me has been imparted to you and that you are a different person from the one who started out.

Scripture can never be plumbed to its depths because there is always more that the Lord can explain and reveal to us as we welcome its power and influence in our lives. Thus, even with all that you have learned in this study, you have not yet finished with the book of Romans! If you walk with the Holy Spirit as your Guide, He will show you more and more in this epistle as you become conformed to the image of Christ.

May the Lord bless you as you continue to study God's Word with the help of our glorious Helper, the Holy Spirit.

# CORRECT ANSWERS WITH NOTES

## LESSON 1 ANSWERS

| Question | Answer | Points |
|---|---|---|
| 1. | **Paul**<br><br>Paul's original name was Saul, and the story of his conversion is told in Acts 9 and Acts 26. Many scholars believe that Paul wrote Romans while staying in Corinth. They point to various indications in both the book of Romans and the book of Acts, including Paul's mention in Romans of several people who were connected with Corinth: Pheobe, Gaius, and Erastus. | 1 |
| 2. | **Apostle**<br><br>Paul describes himself first as a bondservant [Greek *doulos*] of Jesus Christ and only second as an apostle. The word *doulos* is sometimes translated as "slave," but it includes the meaning of a free individual choosing to serve another.<br><br>An apostle is a "sent one." This designation is not limited to the "twelve apostles," as Paul and many others are called apostles in Scripture. In modern speech, we would usually refer to apostles as missionaries because they are "sent out." | 1 |
| 3. | **Gaius**<br><br>Hospitality is a gift, and it can be the source of inestimable blessing. Through his hospitality, Gaius was able to give Paul the time and place to compose this wonderful epistle*. In Romans 12:13, Paul says we should be *"given to hospitality."* In my own story of coming to faith, when I first visited a little Pentecostal church with one of my fellow soldiers and heard the gospel, I probably would have walked out of that church at the end of the service and never gone back again, even though I had raised my hand at the invitation to receive Christ, because I still did not understand what that meant. However, an elderly couple who kept a boardinghouse near the church invited my friend and me back for supper. Because of that, the Lord was able to get a grip on me. That is a very simple, personal example of the importance in ministry of exercising the gift of hospitality. | 1 |
| 4. | **Rome**<br><br>The city of Rome was the capital of the Roman Empire, which was strategic in the evangelization of the known world at that time due to its widespread influence and the strong infrastructure of roads it had built throughout its colonies. This allowed for easier travel not only for armies and merchants but also for Christian evangelists and missionaries. In Romans 1:10, Paul prays that he might have a *"prosperous journey"* (KJV) to Rome. However, when he did make the journey by sea, not only was he a prisoner bound in chains, but he also had to endure numerous stops on the voyage, being shipwrecked, and being bitten by a viper. (See Acts 21, 27—28.) So, was his journey "prosperous"? It was if you believe that prosperity is not primarily about wealth but about being totally equipped to do the will of God. | 1 |
| 5. | **Saints**<br><br>The word *saint* is directly related to the word *sanct*, which is another way of translating "holy." So "to sanctify" means "to make saintly," or "to make holy." Thus, to be sanctified is to be made holy. Holiness always includes within it the idea of being set apart to God. We are all called "saints" because we are set apart to God by our righteousness* in Jesus. | 1 |

| Question | Answer | Points |
|---|---|---|
| 6. | **gospel**<br><br>The word *gospel* occurs thirteen times in the book of Romans. We will go into more detail concerning what this term means as this course progresses. | 1 |
| 7. | **Tertius**<br><br>It is interesting to reflect on how much we owe to letters and to those who wrote them down, as well as those who preserved them through the ages. There are twenty-seven books in the New Testament, and twenty-two of them are letters. I sometimes say that if the early Christians had been lazy about letter writing, we never would have had the New Testament.<br><br>In the opening passage of Romans, Paul expresses his longing to be with the saints of Rome. However, we have to praise God that he *didn't* get the opportunity when he wanted it because then he never would have written this epistle. So, the letter to the Romans is a by-product of his frustration that he was not able to get to Rome when he wanted to. | 1 |
| 8. | **All nations (the Gentiles*)**<br><br>In several places in the New Testament, Paul refers to himself as an apostle to the Gentiles:<br><br>• Romans 11:13: *"For I speak to you Gentiles; inasmuch as I am an **apostle to the Gentiles**."*<br>• Galatians 2:8: *"For He who worked effectively in Peter for the **apostleship** to the circumcised also worked effectively in me **toward the Gentiles**."*<br>• 2 Timothy 1:11: *"To which I was appointed a preacher, an **apostle**, and a teacher **of the Gentiles**."* | 1 |
| 9. | **obedience**<br><br>If you try obeying God in your own strength or in your own ability, it is impossible. The result is frustration. Obedience must proceed out of faith. *"Faith comes by hearing* [that is, from hearing the word spoken], *and hearing by the word of God"* (Romans 10:17). | 1 |
| 10. | a. **called**<br>b. **beloved (or loved)**<br>c. **saints**<br><br>According to the Greek, Paul says that these Roman Christians are "called **saints**" or "holy ones"—not "called *to be* saints," as it is translated in the *New King James Version*—because when God calls you something, you are what He calls you. You may not feel like it. People may not see you that way. But what God calls you is what you are. | 3 |
| 11. | **grace**<br><br>The covenant* of grace does not operate through laws enforced from without but through laws written by the Holy Spirit in the hearts of believers. (See, for example, Jeremiah 31:33.) | 1 |
| 12. | **Lord Jesus Christ**<br><br>In the first eight chapters of Romans, Paul uses the title **Lord** eleven times, the name **Jesus** (His Hebrew name is *Yeshua*) twenty-two times, and the word **Christ** (or *Messiah*) thirty-three times. One reason Romans is so powerful is that it focuses on the center, who is Jesus. Whenever we get off-center and focus on anything but Jesus, the power of the Holy Spirit begins to "leak out" from us, and we have to resort to human energy and human methods. | 1 |
| 13. | **world**<br><br>Again, Rome was the great capital city of the Roman Empire, which dominated much of the known world at that time. Whatever happened in Rome affected the whole of the Roman Empire. | 1 |

| Question | Answer | Points |
|---|---|---|
| 14. | a. **God**<br><br>b. **Son**<br><br>c. **Christ**<br><br>d. **My**<br><br>e. **peace**<br><br>*Evangel* in Greek means "good news." An evangelist, literally, is one who tells the good news. And if you ever hear anything that isn't good news, it isn't the gospel. | 5 |
| 15. | **promised; prophets**<br><br>Paul is dealing with the separation of the old covenant* and the new covenant*. Everything we are preaching in the new covenant, he says, has its origin in the old. To reach the Jewish people, then, it is important to show them the gospel directly out of their own Scriptures, and to show them that this is what was promised from Genesis onward. (See also 2 Peter 1:16–21.) | 2 |
| 16. | **power; holiness; resurrection; dead**<br><br>The power that raised the dead body of Jesus from the tomb was the Holy Spirit. By that action, the Holy Spirit separated Jesus from all other men who had ever died and been buried, declaring Jesus to be the Son of God. As the Spirit of holiness, He also bore testimony to Jesus's perfect holiness. If there had ever been anything unholy in the life of Jesus, at any point, He never would have been resurrected. | 4 |
| 17. | a. **died**<br><br>b. **buried**<br><br>c. **rose**<br><br>Read the following statements aloud, contemplatively: "Christ died for my sins. He was buried. He was raised on the third day." In these three short sentences, you have the kernel of the gospel. Never let yourself be distracted from these great central facts. | 3 |
| 18. | **power; salvation**<br><br>If we are ever prone to be ashamed of the gospel, it is because we have lost sight of the fact that it is the power of God. Furthermore, it is the power of God not for destruction but *"to salvation"* (Romans 1:16), for total deliverance for the human personality—spirit, soul, and body—for those who believe. | 2 |
| 19. | **Jew; Greek**<br><br>Historically, the gospel was presented first to the Jewish people and then to the Gentile world. This was also the order that Jesus indicated for His mission on earth and the Great Commission. (See, for example, Matthew 15:21–28; Acts 1:8.) | 2 |
| 20. | **The righteousness of God**<br><br>The key blessing of the gospel is that it brings us Jesus's righteousness—the righteousness that God accepts. It is only on the basis of His righteousness that we can receive any of the other blessings of God. | 1 |
| | Check your written memory work. If your memory work is word-perfect, 4 points for each verse. (1 point off for each mistake in a verse. If there are more than three mistakes, do not mark any points for that verse.) | 8 |
| | Total Points | ____ /42 |

Fill in the total points for lesson 1 on the "Tally Sheet for Each Lesson" on page 253.

# LESSON 2 ANSWERS

| Question | Answer | Points |
|---|---|---|
| 1. | **The wrath of God**<br><br>We must keep in mind that Romans 1 reveals two opposite sides of the coin with regard to the righteousness* of God and that both sides are very important aspects of God's character. | 1 |
| 2. | **They have been ungodly and unrighteous; they have suppressed the truth in unrighteousness**<br><br>God had made the truth available to humanity, but people chose to suppress it because it did not suit them to face up to it. | 2 |
| 3. | a. **in**<br><br>b. **to**<br><br>It is the combination of two realities—what is internal and what is external—that constitutes this revelation about God. Allow me to swap the order to make this point clear.<br><br>The second reality is the universe, particularly the heavenly bodies with their manifest beauty and order and system, and that includes our wondrous earth. Then there is within man what I call a logical, mathematical faculty that can appreciate the logic* and mathematics of creation. This quality is unique about mankind compared with all other creatures on this earth. | 2 |
| 4. | **Since the creation of the world**<br><br>Paul says that, through creation, God has made the truth about Himself available to all men everywhere. | 1 |
| 5. | a. **His eternal power**<br><br>The first aspect has two parts to it: *eternal* and *power*. We generally have a concept of "power" because we see its effects all around us in different forms, both man-made and human, such as in the running of vehicles or appliances or in the administration of authority exercised by a branch of government.<br><br>The concept of "eternal" may need some additional explanation. As the Creator, God is Alpha. As God the Son, the *"heir of all things"* (Hebrews 1:2), He is Omega. (See Revelation 1:8, 11; 21:6; 22:13.) He spans all time. He proceeds out of eternity, on through time, and into eternity. He is the Eternal, the Uncreated, the Only Begotten of the Father, the Beginning and the End. We need to understand that God has a dual relationship with time: He transcends time, but He also operates within time. God created time, and He works in time, but He Himself is outside of time and before time.<br><br>b. **His Godhead**<br><br>The second aspect of the truth that God has made available about Himself, His Godhead or divine nature, reveals Him as a Being totally other than mankind, totally greater than mankind, and One who is all-powerful. | 2 |
| 6. | a. **glory**<br><br>b. **handiwork**<br><br>c. **speech**<br><br>d. **knowledge**<br><br>Earth, with all its wonders and mysteries, is amazing. Yet, for the most part, we can study and examine these wonders and mysteries at close quarters. The heavens, despite all the new developments in space exploration and travel, are on another level. In Psalm 8, David expresses the questions that arise as he thinks about the marvels of the heavens: *"When I consider Your heavens, the work of Your fingers, the moon and the stars, which You have ordained, what is man that You are mindful of him, and the son of man that You visit him? For You have made him a little lower than the angels, and You have crowned him with glory and honor"* (Psalm 8:3–5). Let's develop an attitude of wonder when we look at creation. | 4 |

| Question | Answer | Points |
|---|---|---|
| 7. | a. | 6 |
| |     **i. The sun** | |
| |     **ii. The moon** | |
| |     **iii. The stars** | |
| |     **iv. All the host (army) of heaven** | |
| | b.  **All the people under the whole heaven** | |
| | c.  **A heritage (inheritance)** | |
| | Scripture has much to say about the heavenly bodies. Since creation, God has intended them to *"be for signs and seasons, and for days and years"* (Genesis 1:14). What Moses is highlighting to the Israelites is the temptation to worship the sun, the moon, the stars, and the heavenly host, and he is telling them to *"take heed."* History is full of cultures that have worshipped aspects of creation, with terrible results, but we are called to worship the Creator, who has invited us into relationship with Himself through His Son. In the book of Revelation, when the sixth seal is opened, we are told that the sun becomes black, the moon becomes like blood, the stars of heaven fall to the earth, and the sky recedes as a scroll when it is rolled up. (See Revelation 6:12–14.) Why would we choose to worship something that is temporal* rather than the One who is eternal? | |
| 8. | **No** | 1 |
| | The so-called "laws" of the universe do not result merely from the random interplay of inanimate forces. The ultimate reality behind the universe is a Person: God. The very word *law** is meaningless without a lawgiver (or lawgivers)—one who enacts and enforces the law. The laws that man detects in the universe are the discernable expression of the faithfulness of the invisible Creator. | |
| 9. | **The Lord** | 1 |
| | Again, for every law that is made, there is a lawmaker (or there are lawmakers) who enact(s) it. The principle of proper explanation is to proceed from the known to the unknown. But when we talk about a law that was not made by anybody, we are proceeding from the unknown—an invalid method of explanation. | |
| 10. | a.  **They did not glorify God as God.** | 2 |
| | b.  **They did not give Him thanks/they were not thankful.** | |
| | From years of observation, I conclude that the moment we cease to glorify God and give Him thanks, we have started on a slippery, downward path. Paul describes this path in subsequent verses as an ever-downward spiral, and the end is a horrible, slimy pit. | |
| 11. | **Fools** | 1 |
| | The Greek word translated *"professing"* in Romans 1:22 means "keeping on saying the same thing again and again." They kept talking about how wise they were; yet, all the time, they were becoming more and more foolish. | |
| 12. | c. **Idolatry** | 1 |
| | The greatest sin is to break the first commandment: *"You shall have no other gods before Me"* (Exodus 20:3). I have traveled in many parts of the world where idolatry is still rampant, and I have seen what a terrible sin it is. There are no words to describe the awfulness of idolatry. | |
| | Can you begin to picture the insult offered to the great, eternal God to depict Him in the form of men, then of flying creatures, then of animals, and finally of reptiles? Notice, too, that the trend is always downward, never upward. Once people have taken those first two steps on the downward path, they will continue downward unless they repent. | |

| Question | Answer | Points |
|---|---|---|
| 13. | **gave them**<br><br>What a terrible phrase! Here is my personal prayer in response: "God, never give me up. I may not appreciate Your dealings with me. I may complain. But, please, never give me up!" Will you join me in saying that prayer? | 1 |
| 14. | **Idolatry**<br><br>The worst that God could ever say about someone is, "Let him alone." Notice that it was in response to Ephraim's (Israel's) idolatry, the same sin mentioned in Romans 1. | 1 |
| 15. | a. **uncleanness; hearts**<br><br>b. **bodies**<br><br>c. **truth; lie**<br><br>d. **creature; Creator**<br><br>God had originally made these ungodly people in His own image, but they changed His image into something vile and degrading. Because they distorted the image of God and defiled it, God said, "All right, I will let you defile your own bodies through lust and impurity." | 7 |
| 16. | a. **Homosexuality**<br><br>Homosexuality has become so prevalent in many societies, with so much acceptance, that even Christians fail to take notice. When we read the story of the destruction of Sodom and ask ourselves, "What sin was God judging them for?" the obvious answer is, "Homosexuality." However, in question 17, we will see that homosexuality is just the fruit, not the root sin.<br><br>b. **Women**<br><br>Paul suggests that the women led the way in homosexuality. As far as Greece is concerned, where Paul was writing from Corinth, that is historically correct. On the island of Lesbos, about the sixth century before Christ, lived a Greek poetess named Sappho, who was what we call a lesbian (the island of *Lesbos* is where the word comes from). She wrote poetry glorifying the homosexual relationship. The poetry was beautiful but corrupt. It is remarkable that sometimes excellent art forms are used to glorify the most ungodly things.<br><br>c. **In themselves**<br><br>As often happens, the men of Greece followed the pattern of the women. Men can be spineless creatures. Often, when women take the lead, men follow them without question. But the results are never God's best intention for humanity. These men received in themselves, in their own bodies, the due penalty of their sin. Sexually transmitted diseases and HIV/AIDS are two of the expressions of this due penalty for sin, but they are by no means the only ones. | 3 |
| 17. | **his own body**<br><br>Men and women need to take into account what Paul wrote in 1 Corinthians 6:18. They cannot practice immorality without doing some kind of damage to their own bodies. In ministering to the sick, I have concluded that if we leave out sexual sin as a common cause of illness, we will probably not deal with the root problems of many who come for ministry. It is not that sexual sin cannot be forgiven, but it must be faced up to and acknowledged for what it is; and the results of it have to be acknowledged as well. Then true repentance can follow, deliverance can ensue, and the healing process can begin. | 1 |

| Question | Answer | Points |
|---|---|---|
| 18. | a. **Pride** | 4 |
| | b. **Fullness of food** | |
| | c. **Abundance of idleness** | |
| | d. **Not strengthening the hand of the poor and needy** | |
| | In Ezekiel 16:49, there is no mention of homosexuality. Isn't that remarkable? Sodom was very much like contemporary Western culture: *"She and her daughter had pride, fullness of food, and abundance of idleness; neither did she strengthen the hand of the poor and needy."* My deduction is that this type of self-indulgent culture will always produce homosexuality. I believe it is this kind of culture in the West that is the root cause of the tremendous upsurge in homosexuality. But homosexuality is not the root sin; it is a fruit of the sin of self-indulgence. | |
| 19. | **As a chaste virgin** | 1 |
| | In the biblical culture of those days, betrothal was not marriage, but it was as binding as marriage, and it was the step to marriage. A woman who was unfaithful in the time of her betrothal was treated like an adulteress. | |
| | I think it is a wonderful testimony to what the blood of Jesus can do that Paul could speak about the church at Corinth as *"a chaste virgin."* When you think about the Corinthians' background, they were pimps, prostitutes, drunkards, extortionists, liars, and thieves. But the blood of Jesus could produce out of them a bride who would be a chaste virgin. Isn't that something! | |
| 20. | **Retain God in their knowledge** | 1 |
| | I believe this diagnoses a problem that is almost universal in the world today. Why do men and women not want to retain the knowledge of God? Because they know that if they did, they would have to give an account of themselves to Him. What I see in humanity at large is people's passionate opposition to the idea that they are subject to God. | |
| 21. | **Minds** | 1 |
| | What could be more terrible than having a debased mind? The previous two judgments to which God gave sinful people over were, first, to physical problems, and, second, to physical sins; but now their minds were warped or twisted out of shape. | |
| | Check your written memory work. If your memory work is word-perfect, 4 points for each verse. (1 point off for each mistake in a verse. If there are more than three mistakes, do not mark any points for that verse.) | 12 |
| | Total Points | ___ /56 |

Fill in the total points for lesson 2 on the "Tally Sheet for Each Lesson" on page 253.

# LESSON 3 ANSWERS

| Question | Answer | Points |
|---|---|---|
| 1. | a. **truth**<br>b. **deeds**<br>c. **partiality**<br>d. **law\***<br>e. **secrets**<br>It is vital to know how God will judge so that we can live accordingly. | 5 |
| 2. | **A mirror**<br>In the tabernacle of Moses, the laver (place of washing) was made of bronze. The women of Israel* gave their bronze mirrors for the making of the laver. The laver typifies the Word of God. Once you have come to the cross and received salvation in Jesus, God's next provision for you is His Word. The fact that the bronze laver was made of mirrors typifies the Word as the mirror, just as James says. And just like the mirrors, when you are reading the Bible, the Bible is reading you and reflecting back how you appear and what in your life needs cleansing and correction. | 1 |
| 3. | **By judging ourselves (according to God's Word)**<br>If we listen to God's voice through His Word, apply it to our lives, repent, and bring our lives into line with it, we have judged ourselves, for this is the standard of divine judgment. If we do this, God will not judge us. | 1 |
| 4. | a. **Eternal life**<br>b. **indignation; wrath**<br>c. **tribulation; anguish**<br>d. **glory; honor; peace**<br>Indignation and wrath are God's reaction; tribulation and anguish are the result—the outworking of judgment on the human race. | 8 |
| 5. | **Teachers**<br>If an increase in knowledge brings with it an increase in responsibility, then it stands to reason that teachers, who hold a lot of knowledge, have a high responsibility and therefore will face more stringent judgment. | 1 |
| 6. | **The conscience**<br>Paul gives us a vivid picture of a court scene going on inside us and explains that the consciences of people without any law can still produce in them the same effect that the law produces. Their consciences do *not* make them righteous*—that cannot be emphasized too much. But they do show them that they need God's mercy. | 1 |
| 7. | **It puffs us up.**<br>Nothing creates pride more easily than having religious knowledge. How many of us are in danger of becoming proud because we have knowledge? We must ask God to protect us from pride as we seek to walk before Him in humility. | 1 |
| 8. | **Ourselves**<br>All too often, we see what we deem as others' errors and sins, but we fail to deal with our own errors and sins first. We must remember that we cannot compare ourselves with other Christians or non-Christians to justify ourselves. If we want to compare ourselves, let us consider Christ's perfection, and that will immediately highlight our need for God's mercy. | 1 |

| Question | Answer | Points |
|---|---|---|
| 9. | **praise**<br><br>The word *Jew* is taken from the name *Yehuda* or *Judah\**. The meaning of *Yehuda* is "praise." In Romans 2:28–29, Paul says that you are a real Jew, a real *Yehudi* (the Hebrew word), only if your praise comes from God and is based not on your outward and external ordinances but on what you are inwardly. | 1 |
| 10. | **Circumcision**<br><br>God has indelibly imprinted on my mind that there is no covenant\* without a sacrifice, and there is no sacrifice without the shedding of blood. In Scripture, if you see a sacrifice, but you don't initially see where the blood is shed, look for it. This applies particularly to the covenant in Genesis 17 where there is apparently no sacrifice, but the mark of the covenant was circumcision. The blood was shed from Abraham's own body, which was a preview of Calvary. It is a fascinating study. | 1 |
| 11. | **heart; Spirit**<br><br>In Romans 8:28–29, Paul is not increasing the number of people who are entitled to be called Jews\*; he is restricting that number to those who fulfill the inward conditions. | 2 |
| 12. | **Repentance**<br><br>Judas Iscariot was remorseful for his sin, but he never changed. Contrast his reaction with the repentance of the Prodigal Son for his sinful lifestyle, which we read about in Jesus's parable in Luke 15:11–32. Scripture tells us, *"He came to himself…. He arose and came to his father"* (vv. 17, 20). That is true repentance. That is the result of an inward change. | 1 |
| 13. | **No (Certainly not!)**<br><br>The word *faith* does not cover merely what we believe intellectually but also our personal commitment to God. So, the word translated as *"unbelief"* in Romans 3:3 is better translated as "unfaithfulness." The unfaithfulness of some of the Jewish people did not nullify God's faithfulness. God remained faithful, even though Israel was unfaithful, because He is a covenant-keeping God. | 1 |
| 14. | **No (Certainly not!)**<br><br>In Romans 3:5, Paul essentially imagines somebody's objection and words it this way: "What you're telling us is that the more unrighteous we are, the more glory that gives to God for His righteousness\*. Therefore, if we want to give glory to God, we should go on being unfaithful." That is the objection. And this is Paul's answer: *"Certainly not!"* | 1 |
| 15. | **No**<br><br>Here is the objection: "If my sin has glorified God by bringing into focus His righteousness, why should I be judged?" That is a perversion of the truth of the gospel. But it is a typical Middle Eastern reaction and a common misrepresentation among both Jews and Muslims. They see the Christian faith as being a way of doing what you want and getting away with it. Paul did not waste much time with those in his day who promoted the idea that this was the gospel he taught, writing, *"Their condemnation is just"* (Romans 3:8). | 1 |
| | Check your written memory work. If your memory work is word-perfect, 4 points for each verse. (1 point off for each mistake in a verse. If there are more than three mistakes, do not mark any points for that verse.) | 12 |
| | Total Points | ___/39 |

Fill in the total points for lesson 3 on the "Tally Sheet for Each Lesson" on page 253.

## LESSON 4 ANSWERS

| Question | Answer | Points |
|---|---|---|
| 1. | **No ("*Not at all.*")**<br><br>Whether we are Jews* or Gentiles*, we have this in common: we are all sinners. But it is particularly hard for Jewish people to see that they are sinners because they set about to obtain their own righteousness* through adherence to the law*. We will deal more with this topic when we study Romans 10. | 1 |
| 2. | **None**<br><br>These words in Romans 3:10–12 are drawn from two passages in the Old Testament: Psalm 14 and Psalm 53. God, by the Holy Spirit, caused this teaching to be recorded twice, once in each of these psalms, in case anybody might miss it the first time. | 1 |
| 3. | **The fool**<br><br>Notice that believing wrong leads you to living wrong. You cannot believe wrong and live right. Likewise, you cannot believe right and live wrong. Our living is the product of our believing. When these people who are mentioned in Psalm 14 said there was no God, they exposed themselves to all forms of evil. | 1 |
| 4. | **The mouth**<br><br>Paul makes four statements to describe what people do with their mouths—all of which are terrible. Similarly, James called the tongue *"an unruly evil, full of deadly poison"* (James 3:8; see also vv. 9–10). | 1 |
| 5. | a. **Destruction; misery**<br>b. **peace**<br>c. **fear**<br><br>Of all the themes in Scripture, "the fear of the Lord" contains some of the most outstanding promises of God's favor and blessing. In fact, I know of no other theme in Scripture that has more blessings to offer than the fear of the Lord. Such fear does not refer to a terror of God, as recorded in Genesis 35:5 and other places in Scripture, but rather to a reverential honoring of and respect for God because of who He is.<br><br>Isaiah 33:6 ends with eight little words: *"The fear of the LORD is His treasure."* The fear of the Lord is not something to be afraid of or to despise. Rather, it is God's treasure that He shares with His people. | 4 |
| 6. | a. **God (Hebrew *Elohim*)**<br>*Elohim* is the primary name for God in the Old Testament that represents God's eternal power and divine nature. It is a plural name that contains the idea of a Godhead and is used about 2,500 times.<br><br>b. **The LORD God (*Yahweh Elohim*)**<br>*Yahweh* in Hebrew is formed from four consonants, Jod-Heh-Vav-Hey, which we transliterate as Y-H-W-H. It essentially means, "He Is Who He Is," although, grammatically, it is more like a personal name.<br><br>c. **His covenant* (and His word)**<br>Once God has committed Himself to a covenant, He never breaks it. A covenant is particularly appropriate to associate with the name *Jehovah*, or *Yahweh*, which speaks of the eternal, unchanging nature of God. | 10 |

| Question | Answer | Points |
|---|---|---|
| 6. (cont.) | **d. The-Lord-Will-Provide** | |

In Hebrew, the word that is translated *"Provide"* literally means "to see." From that meaning, we get the beautiful thought that when God sees, He provides. We also get the wonderful concept that God's first covenant commitment is to provide. This is the root of all His commitment: He provides for His people.

**e. I am the Lord who heals you**

The word that is translated *"heals"* is the basic Hebrew word for physical healing. In modern Hebrew, it is the word used for "doctor." In fact, it would be perfectly correct to translate this phrase as "I am Yahweh [or Jehovah], your doctor."

**f. The-Lord-Is-My-Banner**

This particular episode is invested with a permanent significance because the lesson, as I see it, is this: in our journey to, and in our attempt to enter into, the inheritance God has provided for us, we are always going to face opposition. This is not just something that happened once; it is going to happen from generation to generation. The Lord is going to take our side. He is going to stand with us in the opposition, but we are going to have to participate in these battles.

**g. The-Lord-Is-Peace**

Most of us are familiar with the Hebrew word for "peace": *shalom*. It is the contemporary greeting in Hebrew. That was the name of the altar: The Lord Is Shalom, or Peace. Peace is in a Person—the Lord Himself.

**h. His shepherd (and ours)**

David's use of the word *"my"* indicates the personal nature of his relationship with the Shepherd. He goes on to reveal the significance of a shepherd as one who provides nourishment and refreshment (verse 2), restoration (verse 3), and guidance (verse 3).

**i. The Lord Our Righteousness**

God is going to restore righteousness to His people. But the righteousness that He has promised to restore is in a Person. Our righteousness is not in a system of law or in a religion; rather, as I stated about peace, righteousness is in a Person—the promised Messiah.

**j. The Lord Is There**

Tremendous details are given to us about the construction of the temple: the materials that are used, the dimensions, and so on. Then, when the temple and the city are complete, God's name is given to it: "The Lord Is There." This name brings out, of course, the real purpose for building both the city and the temple—that they should be a dwelling place for the Lord.

| Question | Answer | Points |
|---|---|---|
| 7. | **a. The knowledge of sin** | 3 |

One key purpose for which the law was given was to show human beings the reality and power of sin. First, people need a diagnosis; then, they receive the medicine. This is true psychologically. It is no good for us to explain to people God's way of salvation if they do not realize they have the disease of sin. They have to be convinced that they are sinners before they will recognize and receive God's plan of salvation.

**b. No ("*Certainly not!*")**

Paul is careful to point out there is nothing wrong with the law. The fault is not in the law. In Romans 7:12, he says, "*Therefore the law is holy, and the commandment holy and just and good.*"

**c. The law**

The purpose of the law, therefore, is to bring into the open the total sinfulness of sin—to show it in all its ugliness, all its real colors. There is no source for this revelation but the Bible, and the law is God's diagnostic.

| Question | Answer | Points |
|---|---|---|
| 8. | **a. His flesh**<br><br>The word *"flesh"* in Romans 7:18 does not refer to the physical body; it means the nature we have inherited as descendants of Adam. Thus, the *flesh* refers to our old, Adamic nature. We will come back to this point later in this course.<br><br>**b. No**<br><br>No matter how hard Paul tried in his own strength, he was powerless to do what he knew to be the right thing.<br><br>**c. Sin**<br><br>Do you see what the law does? It pinpoints sin, showing a power at work in us that operates even contrary to our own sincere will and intention.<br><br>**d. Captivity**<br><br>The Greek word for *"captivity"* does not refer to a criminal who has broken the law but to a prisoner of war—someone who has been taken captive and made to fight against the side he is really on. That is Paul's description of his own experience. | 4 |
| 9. | **a. As a tutor**<br><br>The Greek word translated *"tutor,"* *paidagōgos,* is the term from which we get the English word *pedagogue.* It describes a senior slave in the household of a wealthy man whose job was to give that man's children their first basic instructions in right and wrong; and, when they became old enough, to lead them every day to the school or to the tutor who was to teach them. This man was not the teacher; he was the one who took the children to the teacher.<br><br>**b. Christ**<br><br>Whether it is the law of Moses* for the Jews or any law for Gentiles, it gives the first principles of right and wrong. It could not teach us all that we need to know about righteousness. But it became our slave to lead us to the Messiah (Christ), who could teach us.<br><br>**c. Faith (in Christ)**<br><br>Only one Person was ever justified* through keeping the whole law through His sinless obedience: Jesus Christ! That is what qualifies Him to be our Savior and the means of grace by which we are made righteous* through our faith in His atoning* death. | 3 |
| 10. | **a. It kept them under guard (for faith in Christ).**<br><br>In a special situation, the Jews were prepared by being shut up by the law to keep them ready for the Messiah. Being *"kept under guard"* suggests being incarcerated* or kept in custody.<br><br>**b. They would dwell alone.**<br><br>It is one of the most remarkable facts of history that the Jewish nation could be dispersed from her own land in the year AD 70 and, nineteen centuries later, after spending two thousand years living among at least one hundred other nations, could still be a separate, identifiable people. Such retained identity is true only of the people of Israel*. And what kept them separate was primarily the law of Moses.<br><br>**c. No**<br><br>God had to have a people to whom the Messiah could come. He had to prepare a nation carefully and specially to whom He could send His Son—a Son who could obey His parents, keep the ordinances of His nation, and still be faithful to God. It is a tremendous miracle that God was able to do that. | 3 |

| Question | Answer | Points |
|---|---|---|
| 11. | **a. Heaven**<br><br>The laws that God gave Israel were not from any earthly nation. They were directly from heaven.<br><br>b.<br><br>   **i. Just**<br>   **iii. True**<br>   **iii. Good**<br><br>In our world today, nearly all the nations with a code of law that preserves human integrity and morality can trace that code back to the laws God gave Moses. So, the law established a pattern that all other nations could look at to see what it would be like to be a nation governed by laws that are just and true and good. | 4 |
| 12. | **a. The law of the LORD**<br><br>You can read any of the five books of Moses (the first five books of the Bible, called the Torah by the Jewish people) and find inexhaustible lessons to guide you, guard you, and warn you. The same is true of all Scripture. In 2 Timothy 3:16–17, Paul writes, "*All Scripture is given by inspiration of God, and is profitable for doctrine, for reproof, for correction, for instruction in righteousness, that the man of God may be complete, thoroughly equipped for every good work.*"<br><br>**b. Meditating on God's law**<br><br>If you want to be successful, the key is meditating on the right thing. The successful person in this psalm meditates on God's law day and night. That is the reason for his success. When you add the Scriptures beyond the law of Moses, and when you know, for instance, from reading the New Testament, *who* the ultimate Passover Lamb is, meditating on the law becomes an even richer practice. Someone said this about the Old and New Testaments: "The New is in the Old concealed, and the Old is in the New revealed."<br><br>**c. Whatever he does shall prosper.**<br><br>Prosperity means having all that you need to do the will of God. In Deuteronomy 28:11, Moses tells us that the result of hearing and obeying the voice of the Lord is *abundant prosperity* (NIV). In verse 9 of the following chapter, Moses returns briefly to this theme, saying that keeping the words of God's covenant causes us to prosper in all that we do. That leaves no room for failure or frustration in any area of our lives. | 3 |
| | Check your written memory work. If your memory work is word-perfect, 4 points for each verse. (1 point off for each mistake in a verse. If there are more than three mistakes, do not mark any points for that verse.) | 8 |
| | Total Points | ___ /46 |

Fill in the total points for lesson 4 on the "Tally Sheet for Each Lesson" on page 253.

# LESSON 5 ANSWERS

| Question | Answer | Points |
|---|---|---|
| 1. | **No**<br><br>This is a paramount truth that both Jews* and Gentiles* need to embrace. Neither by the law of Moses*, nor by any other laws or set of rules, can anyone be made righteous*. Again, one main purpose of the law* is to diagnose our problem of sin before God reveals His solution. | 1 |
| 2. | **The Law* and the Prophets***<br><br>By referencing the Law and the Prophets, Paul is careful to say, in effect, "I am not innovating. All this is contained in embryo form in the Old Testament. All I am doing is explaining what was implicit in the Law and the Prophets." | 1 |
| 3. | **Jesus Christ**<br><br>The text is better translated as "Yeshua the Messiah" than the Greek alternative, "Jesus Christ," since that term better represents the continuity of Scripture. | 1 |
| 4. | **All**<br><br>There are a number of words in the Bible for wrongdoing, and each one is specific. The Greek word for "*sinned*" in Romans 3:23 means "to miss the mark" or "to come short of the mark." We were all created for the glory of God, and when we live in sin, we fail to fulfill the purpose for which we were created. As a result, somewhere deep inside, we experience frustration. | 1 |
| 5. | **Justification***<br><br>I would prefer to translate "*being justified*" as "having justification offered to us," because we are justified* only when we respond to the offer of justification. Many people view *justified* as a dry, theological word. But it is actually a glorious word for which I will give you a series of possible translations: "acquitted"; "not guilty"; "reckoned righteous"; "made 'just-as-if-I'd' never sinned." | 1 |
| 6. | a. **They will rejoice greatly in the Lord.**<br>b. **Their soul shall be joyful in their God.**<br><br>Where the *New King James Version* says, "*I will greatly rejoice in the* LORD*, my soul shall be joyful in my God,*" other translations say, "*I will have much joy in the Lord. My soul will have joy in my God*" (NLV), "*I am overwhelmed with joy in the* LORD *my God!*" (NLT), "*I delight greatly in the* LORD*; my soul rejoices in my God*" (NIV), and "*I will sing for joy in* GOD*, explode in praise from deep in my soul!*" (MSG). For me, an old word says it best: *exult.* That might be the strongest word possible to convey being intensely happy and telling everybody about it. | 2 |
| 7. | a. **salvation**<br>b. **righteousness***<br><br>Many people know what it is to be saved, but many who are saved do not realize what it is to be justified. First, God clothes you with the garment of salvation. That is wonderful. Maybe we could say that it is a kind of undergarment. Then He wraps the robe of righteousness around you. He totally covers you with this robe of His righteousness. It does not matter from what angle the devil looks at you; all he can see is the righteousness of God. He has nothing he can say against you. That is justification. | 2 |
| 8. | a. **His blood**<br>b. **faith**<br><br>God displayed to the whole universe the sole, sufficient propitiation* or atonement* for all the sins human beings have ever committed, and He demonstrated it by Jesus's life laid down and by His shed blood. God did not do this secretly. He did not do it in a corner. He did it very publicly. | 2 |
| 9. | **In His *forbearance*, God had passed over them.**<br><br>For nearly fifteen centuries under the law of Moses, the Israelites were continually remembering and atoning for their sins. But no sacrifice they ever brought removed their sins. The sacrifices commanded by the law merely covered those sins until the next sacrifice was due. So, for fifteen centuries, God *passed over* sin that had never been properly atoned for. | 1 |

| Question | Answer | Points |
|---|---|---|
| 10. | **He put away sin.**<br><br>In sacrificing Himself, Christ did not just cover sin; He disposed of it. He removed it. He set it aside. Throughout the era of the old covenant\*, God knew what He was going to do through Jesus Christ. For those fifteen centuries, when He passed over sin that had not been properly atoned for, He did it in faith on the basis of the assurance that Jesus would ultimately provide the all-sufficient sacrifice. | 1 |
| 11. | **just; justifier**<br><br>This is the crux of Romans—that God can be both just and justify the sinner. How could He pass over sin without compromising His own righteousness? The answer is set out in Romans. And this is the key verse. God can be perfectly righteous and still forgive sinners. | 2 |
| 12. | **The law of faith**<br><br>The more that religious people know, the prouder they become; and pride is an abomination to God, so He has to do away with it. He does so by this *"law of faith,"* which leaves us nothing to boast of. We cannot claim credit for anything. We did not do anything for ourselves—God did it all. All we can do is receive, by faith, the free gift of righteousness that God offers us. | 1 |
| 13. | **Their faith**<br><br>Again, boasting and pride are incompatible with faith. This is important to remember because many of us are in danger of becoming proud. We do some little thing for God, we find some success in ministry or service, and we think, "Here I am, the one with the answers!" That type of attitude is terribly dangerous. There is no room for pride. It is excluded. | 1 |
| 14. | a. **not worthy**<br>b. **speak a word**<br>c. **faith**<br>d. **believed**<br><br>What accompanies the centurion's faith? Humility. He says, in essence, "I am not worthy. I have no claims. Just say the word." Jesus confirms twice (see Matthew 9:10, 13) that the reason He healed the servant was because of the centurion's faith. | 4 |
| 15. | a. **She fell at His feet.**<br>b. **No; she had to keep asking.**<br>c. **The lost sheep of the house of Israel\* (or people of Israel)**<br>d. **The children's bread**<br>e. **As a little dog**<br>f. **In humility; she replies, *"Yes, Lord, yet even the little dogs under the table eat from the children's crumbs."***<br>g. **Yes; her daughter is delivered from the demon.**<br><br>The conspicuous thing about the Syro-Phoenician woman is her humility. In the West, it is not necessarily an insult to be called a dog; someone can "work like a dog" or be "top dog." But in the Middle East, you could not have a much worse insult. Jesus is putting her in her place, saying, "I am committed by covenant\* to Israel. I made a covenant with the Israelites through Moses that I would be their Healer, but I have no covenant with you, so you are just a little dog." When God seems to be hard, then He is the most merciful when we respond in humility and faith. | 10 |
| | Check your written memory work. If your memory work is word-perfect, 4 points for each verse. (1 point off for each mistake in a verse. If there are more than three mistakes, do not mark any points for that verse.) | 8 |
| | Total Points | ___/39 |

Fill in the total points for lesson 5 on the "Tally Sheet for Each Lesson" on page 253.

# LESSON 6 ANSWERS

| Question | Answer | Points |
|---|---|---|
| 1. | **He believed God.**<br><br>At that point, Abraham did absolutely nothing but believe in God's specific promise to him. And that was how he achieved righteousness\*, as Paul points out. (See also James 2:21–24.) He did not earn it. It was not on the basis of what he had accomplished. Righteousness was credited to Abraham based on his faith alone. | 1 |
| 2. | **None (*"To him who does not work but believes on Him who justified the ungodly…."*)**<br><br>This powerful verse points out that if you want to receive righteousness from God by faith in the same way that Abraham did—and there is no other way—the first thing you have to do is *not do anything*! Paul writes, *"To him who does not work."* You must come to the end of all you can do to earn God's favor, and do nothing but believe. This is the pattern and example of Abraham. | 1 |
| 3. | **As Him who justifies the ungodly**<br><br>In lesson 5, I highlighted the point that in Romans 3:26, Paul tells us God's demonstration of righteousness enabled Him to be both *"just and the justifier of the one who has faith in Jesus."* I indicated that this is the crux of Romans—that God can be just and also justify the sinner. | 1 |
| 4. | **No (Abraham still made mistakes.)**<br><br>I am reassured that Abraham still made mistakes, because if he hadn't, that would put us in a difficult position. We find that after Abraham had received God's promise in Genesis 12, in the ensuing chapters of Genesis, he made some serious mistakes. For example, we read in Genesis 16 that he and Sarah decide they had better get a child through Sarah's maid, Hagar, and they take the initiative out of God's hands. Further on, in Genesis 20, Abraham tells a lie about Sarah and permits her to be taken into a Gentile king's harem (for the second time). That is not the way a husband ought to behave. And yet, God considered him righteous\*, in spite of his mistakes, because he believed God. | 1 |
| 5. | **No (He only did what He saw His Father doing.)**<br><br>In the life of faith, we *never* take the initiative. This is a basic principle that follows Jesus's pattern. The only safe basis for living the life of faith is to let God take the initiative. Each time we do what Abraham did and take the initiative rather than leaving everything in God's hands, we end up in trouble. | 1 |
| 6. | **Satan**<br><br>That is a remarkable statement. Apparently, Satan went to God and said, in effect, "Let me get at those apostles!" Not all translations bring this point out, but it is clear in the Greek that the *you* in this verse is plural: "Sift you apostles like wheat." | 1 |
| 7. | **That his faith should (would) not fail**<br><br>It impresses me about Jesus that He did not pray that Peter would not deny Him. Under the circumstances, given Peter's character at that point, and the tremendous onslaught of the forces of darkness that was to come against him very shortly, it was inevitable that Peter *would* deny Jesus. Jesus is always a realist, for which I am glad. | 1 |
| 8. | **works**<br><br>This verse is another reminder that Paul wants us to be absolutely clear our righteousness cannot come on the basis of our works. | 1 |

| Question | Answer | Points |
|---|---|---|
| 9. | a. **His transgression is forgiven.**<br><br>b. **His sin is covered.**<br><br>c. **The Lord does not impute iniquity to him.**<br><br>d. **There is no deceit in his spirit.**<br><br>The third element is the "negative" side of God's reckoning righteousness to us. He no longer keeps a reckoning of our sins. Thank God! | 4 |
| 10. | **They are for the uncircumcised (Gentiles*) as well.**<br><br>This is a vital question for all who come from a Jewish background, but it goes beyond that because there are other external ordinances of the faith. Some people, for example, compare baptism to circumcision. There are limits to that comparison. We might ask, "Is my faith reckoned to me as righteousness before I am baptized?" My answer is yes. If you sincerely believe in Jesus, and you intend to obey the injunction to be baptized, then your faith is reckoned to you as righteousness from the moment you believe. Afterward, baptism is, in a certain sense, a seal of the righteousness you already have by faith. | 1 |
| 11. | **Before he was circumcised**<br><br>This point is extremely important. Abraham's faith was reckoned to him as righteousness in Genesis 15, but he did not experience circumcision until Genesis 17. There was a considerable period of time between those two events. | 1 |
| 12. | **That he might be the father of *all* those who believe**<br><br>God had promised Abraham that he would be the father of a multitude of nations—not just one nation, Israel*, but all nations—and that, in due course, people from every nation on earth would become his spiritual descendants through faith in his Seed, the Lord Jesus. This was the promise of God to Abraham. Abraham did not have to be circumcised for the promise to be given him; it was given him while he was uncircumcised. | 1 |
| 13. | **The steps of the faith which our father Abraham had while still uncircumcised**<br><br>The only condition for being a descendant of Abraham is faith. God insists upon that. He is tolerant in other areas and allows for many differences. I do not believe God wants all His people to look alike, behave alike, or conform to one single pattern. He enjoys variety. But as for being a descendant of Abraham, God will not waive the condition of faith. We are all descendants of Abraham by faith in Jesus Christ. Faith is the sole requirement. | 1 |
| 14. | **No (It requires faith as well.)**<br><br>Abraham is more than a figure; he is a pattern. He went ahead and laid out the pathway. To be his descendants, we must walk in that pathway. In Paul's words, we must *"walk in the steps of [his] faith."* For people from a Jewish background, circumcision is not sufficient. | 1 |
| 15. | **The righteousness of faith**<br><br>Paul is emphasizing that God made this initial promise solely on the basis of Abraham's faith. It would have been unfair and inconsistent to later add, as a further condition, "But you have to keep the law of Moses*." Paul points out in Galatians 3:17 that the law* was given 430 years later. | 1 |
| 16. | **Wrath**<br><br>*"Where there is no law,"* writes Paul, *"there is no transgression."* Even if somebody has done wrong, unless there is a law, there is no wrath. But when a law is imposed, and it is broken, the reaction of the one who made the law is wrath or anger. | 1 |
| 17. | **No**<br><br>Many people have an incorrect picture of what the law does. We have the idea that keeping the law will draw people closer to God. It will not. Many people who try to get close to God start making all sorts of laws for themselves, and they attempt to keep those laws. What actually happens is that they get farther away from God. We are fighting centuries of religious tradition that tried to persuade us that keeping the law was going to do us good, or even that it was designed to do us good. | 1 |

| Question | Answer | Points |
|---|---|---|
| 18. | a. **So that the promise might be sure to all the seed, not only to those who are of the law, but also to those who are of the faith of Abraham (to include both Israel and Gentiles)**<br><br>God wanted to make sure no one would be excluded from this promise of righteousness; it had to be by faith, so that it might be according to grace. This truth is very simple but very important: none of us has ever earned righteousness from God. We either receive it as a gift by faith or we do not get it at all. There is no alternative way to be righteous before God.<br><br>b. **Boasting (or pride)**<br><br>What does religious legalism invariably produce in the people who practice it? Pride. In the church, we tend to get angry over adultery and fornication and drunkenness. This is right. I am not suggesting that we tolerate those sins. But we tolerate a whole lot of pride, which is a much more serious sin than the others. | 2 |
| 19. | a. **life**<br><br>b. **calls**<br><br>God called Abraham *"a father of many nations"* when Abraham did not yet have a child of his own body. It is important to understand that when God calls a person something, that is what they are. We may not see the evidence, but that does not matter. God called Gideon a *"mighty man of valor"* (Judges 6:12) when he was hiding like a coward. God calls us saints, as we saw in lesson 1. God called me to be a teacher of the Scriptures. What does He call you? | 2 |
| 20. | **No**<br><br>*"Contrary to hope,* [Abraham] *in hope believed"* (Romans 4:18). Who can improve on that expression? There is no way to say it better. Abraham hoped, and yet he had no earthly hope. You, too, may know that experience. You hope, even though there is no hope in the natural; you go on believing. Whatever you do, do not stop believing God. | 1 |
| 21. | **Hopefully, your answer is "Yes."**<br><br>Sometimes people try to persuade themselves that their situation is not all that desperate. Really, it is much better to face the fact that the situation *is* desperate, and say, "There is only one person who can help me, and that Person is God." *That* is faith. | No points |
| 22. | **Yes**<br><br>Abraham received strength in his physical body through faith. Sarah, too, received strength. Her womb was quickened, and, in that respect, she became alive again. This was not a temporary change in Abraham, because, after Sarah died, he married again and had five more children. Christ was raised from the dead by the Holy Spirit, and we, too, can receive new life in our bodies by the same Spirit. | 1 |
| 23. | **Nothing**<br><br>The double-minded, unstable, undecided person gets nowhere with God. Make up your mind from now on that what God says is right and that, if He has promised something, He *will* do it! | 1 |
| 24. | **God**<br><br>How did Abraham give glory to God? Not by his efforts but by believing. So God has provided a way by which we can give Him back the glory that our sin has deprived Him of—by believing. When we believe God, and His promise is worked out in our lives, that gives glory to God. That is the only way we can ever give glory to God—by faith. | 1 |
| 25. | **For *us***<br><br>This glorious statement was written not only for Abraham, but also for us who believe in the gospel of Jesus. | 1 |

| Question | Answer | Points |
|---|---|---|
| 26. | **We were (and we have ascended with Him as well).**<br><br>*Identification** is the key that unlocks what happened at the cross. On the cross, there was a two-way identification. First, Jesus identified with us. He took the sinner's place. He became the last Adam. (See 1 Corinthians 15:45.) He exhausted the evil inheritance that had come upon the whole Adamic race. And He was buried. When He was buried, that Adamic inheritance was terminated. Then He rose again on the third day, the Head of a new race. We must realize and reckon that He was our Representative. | 1 |
| | Check your written memory work. If your memory work is word-perfect, 4 points for each verse. (1 point off for each mistake in a verse. If there are more than three mistakes, do not mark any points for that verse.) | 8 |
| | Total Points | ___/38 |

Fill in the total points for lesson 6 on the "Tally Sheet for Each Lesson" on page 253.

# LESSON 7 ANSWERS

| Question | Answer | Points |
|---|---|---|
| 1. | **By faith**<br><br>In Romans 4, we focused mainly on the example and pattern of Abraham and his faith. Remember that Abraham was justified* by his faith *before* circumcision, or before the giving of the law of Moses*; and God invites both Jews* and Gentiles* to be justified by faith. | 1 |
| 2. | a. **peace**<br><br>For the first time in our lives, we are in harmony with our Creator. And, in a certain sense, because we are in harmony with our Creator, we are in harmony with His creation. Sometimes, after people meet the Lord and receive righteousness* by faith, everything actually looks different.<br><br>b. **Our Lord Jesus Christ**<br><br>We must never lose sight of the fact that it is through Jesus's death on the cross and our identification* with Him in His death, burial, and resurrection that we are justified by faith so that we have peace with God.<br><br>c. **The stones of the field**<br><br>Not everybody has a dramatic experience when they receive salvation, but part of having peace with God is having peace with creation. There is a unique connection between believers and creation. We will explore this idea further when we study Romans 8, which says *"For the earnest expectation of the creation eagerly waits for the revealing of the sons of God"* (verse 19). In verse 21, Paul goes on to explain, *"Because the creation itself also will be delivered from the bondage of corruption into the glorious liberty of the children of God."*<br><br>d. **The beasts of the field**<br><br>When we are justified by faith, everything suddenly becomes different. Forces that were formerly against you are now on your side. Forces you previously could not control no longer frighten you. You have peace. | 4 |
| 3. | a. **access**<br><br>b. **Grace**<br><br>Being justified by faith gives us access into grace that upholds us. We are no longer being carried to and fro, the plaything of forces outside of ourselves, but we are standing firm in the grace of God, and God's grace is upon us.<br><br>c.<br><br>   i. **A chosen generation**<br><br>   ii. **A royal priesthood**<br><br>   iii. **A holy nation**<br><br>   iv. **His [God's] own special people**<br><br>The word *"special"* in 1 Peter 2:9 implies grace, and whenever you hear the word *grace*, it is probably good to think in terms of *favor*. The two words are different ways of translating the same term. The Greek word for grace, *charis*—from which we get the words *charisma* and *charismata*—means beauty, elegance, and charm.<br><br>d. **Life**<br><br>Solomon is talking about a king, but remember that Jesus is not just a king—He is the King of all kings. When He lifts up His face upon us and looks upon us with favor, that is life. | 10 |

| Question | Answer | Points |
|---|---|---|
| 3. (cont.) | **e. A cloud of the latter rain**<br><br>Proverbs 16:15 tells us that God's favor is like *"a cloud of the latter rain,"* and when we realize that the latter rain often represents the outpouring of the Holy Spirit in the last days, we appreciate that God is not giving us only a few drops of favor but rather an outpouring that is ultimately for the sake of the end-times harvest of souls.<br><br>**f. Favor**<br><br>We are protected on every side by the grace or favor of God upon us. It may also be helpful to think of grace in terms of beauty. One of the things that is lacking in many people's religious lives is real beauty; we are content to remain somber and drab. But I think God wants us to be beautiful. In Psalm 149:4, the verse that corresponds to the next question, God says He will *"beautify the humble* [*"meek"* KJV]" with His salvation. What is the beauty that comes on us? It is His *favor.*<br><br>**g. Yes! (The Lord takes *pleasure* in His people.)**<br><br>How we need to hear this truth and receive it into our hearts! | |
| 4. | **a. rejoice; hope**<br><br>We now have hope, in which we rejoice. We may be facing a long, dark tunnel, but there is light at the end. We know that, ultimately, we will share God's glory in eternity forever and ever.<br><br>**b. The hope of glory**<br><br>Once Christ comes in, we have *"the hope of glory."* Hope is an important part of salvation. Romans 8:24, which we will come to later, says, *"We were saved in this hope."*<br><br>**c. As a helmet**<br><br>We must learn to protect our minds; and the helmet is hope—a quiet, serene, confident expectation of good. We rejoice in that hope. | 4 |
| 5. | **a. Tribulations**<br><br>The fourth experiential result of being justified by faith is a very different kind of rejoicing, one that some people want nothing to do with: glorying in tribulations (pressures, tests, trials, and problems).<br><br>**b. Count it all joy**<br><br>You will not merely rejoice in hope of the glory of God, but you will also glory in trials and testings. Paul uses the term *"glory"* (Romans 5:3), while James uses *"joy"* (James 1:2).<br><br>c.<br><br>**i. Perseverance**<br><br>**ii. Patience**<br><br>Essentially, Paul and James give the same reason for why we should be excited by trials that come our way: they produce perseverance and patience. Do you know the only way you can learn endurance? It is by enduring! There is no other way.<br><br>d.<br><br>**i. Perfect**<br><br>**ii. Complete**<br><br>**iii. Lacking nothing**<br><br>Do you wish to be *"perfect and complete, lacking nothing"*? There is only one way to attain that state, and that is the tribulation route. Enduring testing will bring you through to the place where you are *"perfect and complete, lacking nothing."* Again, if you want to achieve that goal, you must take this path. You do not have to arrange the tests; God will take care of that. | 11 |

| Question | Answer | Points |
|---|---|---|
| 5. (cont.) | e.<br><br>   **i. Perseverance**<br><br>   **ii. Character**<br><br>   **iii. Hope**<br><br>When you have already been through a series of tests, and the next test comes, you do not get depressed, wring your hands, and say, "What's happening to me?" You say, "It will be exciting to see how God gets me out of this!" That is hope. You learn only by experience that God will always get you through the situation. It might seem that He is a little slow in doing it, but He will, and you will come out of it. But you do not get that kind of hope without first undergoing testing.<br><br>**f. The love of God**<br><br>What is the ultimate basis of our hope? It is *"the love of God…poured out in our hearts."* What a tremendous phrase! It does not say that *some* of God's love has been poured out in our hearts; it says that *the* love of God—the entire love of God—is poured out into our hearts through the outpoured Spirit. After you have been baptized in the Holy Spirit, I don't think you need to pray for love; rather, you need to draw on the love you already have inside you. It is all available. | |
| 6. | **Death**<br><br>No one can resist death. But when Jesus died and rose from the dead, He proved that love is stronger than death. Love is the strongest force in the universe. Never underestimate its strength. | 1 |
| 7. | **Love**<br><br>Nothing can wear out the love of God. Nothing can crush the love of God; it is uncrushable. It *"bears all things, believes all things, hopes all things, endures all things"* (1 Corinthians 13:7). This is the love that *"has been poured out in our hearts by the Holy Spirit"* (Romans 5:5), and this love gives us hope. | 1 |
| 8. | **a. without strength**<br><br>**b. ungodly**<br><br>**c. sinners**<br><br>**d. enemies**<br><br>This is the full measure of the love of God: Christ died for us while we were still helpless, ungodly, sinners, and enemies of God. This is divine love, wrapped up in the Greek word *agape*. It is unconditional; it makes no demands. Christ did not say to His disciples, "If you will do this or that, then I will pay the penalty for your sins." He did it out of His own will. He was under no pressure or obligation to do so. He owed us nothing. That is the love Paul is talking about. It makes no conditions. It is simply love. | 4 |
| 9. | **As love**<br><br>The apostle John is noted in Scripture as one *"whom Jesus loved."* (See John 13:23; 20:2; 21:7; see also John 19:26.) It is no wonder, then, that it is in one of his epistles that we find this revelation that *"God is love."* This idea is summarized in the same epistle*: *"We love…because He first loved us"* (1 John 4:19). If God had not loved us first, unconditionally, we would not have known what love was and would not have allowed it to work in our hearts, minds, and character. | 1 |
| 10. | **No (*"God does not give the Spirit by measure."*)**<br><br>God does not measure out a ration and say, "This is how much you have earned, and if you do better, I will give you some more tomorrow." That is what I would have done if I had been God. I would have made some conditions or demands. I would have said, "If you straighten out a little bit, and I see some signs of improvement…." In fact, if I had been God, I never would have saved me at all. But I am glad God did not think I was too bad for saving. And when He baptizes us in the Holy Spirit, He pours out His Spirit and, with it, His love—in full measure. | 1 |

| Question | Answer | Points |
|---|---|---|
| 11. | **God** | 1 |
| | Notice the word *"rejoice"* again. This is the climax: rejoicing and exulting—not in an experience, not in a gift, not in a blessing, but in God Himself. | |
| 12. | a. | 3 |
| |    **i. His light** | |
| |    **ii. His truth** | |
| | b.  **As *"my exceeding joy"*** | |
| | David was depressed and mourning because the enemy was oppressing him. That is the reason we, too, often mourn. But God Himself was the supreme joy of David's life. When David was cast down and did not know where to turn, he said, in effect, "I will go to the place of sacrifice and lay my life down on the altar of God. I will abandon myself to Him without reservation and know Him as my exceeding joy." | |
| | Check your written memory work. If your memory work is word-perfect, 4 points for each verse. (1 point off for each mistake in a verse. If there are more than three mistakes, do not mark any points for that verse.) | 8 |
| | Total Points | ___/50 |

Fill in the total points for lesson 7 on the "Tally Sheet for Each Lesson" on page 253.

# LESSON 8 ANSWERS

| Question | Answer | Points |
|---|---|---|
| 1. | a. Y | 6 |
| | b. N | |
| | c. N | |
| | d. Y | |
| | e. Y | |
| | f. Y | |
| | God had given Adam just one commandment, a "negative" command—*"Of the tree of the knowledge of good and evil you shall **not** eat"* (Genesis 2:17)—but no law*. From the time of Adam's transgression, there was no God-given law until Moses. From Moses onward is the period of the law of Moses*. | |
| 2. | **Moses; Jesus Christ** | 2 |
| | The complete system of law came at one time through one man, Moses. The law of Moses was given to only one small section of the human race, maybe three million people, at a certain point in history. It was never given to Gentiles*. Furthermore, the law could be carried out fully in only one place geographically, the land of Israel*, because much of the law entailed actions that could be done only in Israel. | |
| 3. | a. **Earth** | 2 |
| | b. **Heaven** | |
| 4. | a. **First** | 2 |
| | b. **Last** | |
| 5. | a. **First** | 2 |
| | b. **Second** | |
| 6. | a. **A living being** | 2 |
| | b. **A life-giving spirit** | |
| | Notes for questions 3–6: | |
| | Paul sets up a contrast between the first Adam and the last Adam and between *"a living being"* and *"a life-giving spirit."* I have often heard Jesus referred to as "the second Adam," but I do not believe that is what Paul is saying. He gives just two titles to Jesus: *"the last Adam"* and *"the second Man."* | |
| | First, when Jesus died on the cross, He died as the last Adam. In Him, the whole evil inheritance of the Adamic race was exhausted. His sacrifice took into account, and dealt with completely, even the evil of the generations to come. Hebrews 9:14 says that it was *"through the eternal Spirit"* that Jesus *"offered Himself without spot to God."* | |
| | So, through the eternal Holy Spirit, going beyond time, Jesus took on Himself the awful inheritance that had infected the entire Adamic race, including you and me, and dealt with it. When He died, it died. When He was buried, it was buried. It was put away finally and completely. | |
| | And when Jesus rose from the dead, He rose as the second Man, the head of a new race, the Emmanuel race, the God/man race. | |
| 7. | **A living hope** | 1 |
| | Jesus was begotten from the dead by God, and, through faith in Him, *we* are begotten from the dead. We rise out of the depth of sin and the curse of Adam to become members of a new race, of which the Head is Jesus. | |

| Question | Answer | Points |
|---|---|---|
| 8. | a. **image** | 5 |
| | b. **creation** | |
| | c. **created** | |
| | d. **before** | |
| | e. **Him** | |
| | We are often reminded of Christ's *earthly* nature and how He was born of a virgin in Bethlehem. These truths are important because we see Scripture fulfilled and *"the prophetic word confirmed"* (2 Peter 1:19). But it is also very important not to lose sight of Jesus's *eternal* nature, which we find expressed in these verses. None of these statements can be said of Adam. | |
| 9. | a. **head** | 2 |
| | b. **firstborn** | |
| | Jesus is *"the head of the body,"* which is the church, and He is *"the firstborn from the dead."* He was the first to rise in resurrection into a new kind of life—a life that had never existed in the universe before Jesus rose from the dead into that resurrection life. He rose as the Head of the body. Again, He was begotten out of death. Jesus is the last Adam in that He had to seal off the whole evil inheritance of the human race. And He had to rise from the dead as the second Man, the Head of an entirely new race that had never before existed. | |
| 10. | a. **offense [or transgression]; condemnation** | 4 |
| | b. **righteous* act; justification*** | |
| | Adam, by one act of transgression, brought condemnation on the whole race descended from him. He received the command and disobeyed it. Sin entered. Death followed sin. And sin and death have passed over onto all of Adam's descendants, including you and me. But Jesus, through one act of righteousness*, obtained the possibility of *"justification of life ["justification and life"* NIV]" for all human beings. It is the "possibility of justification" because not everyone will receive it. | |
| | The one righteous act—an act that fulfills a requirement of God—was the sacrifice of Jesus Himself upon the cross. | |
| | Note that there are two words for *life* in Greek: *bios*, which generally refers to the course of our natural life on earth, and from which we get the word *biology*; and *zoe*, which refers to God's divine, eternal life and is offered to us who believe. | |
| 11. | a. **disobedience; sinners** | 4 |
| | b. **obedience; righteous** | |
| | Just as surely as Adam's disobedience made us all sinners, Christ's obedience can make us all righteous—not just in theory and not just in theology, but in the way we live, in the very nature that is in us. | |
| 12. | **No; the grace was "much more" and "abounded to many."** | 2 |
| | Although Adam's one act of disobedience brought its consequences upon all of us, we all add our own acts of disobedience. On the contrary, Jesus's one act of obedience brought its consequence—justification—on us, but we have nothing of our own to add to it. It was totally Jesus. So, whereas Adam's guilt was compounded by our guilt, Jesus's righteousness is unique, and we can add nothing to it. | |
| 13. | a. **One** | 2 |
| | b. **Many** | |
| | In the case of Adam, just one act of disobedience brought disaster on us all. But Jesus's one act of righteousness made it possible for us to be forgiven countless acts of disobedience. Do you see the difference? | |

| Question | Answer | Points |
|---|---|---|
| 14. | a. **Death** <br><br> b. **Life** <br><br> Through Adam's one act of disobedience, death reigned over the whole race. We all were subject to death. Yet, when we receive abundance of grace and the gift of righteousness in Jesus, we are delivered from the kingdom of Satan and carried over into the kingdom of God. God invites us to reign with Him—not just in the next world, but also right now. And the manner in which we reign is *life*. | 2 |
| 15. | a. **The law** <br><br> b. **Grace** <br><br> The verb *abound* is the same verb that gives us the noun *abundance*. So, when we read that *"grace abounded much more"* (Romans 5:20), we are reading that an overabundance of grace comes to us through God's mercy. Note also how grace reigns—*"through righteousness"* and *"to eternal life"* (v. 21). Wonderful! | 2 |
| | Check your written memory work. If your memory work is word-perfect, 4 points for each verse. (1 point off for each mistake in a verse. If there are more than three mistakes, do not mark any points for that verse.) | 8 |
| | Total Points | ____/48 |

Fill in the total points for lesson 8 on the "Tally Sheet for Each Lesson" on page 253.

# LESSON 9 ANSWERS

| Question | Answer | Points |
|---|---|---|
| 1. | **Our carnal nature**<br><br>In the context of Romans 6, *"the body of sin,"* the flesh, does *not* mean our physical body. In other places in the New Testament, "the flesh" does mean the actual physical body. But here it means the nature we inherited with our body by descent from Adam. When we are saved, we do not cease to have a body. But the body of sin is put out of action; it is rendered no longer able to function. | 1 |
| 2. | No (Paul is referring to our dying to sin.)<br><br>When Christ comes to live within us, we do not die physically, but the old body of sin, the old Adamic nature, is sentenced to death and dealt with. | 1 |
| 3. | **Circumcision of the heart**<br><br>Again, Paul is *not* saying that we lose our physical bodies by this experience; rather, *"the body of the sins of the flesh"*—the old sinful, Adamic, rebellious nature—is put out of operation. | 1 |
| 4. | **No (*"Certainly not!"* Paul is very emphatic that this is unthinkable.)**<br><br>Paul is thinking like a Jew and using a typical Hebrew phrase, *Haliyla* ("Haleela"), rendered as *"Certainly not!"* Although the King James Bible translates this phrase as *"God forbid,"* the name of God is not in the word; it just means that it is something unthinkable. In other words, "How would you dare to mention or suggest such a thing?" Today, we might say, "Perish the thought!" | 1 |
| 5. | **No**<br><br>When we enter the grace of God through Christ, a dramatic experience takes place: we become dead to sin so that, in the grace of God, we may live to righteousness*. It is a contradiction in terms to talk about living in sin within the grace of God. God does not give grace to people who live in sin. The condition on which we receive God's grace is that we cease to live in sin.<br><br>Admittedly, this state of living in righteousness is progressive as we come into increased revelation and faith, but we do not continue to sin willfully. For further study, the book of 1 John has some interesting, helpful, and challenging comments on sin. | 1 |
| 6. | **No (*"As many of us"* is a limiting statement.)**<br><br>Many Christians underrate the significance of baptism. It is much more important than most people imagine. Paul assumes that every Christian he is writing to has been baptized. | 1 |
| 7. | a. **Believing**<br><br>b. **Being baptized**<br><br>Many people from Pentecost onward have claimed salvation through faith in Jesus without being baptized. But the New Testament acknowledges no such thing, and such people are trespassing on the grace of God. Baptism in water is just as tremendous and life-changing an experience as the baptism of the Holy Spirit. It is not merely some little ceremony you go through to join a congregation. | 2 |
| 8. | **None (He was baptized *"immediately."*)**<br><br>Baptism is so important that when the Philippian jailer got saved, he and his household did not even wait until morning to be baptized; they were baptized in the middle of the night.<br><br>Nowhere does the New Testament open a door to a casual attitude toward baptism. Baptism is an urgent matter. Those who simply go through a ceremony have not grasped the significance of baptism and are missing the real blessing. | 1 |
| 9. | **Christ Jesus (and His death)**<br><br>The only thing *into which* you are baptized in water baptism is Jesus Christ Himself. Do not be content with anything less. Again, we are certainly not baptized into a church or a denomination—only into Jesus. | 1 |

| Question | Answer | Points |
|---|---|---|
| 10. | a. **death** | 2 |
| | b. **life** | |
| | Paul is saying that baptism is death. By being baptized, we are buried with Christ in that watery grave so that we might be resurrected as Jesus was resurrected—not in His own strength but in the supernatural power of the Holy Spirit. The glory of God brought Him out of the tomb. | |
| 11. | **resurrection; death** | 2 |
| | When Paul speaks about being united with Christ *"in the likeness of His death,"* he is speaking about being baptized. It is baptism that cuts us off from our former sins. | |
| | If we have been baptized, *"we also shall be* [united with Christ] *in the likeness of His resurrection."* If you have not been baptized by full immersion following a personal decision to follow Jesus, then you are taking a risk. The promise of resurrection is to those who have been united with Christ—buried with Him by baptism. | |
| 12. | a. **Our old man** | 2 |
| | b. **Through baptism** | |
| | Again, the mystery of identification* is the key that opens up all the riches of the cross. I do not just contemplate Jesus on the cross; I recognize that when He died, I died, too, because He took my place. He was my Representative. He was the last Adam. The total evil inheritance that was due to me and all the descendants of Adam came upon Him. Thus, the way up is identification, and the key is baptism. | |
| 13. | a. **head** | 4 |
| | Jesus's head was injured in several ways: by thorns pressed into His scalp (see, for example, Matthew 27:29), by blows to His face (see, for example, Matthew 27:30), and by His beard being plucked out (see Isaiah 50:6). | |
| | b. **heart** | |
| | Jesus died of a broken heart caused by the rejection of His Father. (See, for example, Matthew 27:46.) But, at the moment He died, the veil of the temple was torn from top to bottom (see, for example, Matthew 27:51), signifying the way was opened up for us to enter into the acceptance that belonged to Jesus by divine eternal right as God's beloved Son. | |
| | c. **foot; head** | |
| | That is the most exact picture you can give in so few words of the appearance of Jesus on the cross. God is telling us through the prophet Isaiah that Jesus bore the punishment of the rebel. | |
| 14. | **No** (*"His visage* [appearance] *was marred more than any man* [completely]*."*) | 1 |
| | We see pretty pictures of Jesus on the cross with a little blood trickling out of His hands or from the wound in His side. That does not begin to represent the reality. Consider all He had been through. There was *"no soundness"* (Isaiah 1:6) anywhere on His body. It had to be that way. It was the out-working of rebellion, the place you and I should have been. | |
| 15. | **The iniquity of us all** | 1 |
| | In Isaiah 53:6, the Hebrew word rendered *"iniquity," avon,* means rebellion and the punishment for rebellion and all the evil consequences of rebellion. On the cross, Jesus, as our Substitute, as the last Adam, became the rebel with our rebellion and endured all the evil consequences of rebellion. On the cross, an exchange took place, and it is the door to God's treasure house: Jesus became identified with our rebellion. | |

| Question | Answer | Points |
|---|---|---|
| 16. | a. **exalted** | 2 |
| | b. **exalted** | |
| | Jesus trusted God. He died in humility, but the Father raised Him up. If the Father had never raised Him up, Jesus never would have come back from the tomb. He humbled himself, and God exalted Him. If you humble yourself, God will exalt you. Don't try to exalt yourself, or you may suffer humiliation. | |
| 17. | a. **We were slaves of sin.** | 2 |
| | b. **We are freed from sin.** | |
| | You can have your past sins forgiven but still be a slave to sin if your old man has not been dealt with. Where Paul says "*freed*," I prefer "cleared" or "justified*." When you die, you are cleared of or justified from sin, because putting you to death is the last thing the law* can do to you. So, when we have died with Jesus, we are justified, freed from and acquitted of sin. The law no longer has a claim against us. We have paid the final penalty in Christ. | |
| 18. | a. **died** | 2 |
| | b. **live** | |
| | Notice that word "*if.*" Earlier, Paul had indicated, "If we have been buried, we will be resurrected." If we have not been buried with Christ, we will not be resurrected with Him. If we have not died with Him, we will not live with Him. We get to choose! | |
| 19. | **sin; God** | 2 |
| | Consider a despicably sinful man who does everything he shouldn't. Now consider that he has a heart attack and dies. Sin has no more power over him and no more attraction for him, and it produces no more reaction from him. That is what it is to be dead to sin. In the same way, you and I, because of what Jesus has done, are to reckon ourselves to be dead to sin. That means sin has no more power over us and no more attraction for us, and it produces no more reaction from us. | |
| | Check your written memory work. If your memory work is word-perfect, 4 points for each verse. (1 point off for each mistake in a verse. If there are more than three mistakes, do not mark any points for that verse.) | 8 |
| | Total Points | ____/38 |

Fill in the total points for lesson 9 on the "Tally Sheet for Each Lesson" on page 253.

# LESSON 10 ANSWERS

| Question | Answer | Points |
|---|---|---|
| 1. | a. **reign** | 2 |
| | b. **unrighteousness** | |
| 2. | a. **God** | 2 |
| | b. **righteousness\*** | |
| 3. | **Sin** | 1 |
| | Notes for questions 1–3: | |
| | Notice the wording that Paul uses in Romans 6:12–14: "reign," "present yourselves," and "dominion." "Reign" speaks of who is king or sovereign in our lives. "Present yourselves" indicates that we have a choice to submit to the right authority. The English word *dominion* is derived from the Latin word for "lord." It tells us that in our new position, received through identifying with Jesus through baptism, we have a new Lord—the Lord Jesus Christ. | |
| | Paul's instructions can be acted on only by people who have passed through the transition he has just described. We must take a firm stand against sin, but not in our own righteousness or our own strength. It must be in Christ's righteousness and empowered by the Holy Spirit. People who have *not* put their faith in Jesus and accepted His substitutionary sacrifice on their behalf are simply not capable of carrying out these instructions. | |
| 4. | **Our wills** | 1 |
| | Just as when you pray, in the Lord's Prayer, "Your will be done on earth as it is in heaven," yielding your will and your desires begins in you, the one praying. | |
| 5. | **Ourselves** | 1 |
| | Having yielded your will to God, yield your physical members to Him as instruments of righteousness. Many translations, including the *New King James Version*, use the word "instruments," but the Greek literally means "weapons." That implies spiritual conflict. The parts of your body are not just instruments, like a hoe or a plow, but weapons, like a sword or a spear, with which you fight. | |
| 6. | **Our bodies** | 1 |
| | It is a question of willing and yielding. You must do it in that order—first will, then yield—because if you do not will, then, by habit, you will yield to sin, since you are used to yielding to sin. But when you have yielded your will to God, you no longer will go on presenting the members of your body as instruments of sin to Satan. | |
| 7. | **By being under grace** | 1 |
| | We appropriate God's grace by faith, and the implication of this truth is powerful. Do not try to have it both ways at the same time because you cannot. If you are under the law\*, sin *will* have dominion over you. This sounds like a shocking statement, but the Bible says it consistently. It is important that you exercise your will rightly, humbly placing your trust in God, because if you do not, Satan will push you around. | |
| 8. | **Spirit** | 1 |
| | In Romans 8:14, Paul says, "As many as are led by the Spirit of God, these are sons of God." So, you have this choice: you can live like a son of God, being continuously led by the Holy Spirit, or you can turn your back on the Holy Spirit and try to keep the law. But you cannot combine the two. This is where people get into a "twilight zone." They are half trusting in grace and half trusting in their own little set of rules that they are keeping. | |

| Question | Answer | Points |
|---|---|---|
| 9. | **We will keep His word (or Word) (which contains His will).** | 1 |
| | Love for God must be united with obedience. Love is obedience to God's Word and to His Spirit's leading. As you just read in John 14:23, Jesus said, *"If anyone loves Me, he will keep My word."* Then He goes on, *"And My Father will love him, and We will come to him and make Our home with him."* We are so used to a motivation of fear for following God: "If you don't do this, you'll get punished." We don't realize that God's motivation toward us—and what He desires from us—is *love*. | |
| 10. | **No ("Certainly not!")** | 1 |
| | This is a different objection from the one at the beginning of Romans 6. That one was, *"Shall we continue in sin that grace may abound?"* (verse 1). This objection is, in effect, "Are we free to commit sinful acts when it suits us, since we are not under a law that says, 'Don't do it'?" | |
| 11. | **Whom we obey** | 1 |
| | When you yield yourself to someone to obey him, you become his slave. So, if, by a decision of your will, you decide to commit a sinful act because you are not under law—let's say an act of immorality—Paul says that by yielding to immorality, you become a slave of immorality. You cannot yield to such a thing without becoming its slave. You have to decide to whom you want to yield: sin or righteousness. | |
| 12. | *"Choose for yourselves this day whom you will serve."* | 1 |
| | Will you serve the true God or will you serve false gods? Since Joshua's day, the choice has never changed. It is not "Choose *whether* you will serve" but "Choose *whom* you will serve." After you are redeemed, your choice is this: will I serve sin or righteousness? Before you were redeemed, you did not have a choice. You could not help sinning; there was no other option. | |
| 13. | **Obeying from the heart** | 1 |
| | The word *"form"* in the phrase *"form of doctrine"* in Romans 6:17 is the same word used for heating and molding metal, causing it to set in a certain shape. In the same way, when people are newly converted and enthusiastic, they are not warm but hot. It is important to mold them properly at the beginning. What form is that hot metal going to be poured into? Into what shape will it be set? It is a passionate concern of mine that people get set in the right form. | |
| 14. | **Slaves of righteousness** | 1 |
| | Here again is the choice. Something is going to control you. Will it be sin or righteousness? If you say, "Righteousness," you will be tested. The devil does not give up as long as he thinks he has a chance of succeeding. He will go on until you come to the place where the temptation no longer means anything to you, where you will not even entertain the thought. At that point, the devil is clever enough not to waste his time. But if you have any double-mindedness, the devil will exploit it. You must make a firm decision to choose righteousness. | |
| 15. | **No (It led to more lawlessness/lawlessness increased.)** | 1 |
| | When we were still under law and under sin, we became more and more lawless. Many of us can trace that process in our own lives because the sin that satisfied us yesterday no longer satisfies today. The devil is always seeking to draw us deeper into sin. | |
| 16. | **Holiness** | 1 |
| | You are going one way or the other—either backward in rebellion or forward in holiness. It is almost impossible to stand still in the spiritual life. Holiness is not something that we hear much about in the church, but it is essential because Hebrews 12:14 says, *"Pursue peace with all people, and holiness, without which no one will see the Lord."* | |

| Question | Answer | Points |
|---|---|---|
| 17. | **No (Sin results in death.)**<br><br>When you were a slave to sin, Paul asks, what did you get? You may have gotten headaches and a "morning-after" feeling and a sense of shame. You may have wondered whether life was really worth living. You may have lived in disagreement, contention, and disharmony with the people closest to you. In the Christian life, we face many temptations and discouragements. We may wonder where we are going, what the problem is, what we are doing wrong, and whether God has forgotten us. But we must never entertain the thought of going back to the old life. Shut that door and throw away the key. It has nothing to offer. | 1 |
| 18. | a. **holiness**<br><br>b. **everlasting life (eternal life)**<br><br>Stop looking back, Paul says, and cultivate looking ahead. You are headed for a life of holiness that does not end with this life but goes on into eternity. It is difficult to walk forward if you are looking backward. So, turn your back on the past. What a privilege to be able to do that! Billions of people on earth today would gladly turn their backs on their pasts if someone would tell them how. | 2 |
| 19. | a. **wages**<br><br>b. **gift**<br><br>Those are the options. If you want your wages—the due reward for what you have done—remember that God is just and that you are a sinner. If you take that option, you will get your wages: death. That is the justice of God. But you can refuse that option and say, "God, I don't want what I deserve. Please give me what I don't deserve—Your free grace gift [Greek *charisma*] that I cannot earn: eternal life. Lord, that is what I want." | 2 |
| | Check your written memory work. If your memory work is word-perfect, 4 points for each verse. (1 point off for each mistake in a verse. If there are more than three mistakes, do not mark any points for that verse.) | 4 |
| | Total Points | ___/27 |

Fill in the total points for lesson 10 on the "Tally Sheet for Each Lesson" on page 253.

# LESSON 11 ANSWERS

| Question | Answer | Points |
|---|---|---|
| 1. | **When he is dead**<br><br>*"Do you not know, brethren (for I speak to those who know the law), that the law has dominion over a man as long as he lives?"* Again, Paul uses the phrase *"Do you not know…?"* numerous times in writing to Christians. In most places today, Christians do *not* know the nature of the law*. Once you are under the law, there is no escape from it except by death. It is a lifetime commitment. | 1 |
| 2. | **a. No**<br>**b. Yes**<br><br>Paul is comparing a Jew's relationship with the law of Moses* to a marriage relationship. The common factor is that both are covenants. The concept of covenant* is extremely important, and I would venture to say that we cannot fully understand our relationship with God unless we understand the scriptural concept of covenant. Please refer to the glossary if you are unsure about the meaning of this term. | 2 |
| 3. | **Israel***<br><br>The law is an illustration for all of us. Coming under the law is like a marriage ceremony in which you marry your fleshly nature. As long as your fleshly nature remains alive, you are not free to marry somebody else; otherwise, you become an adulterer. But Paul gives us good news: when Jesus died on the cross, our first "husband" died, since our old man was crucified with Him, and we are now free to be married to Christ. | 1 |
| 4. | **He is one body, or one flesh, with her (*"The two…shall become one flesh."*)**<br><br>It is helpful to understand that throughout the Greek New Testament, the word *porneia* is used to describe every form of illicit or unnatural sex. The connection with *pornography* is clear in that the word is derived from *porne*—the Greek word for *prostitute*. By looking at pornography, many people commit fornication through their eyes and are thus joined to another. | 1 |
| 5. | **As being one spirit with Him**<br><br>In contrast to sexual union between a man and a prostitute, Paul identifies another kind of union, one that we can have with the Lord. It is not sexual; it is spiritual. This union is a marriage relationship with the Lord. We are joined to Him not in soul or body but in spirit. How are we joined to Him in spirit? By the act of worship. (See John 4:23–24.) That is why worship is the highest activity a human being can engage in. | 1 |
| 6. | **Works of the flesh**<br><br>Do you want such children as are described in this passage? That is what the flesh brings forth. The flesh cannot produce anything acceptable to God. *Corrupt* is the key word to describe our fleshly nature. In Matthew 7:18, Jesus says that a bad or corrupt tree cannot bring forth good fruit. And, in Romans 8:8, Paul says that *"those who are in the flesh cannot please God."* | 1 |
| 7. | **Much fruit**<br><br>The alternative to producing the works of the flesh is to be joined to Christ in a sacred, spiritual union in which you can bear good fruit. Look up Galatians 5:22–23 to read about the fruit of the Spirit. The works of the flesh are totally bad, and the fruit of the Spirit is totally good. | 1 |
| 8. | **No**<br><br>People who bring forth the fruit of the Spirit do not need to be governed by law. They are not under law. They have escaped from their marriage to the flesh under the law, and they are free to be married by the Holy Spirit to the resurrected Christ and to bring forth the kind of fruit appropriate to that union. | 1 |

| Question | Answer | Points |
|---|---|---|
| 9. | a. **vine**<br><br>The key to the Christian life is not effort but union. Most of us are far too busy trying to live for God. But no vine ever brings forth grapes by "trying." What is important for us is a living, personal relationship with God that, without our striving, brings forth the fruit God wants.<br><br>b. **vinedresser**<br><br>The only One skillful enough to prune is the Father. Don't let human beings try to get at you with their pruning shears or axes!<br><br>c. **branches**<br><br>We are the branches when we abide in the Vine. Fruit comes because the life of the Vine is flowing into the branches.<br><br>d. **(Bonus Point) The Holy Spirit**<br><br>As the Holy Spirit flows through the Vine into the branches, the branches bring forth the fruit of the Spirit. | 3 (+1 bonus) |
| 10. | **He is not pruning us because we are unfruitful but because we are already bearing fruit, so that we might bear even more fruit.**<br><br>You may be experiencing God's pruning, and fighting it, wondering what has gone wrong in your life. Nothing has gone wrong. You are not being pruned because you are a backslider or because you are wicked or because you are uncommitted. You are being pruned because you have been bringing forth good fruit, and the pruning will enable you to bring forth even more good fruit. It is part of the process. We must distinguish between God's chastisement and His pruning. | 1 |
| 11. | **No**<br><br>When we are out of relationship with Jesus, we can bring forth nothing good. The key is to abide in Him. Again, it is not effort, but union with Him, that we need to seek. And from that union, the Holy Spirit brings forth the beautiful, luscious grapes that are the fruit of the Spirit. | 1 |
| 12. | **Much fruit**<br><br>In Matthew 12:33 and Luke 6:43–44, there is a similar theme of being known by our fruit. The key to bearing much fruit is to abide in Jesus and allow the Holy Spirit to rise up through us to produce the fruit of the Spirit. Remember, it is not effort but union. | 1 |
| 13. | **The knowledge of sin**<br><br>No one will ever achieve righteousness* with God by keeping a law. The law does not enable people to become righteous*; rather, it brings sin to life and out into full view. It makes us fully conscious of the nature, power, and evil of sin. That is one of the main purposes of the law. | 1 |
| 14. | **Sinful passions**<br><br>That is a startling statement. Most people do not view the law as arousing sinful passions. Note that Paul talks again about bearing fruit, but, in this case, the fruit that he's talking about leads to death. | 1 |
| 15. | **The newness of the Spirit**<br><br>This newness of the Spirit is the theme of Romans 8, and we will begin exploring it in much more detail in lesson 12. | 1 |
| 16. | **You shall not covet.**<br><br>The Greek word translated as *"covet"* also means "lust." I think Paul has lust in mind more than coveting. What the law did, in this one of the Ten Commandments, was to bring the nature and power of lust or coveting out into the open. Paul says, in effect, "Without this commandment, I never would have realized the full and true nature of lust." | 1 |

| Question | Answer | Points |
|---|---|---|
| 17. | **All manner of evil desire** | 1 |
| | Paul says that, far from making him able to overcome coveting, the commandment actually worked in him an *increase* of coveting. If you are having a problem with lust or fear or hatred or resentment, you will not overcome it by rules that forbid you to engage in it. In fact, the more you focus on those rules, the more power that thing will have over you. If you keep saying, "I must not lust, I must not lust," your whole mind will become full of the concept of lust. Again, far from delivering you from lust, those rules will enslave you to it. | |
| 18. | a. **deceived** | 2 |
| | b. **killed** | |
| | James also picks up on the connection between evil desire, deception, and death. In James 1:15–16, he writes, "*Then, when desire has conceived, it gives birth to sin; and sin, when it is full-grown, brings forth death. Do not be deceived, my beloved brethren.*" | |
| 19. | **holy; just; good** | 3 |
| | There is nothing wrong with the law. It is holy, just, and good. The problem is not in the law; it is in us, in our flesh. The function of the law is not to deliver us from sin but to bring us face-to-face with the reality of sin and with the inherent evil and weakness of our own carnal nature. Ultimately, the law brings us to the place where we will turn to God's alternative way, which is the way of faith, not of works. | |
| 20. | **As spiritual** | 1 |
| | After all this, we might be tempted to think that the law is a bad thing. That is not true; the law was perfect, but only Christ could fulfill the law. | |
| 21. | **No** | 1 |
| | Note what the commandment has done by causing us to take sides with God's law and say, "That's what we ought to do." When we discover that the more we try to follow the law, the less we succeed, we reveal that there is something in us that works against our own best intentions. That "something" is sin. So, again, the law has forced sin out into the open. Before that, it lurked, but we were not often conscious of it. Thus, the law serves a God-given purpose—but that purpose is not to make people righteous. Righteousness comes another way. | |
| 22. | a. **Foolish** | 4 |
| | b. **They had been bewitched.** | |
| | c. **By the flesh** | |
| | d. **We come back under a curse.** | |
| | Do you know that you can be bewitched? Paul's readers were Spirit-filled Christians, but they had been bewitched. How did Paul know this? Because they had lost their vision of Jesus on the cross. | |
| | Trying to achieve righteousness with God through self-effort is foolishness, and we have been bewitched when we attempt to do that. Paul reminds us that if we come back under the law, we come back under a curse. The word for this is *legalism**, which you can read more about in the glossary. | |
| 23. | **As a wretched man** | 1 |
| | Paul experienced the conflict between the carnal nature and the spiritual nature to a marked degree. His dead, carnal nature fought the things of God and resisted his best intentions to do good and keep God's laws. Hear his cry of anguish. | |
| 24. | **His "body of death"** | 1 |
| | We have seen numerous times that law empowers sin within us, we are deceived, and we die. | |

| Question | Answer | Points |
|---|---|---|
| 25. | **Jesus Christ our Lord** | 1 |
| | There is a way out of the conflict. The way out is through the cross—the substitutionary sacrifice and death of Jesus. This brings us back to Romans 6:6, which says, *"Knowing this, that our old man was crucified with Him."* Because our fleshly nature was put to death with Jesus, we can be delivered from it and come into the fullness of the freedom of life in the Spirit. | |
| 26. | **Suffering in the flesh** | 1 |
| | That statement used to astonish me. Didn't Jesus do all the suffering on the cross? Why do we have to suffer in the flesh? But although I was put off by the requirement, I was attracted by the consequence: *"He who has suffered in the flesh has ceased from sin."* Wouldn't it be wonderful to have ceased from sin? | |
| 27. | **The will of God** | 1 |
| | I was tremendously attracted by the possibility of living the rest of my life no longer for the lusts of my fleshly nature—that is, the physical body—but for the will of God. As far as I knew my own heart, it was my sincere desire to do the will of God. But the way, it seemed, would be painful, as we see in the next question. | |
| 28. | a. **Deny** | 3 |
| | b. **cross** | |
| | c. **Follow** | |
| | The answer I believe God has shown me—how suffering in the flesh results in ceasing from sin—is extremely practical. In a sense, you have two options: you can suffer God's way or you can suffer your own way, but suffer you will. Anybody who tells you there is no suffering in the Christian life is deceiving you and going flat contrary to Scripture. | |
| | Somebody has defined the cross in two ways. First, it is the place where your will and God's will cross. Every one of us who follows Jesus must come to the place where we say, "Not my will, but Yours, be done." (See Luke 22:42.) Jesus is not the only person who has to say that. And, second, the cross is the place where you die. It is the place of your execution. | |
| | Check your written memory work. If your memory work is word-perfect, 4 points for each verse. (1 point off for each mistake in a verse. If there are more than three mistakes, do not mark any points for that verse.) | 8 |
| | Total Points | ___/48 |

Fill in the total points for lesson 11 on the "Tally Sheet for Each Lesson" on page 253.

# LESSON 12 ANSWERS

| Question | Answer | Points |
|---|---|---|
| 1. | **No**<br><br>The critical phrase here is *"no condemnation."* God no longer condemns you for sin, because you are in Christ. As long as there is any kind of condemnation in your life, you cannot live and function in the Spirit-controlled life described in Romans 8. God's purpose in the previous seven chapters has been to eliminate every possible cause of condemnation. If you have faithfully followed through, and understood and believed God's promises, you should now be able to say, "There is therefore now no condemnation in my life." Self-condemnation is clearly dealt with in 1 John 1:9, so the issue of condemnation for the Christian should be past history. | 1 |
| 2. | a. **Dead**<br>b. **Alive**<br>c. **dead**<br>d. **forgiven**<br>e. **We were under it.**<br>f. **It has been wiped out.**<br><br>Jesus nailed the law* to the cross, and that is where the law ends. Beyond the cross, the law has no claims on you. Remember, the person who has died is justified*. Through Jesus, we have paid the last penalty. | 6 |
| 3. | a. **disarmed**<br>b. **public spectacle**<br>c. **triumphed**<br><br>Jesus spoiled or stripped Satan's principalities and powers—that is, his evil hosts in the heavenlies that seek to dominate and destroy us. | 3 |
| 4. | **No one**<br><br>Paul does not say here, for example, that we are *not* to observe the Sabbath; when you do so is a matter of personal decision. (See also Hebrews 4:1–11.) But we are not to let anybody condemn us with respect to that decision. Being free from condemnation demands a certain amount of confidence because there are a lot of religious people whose favorite occupation is to bring others under condemnation. You must learn where you stand in Christ and say, "I'm not going to let anybody condemn me regarding any requirements of the law, including those that pertain to food, drink, or the Sabbath." | 1 |
| 5. | a. **The law of the Spirit of life**<br>b. **The law of sin and death**<br><br>Two laws in operation against one another are quite common in life. We could consider the law of gravity, which pulls down on an aircraft, and the law of lift, which holds the plane up and stops it from plummeting to the ground. The law of the Spirit of life is infinitely more powerful than the law of sin and death and can never be overcome by it. In the Spirit-led life, the objective is to constantly function under the law of the Spirit of life. | 2 |
| 6. | **It is weak through the flesh.**<br><br>As before, Paul points out that there is nothing wrong with the law. Our carnal nature is the problem. | 1 |
| 7. | **His own Son**<br><br>In the flesh of Jesus on the cross, God finally condemned and disposed of sin. | 1 |

| Question | Answer | Points |
|---|---|---|
| 8. | **He has put it away.**<br><br>By the sacrifice of Himself, Jesus disposed of sin. He put sin out of the way. He terminated its power and its claims. | 1 |
| 9. | **No**<br><br>The sacrifices of the law never took away sin; all the sacrifices did was remind people of their sins and cover those sins until the next sacrifice was due. So, far from disposing of the sin question, the sacrifices of the law constantly and continually brought it up. On the other hand, when Jesus offered His sacrifice of Himself, He put away sin. There remains, therefore, no further sacrifice for sin. Nothing more will ever be needed. It has all been accomplished by Jesus's death on the cross. | 1 |
| 10. | **righteous\* requirement**<br><br>It is not the law that is to be fulfilled but the *requirement* of the law. The Greek word for *"righteous requirement"* comes from the same root as the word that is typically translated "righteous." The word Paul uses in Romans 8:4 is also found in other places in the New Testament, including Romans 1:32; 2:26; 5:16; Hebrews 9:1, 10; and Revelation 19:8. | 1 |
| 11. | a. **love**<br><br>b. **love**<br><br>The key word in both commandments is *"love. "On these two commandments,"* Jesus says, *"hang all the Law and the Prophets"* (Matthew 22:40). Imagine for a moment that I want to hang my jacket up. There is a peg nearby, so I take off my jacket and hang it on the peg. The peg has to be there before I can hang my jacket on it. Jesus is saying that these two commandments were there before the Law\* and the Prophets\* were hung on them. | 2 |
| 12. | **To love one another**<br><br>Incidentally, this applies to financial debt as well—the only thing we are called to owe is love. | 1 |
| 13. | **Fulfilled the law**<br><br>Verses 8 and 10 of Romans 13 both state that love is the fulfillment of the law. It is very clear, and God leaves us no reason to doubt this truth. | 1 |
| 14. | **All of it**<br><br>Any talk about law that does not direct people to love is fruitless discussion. How much fruitless discussion do we have in our churches? I take matter this very seriously. From time to time, I ask myself, "What are you producing by what you teach? If you are not producing love, you are wasting your words, your time, your strength, and the time of all the people." | 1 |
| 15. | a. **heart**<br><br>b. **conscience**<br><br>c. **faith**<br><br>Those are not goals; those are the conditions that make the goal possible. The next verse says, *"Some people have strayed from these things and have turned aside to fruitless discussion"* (1 Timothy 1:6 NASB).<br><br>Again, how many fruitless discussions are conducted among Christians? Why are they fruitless? Because they are not directed toward the goal, which is love. | 3 |
| 16. | **If we have love for one another/By our love for one another**<br><br>Some people complain that the world is judging the church. But Jesus gave the world the right to judge the church by saying, in other words, "If the world doesn't see you loving one another, they have every right to say that you are not My disciples." So, we must fulfill the righteous requirement of the law, which is love. | 1 |

| Question | Answer | Points |
|---|---|---|
| 17. | **God** | 1 |
| | Love is supernatural; it can come only from God. There is no way you can work it up. Religion will not give it to you. It comes only through the new birth. | |
| 18. | **Being born again** | 1 |
| | Your ability to love others comes only from the reality of being born again. Apart from the seed of God's word being planted in our hearts, this kind of love is impossible. What was brought into being by the seed of God's word is fulfilled by the Holy Spirit. | |
| 19. | **The Holy Spirit** | 1 |
| | Love is brought forth from the seed of the Word of God as a new nature within you. And then the whole of the fullness of God's love is poured out into your heart through the Holy Spirit. Once more, it is supernatural. No human effort can ever produce even a counterfeit of the love of God. | |
| 20. | a. **born** | 2 |
| | b. **knows** | |
| | Again, this kind of love can come only from the new birth. It is the supreme distinctive evidence of being born again. | |
| 21. | a. **has** | 2 |
| | b. **keeps** | |
| | The person who loves the Lord is not necessarily the one who prays the loudest and the longest; rather, it is the one who has God's commandments and keeps them. That is the proof of love. | |
| 22. | **We keep His commandments/His word** | 1 |
| | If we do not keep Jesus's commandments, the problem is that we do not love Him. We can say we do, and talk a lot about it, but if we are disobedient, we do not love Him. Love is the motive for obedience, while obedience is the test. | |
| 23. | **No** | 1 |
| | You have not come back under the law, where you are threatened with penalties every time you do something wrong. You are motivated not by fear but by love. Parents can see the wisdom of this. They can make small children obey by threats and shouting and punishment. But when those children become teenagers, they will rebel. Children motivated by love, on the other hand, will still be obedient and want to do the right thing even when they are forty years old. Love is a more powerful motive than fear. And God is wise enough to base His relationship with us not on fear but on love. | |
| 24. | **Our love can increase.** | 1 |
| | Another truth about love that should be a relief to most of us is this: the moment we are born again and even baptized in the Spirit, we are not perfect in love. We have only just started, because love is progressive. The love we have as born-again believers needs to expand, increase, abound more and more. And the more we have of love, the more sensitive we are about what pleases God. | |
| 25. | **The love of God is perfected in us.** | 1 |
| | We perfect the love of God by keeping His word—whether it comes through the Bible, through a prophetic word from a fellow believer, or directly by His Spirit. Trying to "feel" loving is not the way to obtain love. We do not have to try to love. Don't focus on your feelings; instead, focus on obedience. We keep God's word as we are led by His Spirit. | |
| | Check your written memory work. If your memory work is word-perfect, 4 points for each verse. (1 point off for each mistake in a verse. If there are more than three mistakes, do not mark any points for that verse.) | 8 |
| | Total Points | ____/46 |

Fill in the total points for lesson 12 on the "Tally Sheet for Each Lesson" on page 253.

# LESSON 13 ANSWERS

| Question | Answer | Points |
|---|---|---|
| 1. | a. **am giving**<br><br>b. **have given**<br><br>From that point on, legally, the whole land of Canaan belonged to the Israelites. But, experientially, they did not yet hold one inch of it. God brought the children of Israel* into the promised land by two major miracles: the crossing of the Jordan River and the destruction of Jericho. But from that time onward, they had to fight for everything they took. If they did not fight, they did not get it. | 2 |
| 2. | a. **Past**<br><br>b. **Future**<br><br>c. **Present**<br><br>You may have found the exercise in question 2 difficult if you are not familiar with verb tenses, but this *is* important. In Romans 8:5–17, Paul indicates that it is one thing to have legal possession, but it takes determination, faith, and patience to move from the legal to the experiential. | 3 |
| 3. | a. **flesh**<br><br>b. **Spirit**<br><br>The difference in the two ways of living is not just external; it is in the way we think. We could say that some people think like the flesh, and others think like the Spirit. When God changes us, He does not start from the outside; He starts from the inside. Religion starts from the outside and says you have to change your clothes or your lifestyle or whatever. God does not start that way. He starts in the heart. | 2 |
| 4. | a. **death**<br><br>b. **life; peace**<br><br>You will know whether you are spiritually minded if you have life and peace. If you are still anxious, troubled, tormented, and uncertain, you have not yet moved into your inheritance, even though you are entitled to it. We will study Romans 14:17 in due course, but, as an encouragement, read this verse as a complementary passage to Romans 8:6. | 3 |
| 5. | **At enmity with Him**<br><br>You have inside you an enemy of God. This makes a big difference not only in day-to-day life but also in what is done in the name of Christian ministry. Tragically, the majority of Christian seminaries today are educating the carnal mind—God's enemy. It is much the same in many areas of the mission field. We establish facilities to take the less privileged into schools and colleges and educate them, while they have never been converted. In both cases, what we are doing is producing educated enemies of God. Often, such students are the ones who later kick the missionaries out. | 1 |
| 6. | **No**<br><br>That rebel cannot change. Not even God can change him. Once more, what does He do to him? He puts him to death. | 1 |
| 7. | **No**<br><br>As long as you are operating in your natural ability, you may be very religious, even zealous, going to church and participating in religious activities every day of the week, but you cannot please God. | 1 |
| 8. | **Children of wrath**<br><br>Ephesians 2:3 talks about not only our flesh but also our minds as having been at enmity with God, as Paul expresses in Romans 8:7. As a result, we were children subject to God's wrath because we were dead in our sins and transgressions. (See Ephesians 2:1.) | 1 |

200

| Question | Answer | Points |
|---|---|---|
| 9. | **mind(s)** | 1 |
| | True conversion demands a total change of mind. The scriptural word for this is *repentance*—in Greek, *metanoia*, which refers to changing your mind. It is not primarily an emotional experience but a change of the mind and of the will. Repentance is probably the most neglected major doctrine* of the Christian faith in the contemporary church, and the condition of the church shows it. | |
| 10. | **Being transformed by the renewing of your/our mind(s)** | 1 |
| | When will we be changed? When our minds change and are renewed. Much of religion is getting people to change externally, and it does not work. When your mind is changed, however, your external behavior will change automatically. | |
| 11. | **If the Spirit of God dwells in us** | 1 |
| | Many people who have been baptized in the Spirit are not *filled* with the Spirit. There are many areas of their lives that the Spirit has not yet taken over. If a water bottle is held under a fast-flowing waterfall, it will quickly overflow, yet there may still be a lot of bubbles inside the bottle. Many "spiritual" people still have "bubbles" inside them. | |
| 12. | a. **body** | 2 |
| | b. **Spirit** | |
| | Again, when Christ comes to live within you, your old fleshly life dies—not your physical body but your fleshly nature. As far as God is concerned, it is dead. A new life is born into you by the Holy Spirit—not an improved life, not a reformed life, but a new *zoe* (divine, eternal) life. | |
| 13. | a. **old man** | 3 |
| | b. **mind** | |
| | c. **new man** | |
| | Another key word that describes our carnal nature is *corrupt*. That corruption cannot be reversed. Religion is like a refrigerator. It slows corruption but does not stop it. The alternative is to be renewed in our minds and to *"put on the new man which was created according to God, in true righteousness and holiness"* (Ephesians 4:24). | |
| 14. | **Becoming a new creation** | 1 |
| | The new creation is totally of God. It has nothing of the old creation in it. It is new life, a new beginning. If we only realized what we have by way of the new birth, we would get excited about it. But we tend to use the terms *new birth* and *born again* as trite religious phrases, with no conception of what they really mean. | |
| 15. | **Life to our mortal bodies** | 1 |
| | This is the foundational principle of divine healing: the same Holy Spirit power that raised the body of Jesus from the tomb and set Him at God's right hand is at work in our own bodies. Believing that is the basis of faith for any kind of physical healing or miracle that you need. | |
| 16. | **Put to death the deeds of the body** | 1 |
| | Paul says to these "spiritual" Christians, *"If you live according to the flesh you will die."* Because they are nurturing that thing in them that is corrupt, all they will get out of it is corruption. Instead, we are encouraged to put to death the deeds of the body so that we will live. | |
| 17. | **They are led by the Spirit of God.** | 1 |
| | This is the alternative to yielding to the flesh: being led by the Spirit of God. The Holy Spirit is not a theological abstraction. He is not a phrase at the end of the Apostles' Creed. He is a Person. If you want the Holy Spirit to lead you, you must cultivate a personal relationship with Him. Let Him take you by the hand. Listen to His quiet whispers. | |

| Question | Answer | Points |
|---|---|---|
| 18. | a. **The spirit of bondage to fear**<br><br>b. **The spirit of adoption**<br><br>We are no longer slaves but sons. We are not motivated by fear but rather by love as we are guided by the Holy Spirit. | 2 |
| 19. | **The right to become (be) children of God**<br><br>When you are born again, you receive authority. The extent to which you exercise the authority God has given you is the measure of what you have become through the new birth, because authority is useless unless it is exercised. The new birth is the opportunity to develop into something wonderful if you use the authority God has given you. | 1 |
| 20. | **The Spirit Himself (Holy Spirit)**<br><br>Everyone who is born of God has this internal witness. If you don't, you need to check whether you are really born of God. I have been with missionaries, people who were sincere and living good and upstanding lives, who did not know what it was to be born again. It is quite different to have the supernatural testimony of the Holy Spirit that you are a child of God. | 1 |
| 21. | **We are heirs of God and joint heirs with Christ.**<br><br>Being joint heirs does not mean that every one of us gets a little part of the inheritance. It means that, according to the laws of inheritance, we all share in the total inheritance together. That is a tremendous statement! We are heirs to all that Jesus is heir to because we are His younger brothers and sisters. | 1 |
| 22. | **Suffering with Him**<br><br>You cannot become a joint heir without being willing to face suffering. If you reject the suffering, I do not believe you can claim your inheritance. There is a tendency in the church today to dismiss suffering as something that does not belong to the Christian life. I cannot think where people find that in the Bible. Countless statements in Scripture tell us the exact opposite. | 1 |
| | Check your written memory work. If your memory work is word-perfect, 4 points for each verse. (1 point off for each mistake in a verse. If there are more than three mistakes, do not mark any points for that verse.) | 8 |
| | Total Points | ___/40 |

Fill in the total points for lesson 13 on the "Tally Sheet for Each Lesson" on page 253.

# LESSON 14 ANSWERS

| Question | Answer | Points |
|---|---|---|
| 1. | **No**<br><br>Coming from Paul, and considering what he suffered, that is an impressive statement! I encourage you to read 2 Corinthians 11:23–27 to catch a glimpse of the suffering that Paul endured. | 1 |
| 2. | **Through sufferings**<br><br>Christ suffered on our behalf, and the New Testament is clear that suffering is normal and should be expected. In 1 Peter 2:21, we read, *"For to this you were called, because Christ also suffered for us, leaving us an example, that you should follow His steps."* When I look back on my own experiences, I really think I can echo David's sentiments and say, "Lord, be sure my tears are in Your bottle" (see Psalm 56:8), because they are some of the richest parts of my Christian experience. | 1 |
| 3. | **By the things which He suffered**<br><br>Note that the verse from Hebrews talks about *"a Son"* rather than "the only Son." Implicit in this is the idea that all of us who are "sons" can expect to learn obedience the same way. | 1 |
| 4. | **Being illuminated (or receiving revelations)**<br><br>When you are enlightened, you are going to run into conflict. The one will follow the other. Every time you receive a new revelation or new spiritual understanding, you think, "It's wonderful. Now I've got the answer!" But it is like when John, on the island of Patmos, was given the little book to eat by the angel. It was sweet in his mouth but bitter in his belly. When it got down to the process of digestion, it became bitter. (See Revelation 10:8–10.) | 1 |
| 5. | **No**<br><br>Peter reminds us that if we are suffering for doing good, and we endure it patiently, this is commendable to God, but if we suffer for our failings, then that is justified punishment. | 1 |
| 6. | **A far more exceeding and eternal weight of glory**<br><br>What are you and I complaining about? How heavy is our affliction compared with that of Paul? Yet Paul calls his affliction *"light"* (2 Corinthians 4:17). And in Romans 8:18, he says, *"The sufferings of this present time are not worthy to be compared with the glory which shall be revealed in us."* What made the difference with Paul? He had a vision of the glory. If we lose our vision of the glory, we will not benefit from our suffering. | 1 |
| 7. | **At the things which are not seen**<br><br>We are not to use our natural eyes; rather, *"the eyes of [our] understanding being enlightened…[we] may know what is the hope of His calling, what are the riches of the glory of His inheritance in the saints"* (Ephesians 1:18). Suffering will work God's purposes in you while you are looking *"at the things which are not seen."* Paul had a vision of the unseen, and nothing he suffered was worthy to be compared with the glory he saw in the future. If we lose our vision of the eternal, we will still suffer but will receive no benefit from it. | 1 |
| 8. | **The creation**<br><br>Again, human beings are not the only ones suffering. The whole creation is suffering because of Adam's sin, which plunged creation into chaos and futility. Creation will not be redeemed until human beings are redeemed. So, all of creation is waiting for us to be revealed in our resurrection glory. | 1 |

| Question | Answer | Points |
|---|---|---|
| 9. | a. **heavens**<br><br>b. **earth**<br><br>c. **sea**<br><br>d. **field**<br><br>e. **trees; woods**<br><br>There are many passages of Scripture that use wording similar to this, and I find creation more alive to the promises of God than many Christians are! All of nature anticipates the coming of the Lord. The trees are awake, the mountains are awake, the lakes are awake, and the animals are awake—but the church is asleep; it is out of harmony with God and with creation. | 6 |
| 10. | a. **sea**<br><br>b. **rivers**<br><br>c. **hills**<br><br>All creation is longing for the Lord to come and put things right. You see, as I discussed in the introduction to lesson 14, mankind was made the steward of the earth, but, after the fall, we violated the earth. In many areas, we have left it desolate, stripped, bare, and exploited. And the earth is crying out to God, "How long will You let these people trample over me and tear me up and defile me and fill my atmosphere with horrible pollution?" | 3 |
| 11. | **Futility**<br><br>Paul is drawing us into an experience in which we empathize with the whole of creation. Oh, that our hearts would be enlarged! The King James Version renders the Greek word for "*futility*" in Romans 8:20 as "*vanity*." Emptiness. Perhaps the best contemporary word would be *frustration*. But notice that God subjected it "*in hope*," so it is not the end of the story. | 1 |
| 12. | **The glorious liberty of the children of God**<br><br>Once more, only when the children of God come into the freedom of their glory will creation be set free. | 1 |
| 13. | **"*Cursed is the ground for your sake.*"**<br><br>Mankind was the steward of the whole earth, answerable to God; and the fall brought disaster on the entire earth—all that men and women were responsible for. The principle of responsibility is one we run away from today; but, in fact, we are responsible before God for certain things. | 1 |
| 14. | a. **Thorns**<br><br>b. **Thistles**<br><br>Have you noticed that, when Jesus provided redemption from the curse through His crucifixion, the soldiers who had charge of Him gave Him a crown of thorns and a purple robe, which is the color of the thistle flower? That was God's attestation that Jesus was redeeming the earth from the curse. But, remember, the earth's full redemption will not come until mankind's redemption is complete. | 2 |
| 15. | **Labor with birth pangs**<br><br>The earth suffers the effects of man's disobedience. If we consider just two natural occurrences—earthquakes and volcanoes—they are not occurring all the time, but, like contractions when a woman is in labor, they are coming closer together and with greater intensity. | 1 |
| 16. | **We who have the firstfruits of the Spirit**<br><br>May we ask ourselves frankly, "Is that true of me? Do I ever have the experience of the Holy Spirit groaning within me, not for some problem in my life but for the redemption of creation? Do I ever empathize with the creation on which we, men and women, have brought such terrible consequences by our sins, and which consequences we continue to bring?" | 1 |

| Question | Answer | Points |
|---|---|---|
| 17. | **The redemption of our body**<br><br>The aim of the Christian life is not to get to heaven. That is just a stage in the journey. The goal of the Christian life is the resurrection. Only after our resurrection will our redemption be complete, because then the redemption of our bodies will be complete. If all you are aiming to do is get to heaven, you are stopping short of the goal. | 1 |
| 18. | **a. know**<br><br>You might think Paul had never met the Lord. We know he had. But he was saying, "There is a whole lot more of the Lord that I don't know yet. I want to know Him more fully."<br><br>**b. resurrection**<br><br>We all say amen to knowing the power of His resurrection! But here was another part of Paul's goal:<br><br>**c. sufferings**<br><br>Why did Paul want to share not merely the power of Jesus but also His sufferings? I think he did not want Jesus to suffer alone.<br><br>**d. death**<br><br>Jesus laid down His life in sacrifice, and so must we.<br><br>**e. resurrection; dead**<br><br>Here was Paul's goal: sharing in the resurrection from the dead. Again, getting to heaven is a sort of resting stage on the journey. The ultimate goal is the resurrection of the body. | 6 |
| 19. | **The resurrection from the dead**<br><br>Bodily resurrection is the completion of redemption. Jesus redeemed the spirit, soul, and body, but the full outworking of redemption will not be manifested until the resurrection of the body. | 1 |
| 20. | **a. In heaven**<br><br>**b. The Savior, the Lord Jesus Christ**<br><br>**c. They will be transformed to be conformed to Christ's glorious body.**<br><br>When Jesus comes back, our bodies will be changed into the likeness of *"the body of His glory"* (Philippians 3:21 YLT), whereas, at the present moment, we are clothed in what the Greek text calls *"the body of our humiliation"* (verse 21 YLT)—the result of the fall. | 3 |
| 21. | **Jesus Christ**<br><br>Note the reason for this glorious likeness: *"for we shall see Him as He is"* (John 3:2). We won't see Him in His earthly body but in His glorious resurrection body, and we will be transformed into His likeness. | 1 |
| 22. | **As the beginning of sorrows**<br><br>The Greek word for *"sorrows"* literally means "birth pains"; this refers to the birth pangs of a new age. | 1 |
| 23. | **Because our redemption draws near**<br><br>That is the climax—not just our personal redemption, but also the redemption of creation. All creation is groaning and experiencing birth pangs, longing for redemption. As we have been discussing, God's purpose is that we *"who have the firstfruits of the Spirit"* (Romans 8:23) should not be wrapped up in our personal problems and church quarrels, but rather groaning together with all of creation for the glorious vision of what God has in mind, and giving ourselves in prayer to bring it about. | 1 |

| Question | Answer | Points |
|---|---|---|
| 24. | **It is future-focused.** | 1 |
| | Notice, again, that hope turns toward the future; faith is in the present. But, Paul says, *"We were saved in this hope* [or by hope]." In other words, hope is an essential part of being saved. Without hope, we do not have valid salvation. | |
| 25. | **Perseverance** | 1 |
| | Paul goes on to point out that hope produces perseverance. He says, *"If we hope for what we do not see, we wait eagerly for it with perseverance."* And perseverance, again, is essential to salvation. Many different passages of Scripture emphasize that we have to persevere in our faith and in living the Christian life until the consummation of that faith. So, once more, hope is essential to salvation. | |
| 26. | **Christ in you (the hope of glory)** | 1 |
| | This glorious mystery is revealed in three short words. What is it? *"Christ in you."* This is the most exciting thing that can ever be revealed to humanity: Christ, the eternal Son of God, by the Holy Spirit, can be in us—in us as individuals; among us as the people of God. This is the secret that God has reserved for us. Don't you feel privileged? Don't you get excited when you think about it? But have you realized what it means to have Christ in you? It means you have the hope of glory. | |
| 27. | **Not knowing what we should pray for as we ought** | 1 |
| | Our weakness is that we are not enlarged enough in our understanding and our feelings to respond to the challenge of knowing how to pray. When we consider what Paul was just saying about groaning for the whole creation, it is perfectly true—we do not know how to do it. | |
| 28. | **He makes intercession for us (with groans which cannot be uttered).** | 1 |
| | The Holy Spirit is a Person; and, when He comes to live within you, if you know how to relate to Him, you can release Him to pray in you and through you. This is one aspect of the gift of tongues—the Holy Spirit praying through us. | |
| 29. | **The will of God** | 1 |
| | In Song of Solomon 5:2, the bride of Christ says, *"I sleep, but my heart is awake."* You can have Someone inside you who never goes to sleep, never gets tired, never is perplexed, and always knows how to face a given situation and give the right prayer according to the will of God. That is God's remarkable provision through the Holy Spirit. | |
| | Check your written memory work. If your memory work is word-perfect, 4 points for each verse. (1 point off for each mistake in a verse. If there are more than three mistakes, do not mark any points for that verse.) | 8 |
| | Total Points | ____/52 |

Fill in the total points for lesson 14 on the "Tally Sheet for Each Lesson" on page 253.

# LESSON 15 ANSWERS

| Question | Answer | Points |
|---|---|---|
| 1. | **God chose us.**<br><br>We have total security based on God's choice of us. If we had chosen Him first, there could have been an instability due to our thoughts or feelings at any particular time. But God is unchanging, so we can have full confidence in Him, especially in moments of uncertainty. Note the reason for our selection and appointment: to bear enduring fruit. | 1 |
| 2. | **God's own will**<br><br>The previous verse, James 1:17, says, *"Every good gift and every perfect gift is from above, and comes down from the Father of lights, with whom there is no variation or shadow of turning."* The new birth is a gift from above, and, again, God does not change, so we can have complete confidence in His goodness toward us. | 1 |
| 3. | a. **love**<br>b. **called**<br><br>You cannot just say that anything that happens to you is God's working everything together for good, because this promise applies only to those who love God, who are called, and who are walking in God's purposes. If these things are true of you, then everything that happens to you is the outworking of God's plan, no matter what may appear to be the case. | 2 |
| 4. | a. **hedge**<br>b. **wall**<br><br>Many times, when God's children begin to go astray, God builds a hedge in front of them so there is no way through. That is also God's working everything for good to you. Then, no matter what happens—and it may appear to be a disaster—you can know that God is making it happen for your good. | 2 |
| 5. | **Stage 1: foreknew**<br><br>The origin of everything created is God's foreknowledge, which existed before creation took place. What a staggering thought! God did not act in ignorance; He did not experiment. He knew in advance what kind of people we would be, how He would deal with us, and how He could work out His plan for us and through us. | No points |
| 6. | **Stage 2: chose**<br><br>We just saw in 1 Peter that we are chosen according to the foreknowledge of God. It is important to see that God's choice of us is based on His knowledge of us. He chooses us because He knows us in advance. He knows what we are like; He knows what He can make of us. | 1 |
| 7. | **Stage 3: predestined**<br><br>People can twist the doctrine* of predestination. We are not predestined to be saved; we are predestined to be conformed to the image of Jesus. When people say they are predestined to be saved, yet there is no evidence of transformation in their lives, we may question it. But when we see somebody being conformed to the image of Jesus, the only explanation is that God predestined it. So, don't let the doctrine of predestination become a stumbling block to you. Again, it is sometimes taken and twisted and used almost to beat God's people with. But it is a glorious truth if we accept it in the right way. | 1 |

| Question | Answer | Points |
|---|---|---|
| 8. | **Stage 4: called**<br><br>The word *call* also means "invite." At this point in our lives, when God calls us, we are confronted with eternity. It is a solemn and sacred moment. God never changes His mind. He never withdraws His gifts or changes His calling. You have been issued a calling that is secure. The Creator of the universe is the Author of this calling, and His authority is behind it.<br><br>To what are we called? Fellowship with the Godhead. (See 1 John 1:3.) You may not know it, but you are also called to a certain task. *That calling is holy.* Fulfilling your calling should be the first priority in your life. Your calling, whatever it is, is sacred—whether it is to be a homemaker or a physician or a missionary or whatever. God planned it in advance. You do not have to work it all out; you simply have to walk in the good works *"which God prepared beforehand that* [you] *should walk in"* (Ephesians 2:10). | 1 |
| 9. | **Stage 5: saved**<br><br>Having called us, God saves us when we respond to Him. There is a definite moment in time when you respond to the call, and God saves you. You pass out of death into life, out of condemnation into the righteousness* of God. It is the greatest single translation that can take place in a person's life. It is our response to God's call—getting plugged in to God's eternal plan. | 1 |
| 10. | **Stage 6: justified***<br><br>When you accept Jesus and His propitiatory* sacrifice on your behalf, you are not only saved but also justified—reckoned righteous*. You are not merely clothed with a garment of salvation, but you are covered with a robe of righteousness—God's righteousness. (See Isaiah 61:10.) | 1 |
| 11. | **Stage 7: glorified**<br><br>Notice that, like each of the previous six stages, *glorified* is in the past tense. It is not something that will happen after we die; it is done now through our faith in Jesus. This is exciting—but few Christians seem to realize it! We are made alive, resurrected, then enthroned. That is the final stage of God's plan. He has invited us to share the throne of glory with Him right now in this present age. | 1 |
| 12. | **No**<br><br>Paul does not say that nobody is against us; he says, in effect, "What does it matter who is against us?" You have probably heard this simple saying: "One plus God is a majority." That is true in any circumstance—one plus God is a majority. | 1 |
| 13. | **own Son**<br><br>What a tremendous truth! If you want to know how committed God is to you, look at the cross. God gave His only Son to die in agony and shame on your behalf. If God did that, Paul says, then, very logically, there is nothing good that He will withhold from you. So, when you are in times of darkness, temptation, and doubt, don't try to reason it out; just turn to the cross and say, "That is the measure of God's love and commitment to me. I may not understand what is going on, but I am God's child, and I know He is totally committed to me." | 1 |
| 14. | **No**<br><br>God says, "I have justified you. The price has already been paid by the death of My Son." If God has justified us, who can make us feel guilty? He has done everything to keep us from coming under condemnation. So, don't get involved in arguing with the devil about his accusations.<br><br>But people do condemn us, and we are prone to condemn ourselves too. Sometimes even Christians wound one another by words spoken from the old man, and we become each other's accusers. How many times, when praying about people, have I accused them before God? What insolence and arrogance! I am accusing before God somebody whom He Himself has undertaken to justify, somebody for whom Christ died. | 1 |

| Question | Answer | Points |
|---|---|---|
| 15. | **(Jesus) Christ**<br><br>Jesus paid the full penalty by His own death, and He rose from the dead so that He might be our Intercessor forever. Notice that in Romans 8:26, we learned that the Holy Spirit makes intercession for us, and now we learn that Jesus also makes intercession for us. Can you appreciate how totally committed God is to seeing you through all the way from foreknowledge to glorification? | 1 |
| 16. | **He always lives to make intercession for us.**<br><br>Think of the periods of Jesus's ministry. Thirty years of perfect family life. Three and a half years of public ministry. And nearly two thousand years of intercession. What does that tell us about our own priorities? | 1 |
| 17. | **Advocate**<br><br>When we do sin, we have the most expert Advocate in the universe pleading our case. There is no reason ever to feel condemned. God is on our side. Jesus is at the right hand of God as our Advocate. God has undertaken to justify us and will not tolerate condemnation of us. | 1 |
| 18. | **We are.**<br><br>Lots of weapons will be formed against us, but they will never succeed. God does not say *He* will condemn every weapon and tongue used against us, but that *"you"* will. He has given us the basis to do it—our righteousness from God through Jesus our Savior. | 1 |
| 19. | **No**<br><br>Having dealt once again with the matter of condemnation and guilt, we come now to the beautiful, glorious climax. Notice, however, that you cannot get there if you are living under condemnation. The climax of our relationship with the Messiah is inseparable and eternal unity in the Spirit. Jesus is the goal. He is the beginning; He is the ending. He is the first; He is the last. He is the Alpha; He is the Omega. You have not arrived until you have union with Jesus in the Holy Spirit. | 1 |
| 20. | a. **Tribulation**<br>b. **Distress**<br>c. **Persecution**<br>d. **Famine**<br>e. **Nakedness**<br>f. **Peril**<br>g. **Sword**<br><br>Paul would not have listed these threats if they could never happen to us. It would have been a waste of words. We may encounter any or all of these difficulties, but one thing they can never do is separate us from the love of God. | 7 |
| 21. | ***"We are killed all day long; we are accounted as sheep for the slaughter."***<br><br>Paul is quoting verse 22 of Psalm 44, a very somber psalm. In it, the sons of Korah were speaking to God's people under the old covenant*, but I have a deep inner conviction that these words will be true of the church as well. God has not promised to keep us from persecution. In fact, Jesus and some of the New Testament writers warn us to anticipate it.<br><br>All around this earth, our brothers and sisters are being imprisoned, beaten, and persecuted, and they are laying down their lives; but thank God they are not being separated from the love of God. Paul promises here that persecution can never separate us from God's love. | 1 |
| 22. | **Yet/But**<br><br>Paul is reminding us that any and every trial which may come upon us is not the end of the story, that there is more to come. Conjunctions like "yet," "but," and "nevertheless" in Scripture often alert us to a positive alternative that God wants to encourage us with. | 1 |

| Question | Answer | Points |
|---|---|---|
| 23. | **more; conquerors**<br><br>What does it mean that *"we are more than conquerors"*? It means that we come through the test or battle with more than we had when we went into it. We have not merely won but have also gained spoil. That is being more than a conqueror, and that is what Paul promises us that we will do. In all these things, we overwhelmingly conquer. | 2 |
| 24. | a. **death; life**<br>b. **angels; powers**<br>c. **present; come**<br>d. **height; depth**<br>e. **created**<br><br>It is something when a person is *"persuaded"* (Romans 8:38) or *"convinced"* (NIV, NASB). It carries conviction and makes an impact on people. Of what is Paul persuaded? That nothing can ever break or terminate our eternal and inseparable union with Jesus, our Savior, our Messiah, through the Holy Spirit. Christ is the Beginning, and He is the Ending. | 9 |
| 25. | **Hidden with Christ in God**<br><br>We have a hidden life, a life beyond the veil of time and eternity. Remember that in the tabernacle and the temple, there was a veil between the Holy Place and the Holy of Holies (or Holiest of All), where God's presence dwelled. Hebrews 6:19 tells us, *"This hope we have as an anchor of the soul, both sure and steadfast, and which enters the Presence behind the veil."* | 1 |
| 26. | **We will appear with Him in glory.**<br><br>Jesus Christ is our life. He is all we need. Do you remember that when we considered *"the mystery which has been hidden from ages and from generations, but now has been revealed to His saints"* (Colossians 1:26), we learned that Christ in us is *"the hope of glory"* (verse 27)? Paul is telling us that when Christ appears, our hope will be fulfilled, and we will appear with Him in glory. | 1 |
| 27. | **all**<br><br>When we have Christ, we have everything. He is all we need. He is the Beginning and the Ending, the Author and the Finisher. The only appropriate way to respond to these glorious truths is to take time to pour out your heart in praise and thanksgiving to God. | 1 |
| | Check your written memory work. If your memory work is word-perfect, 4 points for each verse. (1 point off for each mistake in a verse. If there are more than three mistakes, do not mark any points for that verse.) | 8 |
| | Total Points | ___/51 |

Fill in the total points for lesson 15 on the "Tally Sheet for Each Lesson" on page 253.

# LESSON 16 ANSWERS

| Question | Answer | Points |
|---|---|---|
| 1. | **Pride** <br><br> Pride produced rebellion. And when we examine the roots of many problems we face today, we see that they are the same as they were in ancient times. They have not changed. The sins that most preachers deal with in church are just branches on a trunk. The trunk is sin, but the roots of that trunk are rebellion. That is where the whole problem began, and when you really want the problem settled in your individual life, that is where you have to go: to the roots. | 1 |
| 2. | a. **heaven** <br> b. **throne** <br> c. **congregation** <br> d. **clouds** <br> e. **Most High** <br><br> In this passage from Isaiah, we read the name *Lucifer*, which is the name that Satan had before he fell. Lucifer means "the bright one," "the shining one," "the glorious one." <br><br> Here we find the very heart and root of the problem. In Isaiah 14:13–14, one phrase is repeated five times: "*I will.*" As it was with Satan, it is man's will set in opposition to God that is the root of all problems. | 5 |
| 3. | a. **Zion** <br> b. **Greece** <br><br> To me, the "sons of Zion" are biblical Zionists who live by one basic text that opens the Bible: "*In the beginning God…*" (Genesis 1:1). For them, everything has its source and origin in God. God is the ultimate: His promises and His decrees will ultimately determine the course of human history. As I understand it, God counts these people worthy to inherit the land of Israel*. <br><br> Through my classical education at Eton, I started learning Latin when I was nine and Greek when I was ten. I spent the next fifteen years studying Latin and Greek, the last five of those years at Cambridge University studying Greek philosophy. I want to say that my fellow students and I were mostly "sons of Greece," despite the fact that we were all theoretically Christians. I never heard about being "born again" until I was twenty-five, but we respected Christ and Christianity. Alongside that, we also respected the Greek poets, tragedians, and philosophers and were under the powerful influence of humanism. <br><br> I would add that we need to be delivered from slavery to the classics before we will see real revival. | 2 |
| 4. | **Greece** <br><br> If you analyze history, Babylon has had very little real influence on Western history. Medo-Persia has had relatively little influence. Rome has had a great influence, but you need to remember that although Rome defeated Greece militarily, Greece defeated Rome philosophically; the Romans came under the thinking of the Greeks. <br><br> So, the procreative life that issued from that historical background was *the life of Greece*. It is hard for people who are not familiar with it to realize how much the thinking and culture of Europe and the countries that have been influenced by Europe have been under the dominion of Greek thought. | 1 |
| 5. | **Woe** <br><br> This verse describes a total turning upside down of the truth. It is a complete rejection of all absolute values, and that is what we find today—we are surrounded by people who call evil good and good evil, bitter sweet and sweet bitter, and light darkness and darkness light. Wherever you look today, that is what you see. Without doubt, that is *humanism*. | 1 |

| Question | Answer | Points |
|---|---|---|
| 6. | **Woe**<br><br>The passage is clear that God will not tolerate the proud. Many people quote Proverbs 16:18 as, "Pride goes before a fall," but that is not what it says. The hard truth is that *pride goes before destruction, and a haughty spirit before a fall.* | 1 |
| 7. | **A throne of iniquity (or lawlessness)**<br><br>That is a throne that is set up in opposition to God. It is a throne that makes laws that are unlawful, that makes what is lawful unlawful and what is unlawful lawful. The European Union is well on the way to doing that. They are determined to make abortion law and to force homosexuality on people. They are not just legalizing it, but they are creating a legal situation in which it will be unlawful *not* to do it. If you can't see that, you need to wake up. | 1 |
| 8. | a. **Justice**<br>b. **righteousness***<br>c. **truth**<br>d. **equity**<br><br>When I listen to media reports on the situation in Israel, this is what I always end up with: *"Truth is fallen in the street."* There is no more room for truth. People are practicing lies. Isaiah 59:14 goes on to say, *"Equity cannot enter."* There is no room for fair judgment; justice is warped. | 4 |
| 9. | **He makes himself a prey.**<br><br>There will come a time when all you'll have to do is live righteously and you will become a prey, because the whole system is set against righteousness. | 1 |
| 10. | **God's**<br><br>This is an outworking of God's sovereignty. God chooses, not because we earn it or deserve it, but just because He chooses. Do you trust God? Do you trust God to choose? Do you trust His timing? If you trust Him to give, do you also trust Him to take away? It is illogical to trust God only to give and not also to take away. These are very important questions for your life. When you can come to the point of trusting God, you will be a far more peaceful person. | 1 |
| 11. | **His mercy**<br><br>Ultimately, God's choice depends not on our own effort, not on our own cleverness, but on His mercy. You may scarcely have faced this issue, but the results that really matter in your life do not come from all your efforts or all your cleverness; they come because God is merciful. We can trust God's mercy much more than we can trust our own cleverness. | 1 |
| 12. | **Christ**<br><br>Many of us are familiar with this Scripture but have not really applied it to our lives. We are somehow still trusting in keeping a set of rules to achieve righteousness with God—and that does not work. | 1 |
| 13. | a. **Confess**<br>b. **Believe**<br><br>The need for this twofold response is the most important truth you must receive and accept in your entire life. Many people want to know, "How can I be saved?" This is the answer. | 2 |
| 14. | **The election of grace**<br><br>The last phrase says, more literally, "according to the choice of grace." It all depends on God's grace and His choice. | 1 |
| 15. | **goodness; severity**<br><br>A lot of preaching deals only with God's kindness. But there is another side to God—His severity. The way we relate to God will determine which side of Him we see. | 2 |

| Question | Answer | Points |
|---|---|---|
| 16. | **No (They are irrevocable.)** <br><br> Once God has given something, He never withdraws His gift. Once God has called someone, He never withdraws His calling. | 1 |
| 17. | **God/The Lord** <br><br> Humanism states that man is the measure of all things, but Scripture is very clear that everything starts with God, is maintained with God, and ends with God—and that glory will be His forever. | 1 |
| | Check your written memory work. If your memory work is word-perfect, 4 points for each verse. (1 point off for each mistake in a verse. If there are more than three mistakes, do not mark any points for that verse.) | 4 |
| | Total Points | ____/31 |

Fill in the total points for lesson 16 on the "Tally Sheet for Each Lesson" on page 253.

# LESSON 17 ANSWERS

| Question | Answer | Points |
|---|---|---|
| 1. | **brethren** <br><br> What an amazing statement! There might be only two men in the Bible who felt that way. One is Paul, and the other is Moses—two of the men God used as much as anyone else to fulfill His purposes. And one of the conditions for doing what God wants done is having a burden for the well-being of His people. | 1 |
| 2. | a. **The Gentiles\*** <br><br> b. **He should be killed.** <br><br> Through the centuries, Paul has been viewed with hostility by the Jewish people. One reason is that they consider him to be a source of anti-Semitism. Even in his own lifetime, he was persecuted bitterly by his own people because he was taking the gospel to the Gentiles. When we study the life of Paul as revealed in the New Testament, we find that the main reason he was persecuted was that he was taking something the Jewish people felt belonged exclusively to them and giving it to people the Jews\* considered inferior and unworthy. | 2 |
| 3. | a. **adoption** <br><br> The first distinctive privilege is the Jewish people's adoption as sons. When the Lord told Moses in Exodus 4:22–23 to tell Pharaoh to release Israel\*, He said, *"Israel is My son, My firstborn.... Let My son go that he may serve Me. But if you refuse to let him go, indeed I will kill your son, your firstborn."* All the Egyptian firstborn sons were indeed killed on the night of the Passover, but not those of Israel—God's son, His firstborn, firstborn among the nations. <br><br> b. **glory** <br><br> The second special privilege Israel enjoyed is *"the glory"*—the manifest presence of God visible in various forms, including as a cloud and as fire. <br><br> c. **covenants** <br><br> Third, all the covenants of the Bible, from Noah onward, were revealed to the patriarchs and to Israel. <br><br> d. **law\*** <br><br> Fourth was the giving of the law to Moses on Mount Sinai. <br><br> e. **service** <br><br> The fifth privilege refers to the service that Israel performed in the tabernacle of Moses and in the first and second temples. <br><br> f. **promises** <br><br> Sixth, a great number of promises were given to Israel. For an example, read Deuteronomy 28, where God lays out the blessings for obedience and the curses for disobedience. <br><br> g. **fathers** <br><br> The seventh privilege refers to the patriarchs: Abraham, Isaac, and Jacob. <br><br> h. **Christ** <br><br> And, eighth, the Messiah, who came *"according to the flesh"* from the fathers. According to His human nature, Jesus was from the tribe of Judah\*. <br><br> Paul says this of Jesus in Romans 9:5: "[He] *is over all, the eternally blessed God. Amen."* This is one of various places in which Paul gives the title "God"—in Greek, *Theos*—to the Lord Jesus Christ. | 8 |
| 4. | **No** <br><br> Paul explains that God's word accomplished its purpose, and we will look at the reasons he gives in the following questions. | 1 |

| Question | Answer | Points |
|---|---|---|
| 5. | **No** | 1 |
| | It is very important that we understand this. Paul is saying, in an exceptional use of the word *Israel*, that not all people who are Israelites by natural birth are accepted as Israel by God. And he goes on to present two cases in which God did not include all who might have been included but separated out the sons to whom He gave the title *Israelite*. | |
| 6. | a. **Abram's descendants** | 13 |
| | The promise was not just to Abram (Abraham) but was reiterated to Abraham when God renamed him as being a *"covenant between Me and you and your descendants after you in their generations, for an everlasting covenant"* (Genesis 17:7). | |
| | b. **Hagar** | |
| | Romans 9:8–9 indicates that Hagar's children are children of flesh, not of promise. Galatians 4:21–25 reveals some important symbolism about this, including that the covenant* of the law from Mount Sinai *"gives birth to bondage, which is Hagar"* (verse 24). | |
| | c. **Ishmael** | |
| | Of the two sons of Abraham, God excluded the older one, Ishmael, and chose the younger one, Isaac. Ishmael's descendants are excluded, and the only ones counted as descendants of Abraham are the ones descended from Isaac. (See Romans 9:7.) | |
| | d. **A covenant** | |
| | Although people often don't understand the gravity of a covenant, to God, a covenant is absolute and binding. In Psalm 105:8–10, we read, *"He remembers His covenant forever, the word which He commanded, for a thousand generations, the covenant which He made with Abraham, and His oath to Isaac, and confirmed it to Jacob for a statute, to Israel as an everlasting covenant."* | |
| | e. **A son** | |
| | It is significant that, at a time when Abraham and Sarah were old and childless, God promised Sarah a son because she was the freewoman through whom God's promise that Abraham was to be the father of many nations was to be fulfilled. | |
| | f. **An everlasting (eternal) covenant** | |
| | In numerous places in the Bible, God indicates that His covenant is not just for time but also has eternal implications. Galatians 4:26 contains an element of this implication when it talks of the heavenly Jerusalem that *"is the mother of us all"* (who are children of the promise through faith). | |
| | g. **Because she was barren** | |
| | God's promises are not without opposition. It is interesting to note that Abraham, Isaac, and Jacob all had wives who were barren: Sarah was barren until she was ninety, Rebekah was barren, and Rachel was also barren. (See Genesis 29:31.) But God intervened in each instance, and the women bore children according to God's promise. | |
| | h. **The younger (Jacob)** | |
| | For Esau, the older son, to serve Jacob, the younger son, is contrary to the normal tradition of the Middle East, where the eldest is the senior son with the preeminence. Not so here. For the second time, God excluded the older son and chose the younger. Paul uses every resource of language to emphasize that it was God's choice that was decisive. It did not depend on anything Esau or Jacob had done. In fact, even before they were born, while they were still in their mother's womb, God said, "I reject Esau and choose Jacob." (See Romans 9:13.) Paul is emphasizing that everything depends on God's choice. | |

| Question | Answer | Points |
|---|---|---|
| 6. (cont.) | **i. Israel**<br><br>The name *Jacob* is usually interpreted as "supplanter," and the name *Israel* means either "a prince with God" or "one who wrestles with God." As with his grandfather Abram, the change of Jacob's name was a crisis in his life, having a decisive effect on his ongoing destiny* and the development of his character. In other words, a name is connected with character and destiny.<br><br>**j. The twelve patriarchs**<br><br>In Romans 9:5, we saw that one of the privileges of Israel was *"the fathers,"* and I have listed Abraham, Isaac, and Jacob in that regard; but, in the book of Acts, Jacob's (or Israel's) sons are also listed as patriarchs.<br><br>**k. Tribes**<br><br>The families of the twelve sons of Jacob (Israel) became the twelve tribes of Israel. When Joseph went down to Egypt, and his family went to live in Goshen, Israel (Jacob) blessed Ephraim (the younger son of Joseph) above Manasseh (the older)—another example of God's election. These two sons became two half-tribes of Israel, so there is no tribe of Joseph. When the nation of Israel split, the tribes of Judah and Benjamin remained in the south as the kingdom of Judah, and the other ten tribes separated themselves as the kingdom of Israel.<br><br>**l. Faith**<br><br>This principle goes right back to the history of the patriarchs, when it was not natural descent, but embracing the promise of God's word, that determined who was to be accepted by God as His people. To be a true Israelite, you first had to be descended from Abraham, Isaac, and Jacob; but that, in itself, was not sufficient. To be one of God's chosen people, you also had to receive the seed of God's word by faith in your heart.<br><br>**m. Christ**<br><br>If it is a requirement for you to have faith and to be in Christ to be Abraham's seed, can you understand how Paul is limiting the use of the word "Israel" and the "children of the promise"? | |
| | Check your written memory work. If your memory work is word-perfect, 4 points for each verse. (1 point off for each mistake in a verse. If there are more than three mistakes, do not mark any points for that verse.) | 4 |
| | Total Points | ___/30 |

Fill in the total points for lesson 17 on the "Tally Sheet for Each Lesson" on page 254.

# LESSON 18 ANSWERS

| Question | Answer | Points |
|---|---|---|
| 1. | **Israel***<br><br>To paraphrase this verse, we might say, "Not all who are descended from Israel are Israel." Paul is not talking about people who are not descended from Abraham. He is saying that God does not accept all of those who are descended from Abraham as His people. So, rather than extending the meaning of *Israel*, Paul is reducing it. He is saying that some people who would be called Israel really do not qualify. This is a rare use and not the normal use of *Israel*. | 1 |
| 2. | **As the Israel of God**<br><br>Most people today interpret the phrase *"the Israel of God"* as the church. I think that is a mistake. In these two verses, Paul is talking about two different categories of people: first, Gentiles* who previously had no relationship with God but who have now come into a relationship with Him by becoming *"a new creation"*; and, second, Israelites who have been completed by their relationship to the Messiah and who have thus become *"the Israel of God."* In this sense, Paul is applying the word *Israel* only to those Israelites who are not merely Israelites by birth but who have also received the seed of the promise of God's Word and experienced the new birth in Christ. | 1 |
| 3. | **He has formed them for Himself.**<br><br>The word *"formed"* is used of a potter molding a vessel. God had been molding the Israelites for fifteen centuries. They were a people He had already formed for Himself, but they needed to be completed by their acknowledgment and acceptance of the Messiah. | 1 |
| 4. | **A servant**<br><br>Unlike the Gentiles receiving something new, the Jewish people had had God's promises for many centuries. To them, Jesus was, in Paul's words, the *"servant"* who would confirm the promises they already knew and were expecting to see fulfilled. | 1 |
| 5. | **The Gentiles**<br><br>The difference is clear. Again, the Jewish people had many promises already given to them that had to be fulfilled. The Gentiles had no promises. They did not depend on God's faithfulness to fulfill His promises; they depended only on His mercy. This is the distinction between those who come into the new creation out of nothing, and those who have been completed because they have already received God's promises. | 1 |
| 6. | **inwardly**<br><br>As we saw in our discussion of Romans 9:6 (see question 1), Paul is not extending the use of the term *Jew* here but restricting it. He is saying that it is not sufficient merely to be a Jew outwardly, merely to have natural descent, merely to have physical circumcision. God is looking for the circumcision of the heart, an internal "setting apart," in the Spirit, that produces praise. | 1 |
| 7. | **Nathanael**<br><br>Nathanael was a true Israelite not merely because he was an Israelite by natural descent, but because he had the inner attitude of heart that God requires. So, a true Israelite—in the words of Galatians 6:16, *"the Israel of God"*—is not a Gentile who has come to Christ but an Israelite whose background in the promises of God extending over many centuries has been completed through faith in the Messiah. | 1 |
| 8. | **Israel after the flesh**<br><br>The literal translation is "Look at Israel according to the flesh." Paul is saying, "Look at those who are Israelites only by natural descent and who do not fulfill the inner conditions of the heart." That is why they went into idolatry. They were still Israelites by natural descent but were not accepted by God because of their inner heart condition. | 1 |

| Question | Answer | Points |
|---|---|---|
| 9. | **Assemble them**<br><br>Since these words were written before the Babylonian captivity of Israel, Isaiah was predicting a second regathering—not the regathering from Babylon but a subsequent one. The fact that many places are mentioned from which the Jews* never returned after the Babylonian captivity is also evidence that God did not have in mind the return from Babylon. On the other hand, every statement in this passage has been fulfilled exactly concerning the regathering of the Jewish people in recent years. God is fulfilling His promises to Israel as a nation. | 1 |
| 10. | **The land that He gave to their fathers**<br><br>Only one land agrees with that description—the land God gave the forefathers of Israel and Judah*. God was saying, "I will bring them back, and they will possess it." They never possessed the land after the Babylonian captivity. In fact, they became, as it were, tenants on the land at the discretion of a Gentile empire, tenants who would be uprooted and driven out by the Romans in AD 70. Nothing in that period answers to these words.<br><br>But again, everything in this passage of Jeremiah has been fulfilled and is being fulfilled in our day. Israel, as an independent nation, came into existence in 1948, and I happened to be there to witness it. | 1 |
| 11. | a. **Gather Israel**<br><br>b. **Keep Israel (as a shepherd does his flock)**<br><br>As I mentioned, this promise is being fulfilled in our day. I have had the privilege of serving as God's messenger in at least twenty nations and making this proclamation: "Hear, O nations, the Lord who scattered Israel *is* gathering him and *keeping* him as a shepherd does his flock." (Jeremiah 31:10 updated to present tense because it is happening now.) | 2 |
| 12. | **No**<br><br>This means that as long as we can go outside and look up into the sky and see the sun, moon, and stars in their divinely appointed order, or as long as we can stand on the border of the sea and look at the waves roaring, by those things alone we can know that Israel is still a nation before the Lord, with whom He is dealing. | 1 |
| 13. | a. **rejoice**<br><br>b. **plant**<br><br>The *"great calamity"* (Jeremiah 32:42) of the exile God brought on Israel is historical fact. It was not metaphorical or spiritual. It was real; it happened. The pages of history record it. God says, "In the same way I brought calamity upon them, I am going to bring all the good that I have promised them." That good is not going to be metaphorical or spiritual; it will be real in the annals of history. | 2 |
| 14. | **God will be hallowed in Israel.**<br><br>God is saying, "My name will be hallowed, and My holiness will be demonstrated, in what I do in you." God uses the saving of the Gentiles to provoke Jews to jealousy. (See Romans 10:19; 11:11.) But here we see that what God does in Israel will be a witness to the Gentiles. Note that God uses the one to get the attention of the other. | 1 |
| 15. | a. **despised; nation**<br><br>How applicable these promises are to our own day when people continue to sneer and say Israel is not worthy to be considered a nation. A number of religious Christians say the Jews did not recognize their Messiah but crucified Him, and that God is therefore done with them. Many nonreligious people call the Jews a hateful, bullying people who do not own the land of Israel and deserve to be annihilated—and will be.<br><br>b. **No**<br><br>It impresses me that the Bible is so perceptive. It looked ahead with divine, telescopic sight and saw how things would be after the words were actually written, thousands of years in the future. God says here, "I will never abandon the Jews." So, replacing Israel with the church in the promises of God discredits not only Scripture but also God's faithfulness. | 3 |

| Question | Answer | Points |
|---|---|---|
| 16. | a. People in the church (of Sardis) | 8 |
| | b. Dead | |
| | c. | |
| |     i. Be watchful | |
| |     ii. Strengthen the things which remain | |
| |     iii. Remember how they had received and heard | |
| |     iv. Hold fast | |
| |     v. Repent | |
| | d. Jesus would come upon them as a thief (and they would not know what hour He would come upon them). | |
| | That warning does not differ in many ways from God's words of warning to Israel. Can you see that if God were to break His covenant* with Israel, then we couldn't depend on Him to uphold His covenant with the church, because there has been just as much unfaithfulness in the church as there has been in Israel? | |
| 17. | a. | 4 |
| |     i. The Amen | |
| |     ii. The Faithful and True Witness | |
| |     iii. The Beginning of the creation of God | |
| | b. Lukewarm | |
| | That is plain speaking! Could His message be applied to sections of the church today that are neither cold nor hot? I think it could. And yet, in the names of Jesus listed, we read of *the Faithful and True Witness.* Faithfulness is part of God's character that He cannot escape in spite of our unfaithfulness. Paul writes to Timothy, *"If we endure, we shall also reign with Him. If we deny Him, He also will deny us. If we are faithless,* **He remains faithful***; He cannot deny Himself"* (2 Timothy 2:12–13). | |
| | Check your written memory work. If your memory work is word-perfect, 4 points for each verse. (1 point off for each mistake in a verse. If there are more than three mistakes, do not mark any points for that verse.) | 8 |
| | Total Points | ___/39 |

Fill in the total points for lesson 18 on the "Tally Sheet for Each Lesson" on page 254.

# LESSON 19 ANSWERS

| Question | Answer | Points |
|---|---|---|
| 1. | **No ("Certainly not!")**<br><br>Paul backs up his answer with a quote from Exodus 33:19: "*Then He said, 'I will make all My goodness pass before you, and I will proclaim the name of the LORD before you. I will be gracious to whom I will be gracious, and I will have compassion on whom I will have compassion.'*" What he is indicating is that Israel* has known this truth since Mount Sinai, so they shouldn't raise any objection. | 1 |
| 2. | **No**<br><br>It is God's choice alone that determines to whom He shows mercy and compassion. For the rest of Romans 9, Paul continues to deal with people's objections. | 1 |
| 3. | **Hopefully, your answer is "No"!**<br><br>You can have justice if you want it because God is just. He gives justice according to a plumb line or level—it is as exact as that. There is not a single variation, not one millimeter off, in God's justice—if that is what you want. But none of us can afford to ask for justice. | No points |
| 4. | **Death**<br><br>As we have discussed, wages are what you deserve. If you want your wages, God will not withhold them. Come with your hand held out, and you will get them. But the wages of sin is death. The alternative is the free gift of God: eternal life. You cannot earn that. You will never deserve it. So, you must decide: do I want my wages, or do I want my gift? | 1 |
| 5. | **The wicked**<br><br>This verse could equally be translated, "The Lord has made everything for His own purpose, yes, even the wicked for the day of doom." | 1 |
| 6. | **Pharaoh**<br><br>We have no problem believing that God called Moses from the burning bush to lead Israel out of Egypt, but Scripture is clear that God also chose Pharaoh to bring resistance to those efforts. | 1 |
| 7. | **a. That He may show His power in Pharaoh**<br>**b. That His name may be declared in all the earth**<br>We may be tempted to feel sorry for Pharaoh, but let's study the whole record:<br>  1. Pharaoh hardened his own heart *six times* before God did anything. (See Exodus 7:13, 22; 8:15, 19, 32; 9:7.)<br>  2. Then the Lord hardened Pharaoh's heart *once*. (See Exodus 9:12.)<br>  3. Pharaoh hardened his own heart *again*. (See Exodus 9:34.)<br>  4. Finally, the Lord hardened Pharaoh's heart *four* more times. (See Exodus 10:1, 27; 11:10; 14:8.) | 2 |
| 8. | **The iniquity of the Amorites was not yet complete.**<br><br>The Amorites were already a wicked, idolatrous, perverted people. But God tells Abraham that their wickedness has not yet become fully ripe. He is saying that when their iniquity was fully ripe, He would cast in His sickle and reap them, and Abraham's descendants would take the land. So, when you look at what is happening in the world today, realize that it is wicked but not fully ripe. When it is fully ripe, God will cast in the sickle and reap. (See Revelation 14:14–20.) | 1 |
| 9. | **He wills**<br><br>Paul's wording is a little unsatisfying to some people because they have lost sight of God's sovereignty. In a world where humanism is so prevalent, it can be difficult to appreciate just how great and powerful God truly is. And He has the prerogative to have mercy on some and to harden others. | 1 |

| Question | Answer | Points |
|---|---|---|
| 10. | **He formed man with it.**<br><br>God is the original Potter who formed man from the dust of the ground. In Romans 9:20, Paul returns to this theme of *"the thing formed"* and *"him who formed it."* Many people are asking God the same question today: "Why have You made me like this?" The answer remains the same: God has the right to decide. God knows His business, and we should not try to instruct Him. | 1 |
| 11. | **The potter**<br><br>We cannot deny that it is the potter who chooses what to make with the clay. The same clay could be used for a beautiful urn or a functional sewage pipe, and the potter is the one who decides. In this verse, God is the molder of the vessels. | 1 |
| 12. | a. **To show His wrath**<br><br>b. **To make His power known**<br><br>When you see the wicked flourishing, think of God's patience. He endures wickedness because His purposes are being worked out. Second Peter 3:15 says that our Lord's *"longsuffering,"* or patience, brings salvation. That is one thing that amazes us—how long God endures wickedness. It is a question and frustration we all face: "How can God let that kind of thing go on?" Again, the answer is that God knows His business, and He endures wickedness for the sake of His elect. Once His purposes are worked out in His chosen ones, He will deal with the wicked. | 2 |
| 13. | a. **wrath; destruction**<br><br>b. **mercy; glory**<br><br>*The Living Bible* says that you and I are vessels *"made for pouring the riches of His glory into"* (Romans 9:23). God is fashioning you to become a vessel of glory. Why does God permit wickedness? Because He is making you the kind of vessel that will hold His glory.<br><br>You can see that the theme of God's choice and foreknowledge goes all through these chapters. Unless you can grasp this theme, you will miss the message. | 4 |
| 14. | a. **Jezreel**<br><br>The name means "God will sow."<br><br>b. **Lo-Ruhamah**<br><br>The name means "No mercy."<br><br>c. **Lo-Ammi**<br><br>The name means "Not my people."<br><br>d. **"My people."**<br><br>e. **"Mercy is shown."**<br><br>f. **sow**<br><br>g. **mercy**<br><br>h. **My people**<br><br>We must remember that God is regathering the Israelites to the place where it was said, *"You are not my people"* (Hosea 1:10), so that He might declare to them that they *are* His people. He is showing mercy on them, and He is "sowing [them] for Himself in the earth." | 8 |
| 15. | **The remnant (of the children of Israel)**<br><br>Verse 27 refers not to *a* remnant but to *the* remnant—the chosen, foreknown remnant. If God had not left Israel a remnant, they would have been wiped out. We see at the end of Romans 11 that *"all Israel will be saved"* (verse 26). But we have to put these two passages together: all Israel by then will be the chosen remnant. So, these two Scriptures explain one another. | 1 |

| Question | Answer | Points |
|---|---|---|
| 16. | a. **No**<br>b. **Yes**<br>c. **Yes**<br>d. **No**<br>e. **Faith**<br>f. **law\***<br><br>The Israelites tried to earn God's righteousness\*, whereas God's righteousness can be received only by faith. Because the Israelites tried to earn it, they did not receive it by faith. The Jews\* who sought to achieve righteousness by keeping the law failed. Yet the Gentiles\*, who knew nothing about the law and were not interested in righteousness, achieved righteousness through faith in Christ. | 6 |
| 17. | **They did not seek it by faith (but by the works of the law).**<br><br>This is the paradox: the Jews failed because they rejected the Messiah—the stone God had laid down on which to build His kingdom. Israel is the pattern, but the same situation applies to many churchgoing Christians. If we think we have to earn righteousness or salvation, we will not receive it by faith, because the two approaches are mutually exclusive. The truth is, righteousness cannot be earned. | 1 |
| 18. | a. **sanctuary**<br>b. **offense**<br><br>Jesus is either a sanctuary, if you believe in Him and receive Him by faith, or a stone over which you stumble and fall, if you do not believe. Jesus is always that way. Either you enter by faith into the sanctuary, or you trip over the stone of stumbling. The issue is this: you cannot achieve God's righteousness by your own efforts. Paul ends Romans 9 with this wonderful encouragement: *"Whoever believes on Him will not be put to shame"* (v. 33). | 2 |
| 19. | a. **A stumbling block**<br>b. **Foolishness**<br><br>The cross is an offense (see also Galatians 5:11) and a stumbling block because it undercuts all human pride and self-righteousness. It leaves us with no claim of our own; we can only trust in the undeserved mercy of God. | 2 |
| | Check your written memory work. If your memory work is word-perfect, 4 points for each verse. (1 point off for each mistake in a verse. If there are more than three mistakes, do not mark any points for that verse.) | 8 |
| | Total Points | ____ /45 |

Fill in the total points for lesson 19 on the "Tally Sheet for Each Lesson" on page 254.

# LESSON 20 ANSWERS

| Question | Answer | Points |
|---|---|---|
| 1. | **That they may be saved** | 1 |
| | The most important thing for Jew *or* Gentile is to be saved—to know that *you* are saved. That is why I have certain reservations concerning all the excitement about the restoration of Israel* and Judah* to their homeland because, sometimes, sound Christians begin to think and act as though all that matters is that you are Jewish. It is not! Jews* and Gentiles* *all* need to be saved. | |
| 2. | **Knowledge (of God's way of salvation)** | 1 |
| | If you know the Jewish people, you will realize how unpopular this statement would make you with them. If there is one thing they do not want to hear, it is that they do not know. We can understand, then, why Paul was *persona non grata* with them. | |
| 3. | **Submit to the righteousness* of God** | 1 |
| | Notice the phrase *"have not submitted."* What problem does that phrase indicate? Pride. It is also a problem for every one of us. It is humbling to have to acknowledge, "I have no claim on God except His undeserved mercy and the fact that Jesus took my place and died on the cross for me." We must submit to that truth. | |
| 4. | **No** | 1 |
| | Jesus did not come to destroy the Law* and the Prophets* but to fulfill them. (See Matthew 5:17.) Matthew and John are careful to point their readers back to the prophetic Scriptures about the Messiah. Matthew uses the phrase *"might be fulfilled"* ten times (Matthew 1:22; 2:15, 23; 4:14; 8:17; 12:17; 13:35; 21:4; 26:56; 27:35), and John uses it seven times (John 12:38; 15:25; 17:12; 18:9, 32; 19:24, 28). Jesus says it more emphatically: *"Then He said to them, 'These are the words which I spoke to you while I was still with you, that **all things must be fulfilled** which were written in the Law of Moses and the Prophets and the Psalms concerning Me'"* (Luke 24:44). | |
| 5. | **Law* as a means of obtaining righteousness** | 1 |
| | Where the *New King James Version* says *"the law,"* the word *"the"* has been inserted by the translators. Primarily, Paul speaks about the law of Moses*. But the law of Moses is merely a pattern of any law. Christ is the end of law as a means of obtaining righteousness for everyone who believes. That is a far-reaching statement! If you believe in Jesus, then the death of Christ on the cross has terminated law—not only the law of Moses but any law—as a means of achieving righteousness with God. | |
| 6. | **The whole law** | 1 |
| | If you keep the whole law, entirely, all the time, you need no other righteousness. But no one besides Jesus has ever kept the whole law entirely, all the time, so we cannot depend on that. You cannot split the law up into little sections and say, "I'll keep this part but not that part," because it is one single system. You either observe it all the time, or you do not achieve righteousness by it. | |
| 7. | **The righteousness of faith** | 1 |
| | What Moses said, and what Paul takes up as a theme in Romans 10, is that the righteousness of faith depends not on something that still has to be done but on something that has already been done. You do not have to go up to heaven; you do not have to descend into the abyss. Christ came from heaven. He went down into the abyss. (See Romans 10:6–7.) He has finished the atonement*. It is settled. You do not have to do it, and it does not have to be done again. | |

| Question | Answer | Points |
|---|---|---|
| 8. | a. **The mouth**<br><br>b. **The heart**<br><br>Notice that, in our obtaining righteousness by faith, two parts of the human personality must be involved: the mouth and the heart. In Romans 10:8–10, Paul mentions each of these parts three times. The first two times, he talks about the mouth first and the heart second. The last time, he mentions the heart and then the mouth. This is significant. It is not easy to know what is in the heart of a person. In fact, the only One who really knows a person's heart is the Lord. But if you want something in your heart, how do you get it there? By repeating it with your mouth. It may seem as though nothing is happening, but, after a while, it happens. | 2 |
| 9. | **The word of faith**<br><br>Obtaining righteousness on the basis of faith comes through a word—the word of the gospel. The message of the gospel is the only key that opens to us the door to the righteousness of faith. Think how important that makes it. Until this message is proclaimed, even people who long to attain righteousness cannot.<br><br>What an obligation we have, therefore, to proclaim the gospel to the whole human race! We are not just to sit in church on Sunday mornings and sing a few hymns. That does not discharge our debt to humanity. | 1 |
| 10. | a. **Confess; mouth**<br><br>b. **believe; heart**<br><br>That is the clearest single statement in one verse of how to be saved: confess with your mouth Jesus as Lord and believe in your heart that God has raised Him from the dead. Notice that if you do not believe in Jesus's resurrection, you cannot be saved. | 4 |
| 11. | a. **righteousness**<br><br>b. **salvation**<br><br>The English word for *confess* is derived from a Latin word that means "to say the same as." That is also the meaning of the word in the Greek text of the New Testament. So, confession for us as Bible-believing Christians means saying the same thing with our mouths that God has said in His Word. If I am sick, but God's Word says that "[Jesus] *Himself took our infirmities and bore our sicknesses*" (Matthew 8:17) and that "*by His stripes* ["wounds" NIV, NASB] *we are healed*" (Isaiah 53:5), then I need to choose with whom I will side—God's Word or the symptoms. And this is not a system; you cannot make it "work." It is one thing to believe in the mind; it is another thing to believe in the heart. Again, how do you get God's Word to the heart? By way of the mouth. | 2 |
| 12. | **No**<br><br>God's plan of salvation is open to everybody who believes in Jesus. | 1 |
| 13. | **All who call upon Him**<br><br>Paul is quoting from Joel 2:32, where the alternative reading in the *New King James Version* is, "*Whoever calls on the name of the LORD shall be* [delivered]." Deliverance is part of our salvation, and this was the verse that gave me the key to pray for my deliverance from depression. | 1 |
| 14. | **beautiful; peace; glad; good**<br><br>This is a wonderful picture of one who carries the message of the gospel. It is a quote from Isaiah 52:7, which goes on to say of such an evangelist, "*Who proclaims salvation, who says to Zion, 'Your God reigns!'*" | 4 |

| Question | Answer | Points |
|---|---|---|
| 15. | **No**<br><br>Paul is quoting the first verse of Isaiah 53, the chapter that contains the most complete prophetic unveiling of the atonement of Jesus Christ. That verse gives a warning: not everybody will believe. The problem is not that God has not provided the solution but that not everyone accepts it with faith. | 1 |
| 16. | **Yes**<br><br>It is not because the Jewish people have not heard. In Romans 10:18, Paul goes on to quote Psalm 19:4 about the testimony of the sun, moon, and stars, which he applies to the message of the gospel. We also dealt with this theme in lesson 2, where we concluded that God's invisible attributes are clearly seen in creation. | 1 |
| 17. | a. **God**<br><br>b. **Idolatry** (*"What is not God"*; *"foolish idols"*)<br><br>c. **Jealousy**<br><br>d. **A foolish nation**<br><br>In Romans 10:19, Paul asks rhetorically, *"Did Israel not know?"* He then points us back to Deuteronomy 32:21, where we read that due to the Israelites' idolatry, God chose to provoke them and move them to anger. What is *"a foolish nation"*? The Gentiles. The Gentiles are a foolish nation by comparison with Israel, who had a heritage of fifteen centuries of God's instruction. The Israelites were set apart. So, now God angered the Jews by accepting peoples they despised. | 4 |
| 18. | a. **found; manifest**<br><br>b. **disobedient; contrary**<br><br>Paul is saying, then, with his fellow Jewish people in mind, "We were warned. We can't say it would never happen to us because our own prophets told us it would. Our own Moses said that God is going to make us jealous by people who haven't even been the people of God—people who are on a different level from us spiritually. We haven't obeyed God, but, as prophesied by Isaiah, God has been found by those who weren't even looking for Him." | 4 |
| | Check your written memory work. If your memory work is word-perfect, 4 points for each verse. (1 point off for each mistake in a verse. If there are more than three mistakes, do not mark any points for that verse.) | 8 |
| | Total Points | ____/40 |

Fill in the total points for lesson 20 on the "Tally Sheet for Each Lesson" on page 254.

# LESSON 21 ANSWERS

| Question | Answer | Points |
|---|---|---|
| 1. | **No (***"Certainly not!"***)**<br><br>In Greek, there is a form of question that expects the answer *no*. That is the form Paul uses here. This crucial question keeps coming up in the book of Romans and remains one of the primary questions in the church today. | 1 |
| 2. | **Himself**<br><br>If we need proof that God has not rejected the entire people of Israel*, we need to look no further than Paul, who points out his lineage from Abraham, through Isaac and Jacob/Israel, and then through Benjamin. | 1 |
| 3. | **Those whom He foreknew**<br><br>We come back to that decisive factor—that those whom God has chosen and foreknown are His people. | 1 |
| 4. | **Elijah**<br><br>The King James Version says, "[Elijah] *maketh intercession to God against Israel*" (Romans 11:2). That phrase has always gripped me. Here was a prophet of God making intercession *against* God's people. I believe this was a weakness in Elijah, since I do not believe we should ever make intercession against the people of God. I can empathize, though; I have often felt like doing it myself. But we should not yield to the temptation. | 1 |
| 5. | **No**<br><br>On Mount Sinai, the Lord corrected Elijah and told him he was not the only one left who served the Lord. Notice again the emphasis on God's grace. To paraphrase, God said, "Those seven thousand men have not kept themselves; I have kept them. I have reserved them for Myself. They are My reserved remnant." | 1 |
| 6. | **A remnant**<br><br>The literal translation of the final phrase in Romans 11:5 is "according to the choice [or election] of grace." So, we come back to the theme that grace makes God's sovereign choice, and God's choice settles who His people are to be. God has a remnant in both Israel and the wider church. That is one reason it is important to study the facts about Israel: the same principles apply to us. | 1 |
| 7. | **Hopefully, you think it is!**<br><br>Paul points out that there is among the Jewish people a remnant of believers according to the election of grace. There has never been a time, from the first century to the present day, when there have not been Jewish people who believe in Jesus as their Messiah. Sometimes the remnant has been small. At this time, it is increasing rapidly. And, soon, according to the election of grace, it will no longer be just a small remnant. | No points |
| 8. | **No**<br><br>This point is extremely important. If you can earn it, it is not grace. If you deserve it, it is not grace. God's grace is not earned, and it is not deserved; it is received only one way—by faith. Jesus alone *deserved* the empowering presence of grace because He "*knew no sin*" (2 Corinthians 5:21). | 1 |
| 9. | **No**<br><br>You may not even boast about the fact that you have faith, because "[faith is] *not of yourselves; it is the gift of God*" (Ephesians 2:8). God gave you the faith by which to receive His grace. Grace begins where human ability ends. God is continually thrusting us out beyond the level of our own abilities so that we may move out into His grace. | 1 |

| Question | Answer | Points |
| --- | --- | --- |
| 10. | **Grace**<br><br>The writer of Hebrews exhorts us to come boldly to God so that we may obtain two things: mercy and grace to help in time of need. I am convinced that everybody who comes to obtain mercy and grace receives those things. The only reason people do not receive mercy and grace is that they do not come. God has made them available to every one of us. | 1 |
| 11. | **known**<br><br>God never forced Abraham to do anything; He chose him because He knew him, and He knew He could trust him to do what He was calling him to do. What did He ask of Abraham? To teach his children and his household the ways of the Lord so that God might bring upon Abraham the promise He had made of a son and of a great people to be descended from him. | 1 |
| 12. | **Blindness (spiritual)**<br><br>The elect—those whom God foreknew and chose—have obtained salvation. The rest, Paul says, have been blinded. Note that it was God, and not the devil, who gave them *a spirit of stupor* (Romans 11:8). This was the result of God's people, the Jews\*, hardening their hearts against Him and rejecting His truth. | 1 |
| 13. | a. **Spirit; Lord**<br><br>b. **spirit; Lord**<br><br>Can you absorb that? God permitted a distressing spirit to have access to Saul because he *"rejected the word of the Lord"* (1 Samuel 15:23). Satan does not have power to do anything God does not permit him to do. But God can permit Satan to release a distressing spirit against us if we persistently reject the truth. | 4 |
| 14. | **People did not receive the love of the truth.**<br><br>Isn't that an urgent warning? If we do not *"receive the love of the truth,"* God will deal with us, and we will come under deception. | 1 |
| 15. | **Strong delusion (that they should believe the lie)**<br><br>When a deluding spirit comes upon any person, that person can no longer see the truth. God is already permitting a deluding spirit to come on various sectors of the church that have rejected the revealed truth of God, especially on the ministers and leaders responsible for those errors. | 1 |
| 16. | **stumbled; fall**<br><br>I think that it would be legitimate, in view of what follows, to add the word "irretrievably" to the end of the question *"Have they stumbled that they should fall?"* Has Israel stumbled that they should fall irretrievably? Again, the answer is "Certainly not!" Although Israel's fall has lasted for a long while, it is temporary, not permanent. | 2 |
| 17. | **Salvation has come to the Gentiles\*.**<br><br>This is one of those amazing mysteries of God—that Israel's rejection of their Messiah and His crucifixion and resurrection opened the way for salvation to come to the entire Gentile world. | 1 |
| 18. | **The lost sheep of the house of Israel**<br><br>Jesus instructed His disciples to go only *"to the lost sheep of the house of Israel"* because God had ordained the Jewish people to receive the first offer of the gospel. | 1 |
| 19. | **All the nations**<br><br>*"Nations"* refers to the Gentiles. Israel had been given the first offer and had refused it. The people of Israel wanted the kingdom, and they believed it was for them, but they lost the kingdom because they rejected the King. Because of their refusal and rejection of the Messiah, the opportunity for salvation was extended to all other nations. | 1 |

| Question | Answer | Points |
|---|---|---|
| 20. | **A nation bearing the fruits of the kingdom**<br><br>What was the "*nation*" Jesus mentioned to which the kingdom was offered? Not America or Great Britain or Russia. The church is that new nation—and, according to 1 Peter 2:9, it is "*a holy nation.*" But the church qualifies as the custodian of the kingdom only as long as it brings forth fruit. | 1 |
| 21. | **"*Lord, will You at this time restore the kingdom to Israel?*"**<br><br>Some people say the kingdom will never be restored to Israel. But, if that were true, Jesus would have answered the disciples, "It will never be restored." (Contrast Acts 1:7–8.) Perhaps the emphasis also needs correcting—that Israel will be restored to the kingdom of the Messiah. | 1 |
| 22. | a. **times; seasons**<br>b. **power**<br>c. **witnesses**<br><br>Since the offer of the kingdom has now been extended to all nations, it has to reach all nations—every part of the earth—before the age can close. We receive power from the Holy Spirit to be witnesses to the gospel of Christ. (See Acts 1:8.) The church age began with a major outpouring of the Holy Spirit, and it is closing with a major outpouring of the Holy Spirit. If we do not realize that the outpouring of the Holy Spirit is given for the sake of the harvest, we will miss the purposes of God.[2] | 4 |
| 23. | **The end will come.**<br><br>Again, once Israel forfeited the kingdom of God, and the message could be sent to the nations, this course was set in motion: the age cannot close until all the nations have received the message. That is what Paul means when he says that through the fall of the Jewish people, salvation has come to the nations. | 1 |
| 24. | **Yes (It will bring even more riches.)**<br><br>If the blessing of salvation has come to the nations through Israel's transgressions, what will come when Israel is restored? You can see how completely we are missing the purposes of God if we do not align ourselves with His plan for the restoration of Israel, because the fullness of God's blessing will not come to other nations until Israel is restored. | 1 |
| 25. | **To save some of them**<br><br>Paul wants to bring forth a Gentile church that will so enjoy the blessings of God and demonstrate the presence of God that the Jews will say, "We want what they have." But, how often, honestly, has the church done anything to make the Jews jealous? | 1 |
| 26. | **Life from the dead**<br><br>What an exciting verse! When the Jews themselves are reconciled, what will it be but "*life from the dead*"? That is a profound statement. I see the Gentile civilization we live in today committing suicide: destroying the earth, destroying themselves, building armaments that can wipe out the human race many times over. What is going to change all this? The restoration of Israel to their Messiah. That will produce cosmic changes. It is the hope of the earth. | 1 |
| 27. | a. **firstfruit; lump**<br>b. **root; branches**<br><br>The first comparison is taken from a ceremony from the law of Moses*. If you dedicated something to the Lord, you were offering a little piece of it to Him, and the whole thing became holy. So, if the firstfruits of Israel have been offered to the Lord, that means the whole nation is holy. | 4 |

---

2. See Derek Prince, *The Harvest Just Ahead* (Charlotte, NC: Derek Prince Ministries–International, 2011).

| Question | Answer | Points |
|---|---|---|
| 28. | **A wild olive tree**<br><br>The people of Israel were cultivated through the patriarchs and through the Scriptures. The Gentiles, by comparison, were wild branches. They were invited to partake of the root (a common description of the Messiah) and the sap (a picture of the Holy Spirit), both of which are holy.<br><br>I believe we need to be excited about our roots today because Paul says we have been grafted into the good olive tree, and its roots are Abraham. Again, I never feel inferior, and you don't need to feel inferior either. If you are in Jesus, whatever you were, you now have the best ancestry. You are the seed of Abraham, and that is better than being a member of a royal family of Europe, the Middle East, or anywhere else. | 1 |
| 29. | **No**<br><br>Remember, if you are a Gentile, you did not originally belong to that olive tree, but some of the branches were unbelieving and got broken off, so you have been grafted into the tree. You do not support the tree; the tree supports you. So, do not be arrogant toward the people of Israel. | 1 |
| 30. | **God might not spare them either.**<br><br>Again, Paul is warning Gentiles not to be arrogant about being grafted into the olive tree at the expense of the natural branches. Remember, the requirement for belonging to the kingdom of God is to bear fruit. Without fruit, you forfeit the kingdom. God doesn't show partiality. (See Acts 10:34.) Israel forfeited the kingdom because they did not bring forth fruit. Any group on earth that does not bring forth fruit will also forfeit the kingdom. Is that a danger for some sectors of the church? I would have to say that it is a very real, imminent danger. | 1 |
| 31. | a. **Goodness**<br><br>b. **Severity**<br><br>The language here is plain. You stand by faith as long as you continue in God's goodness and bring forth fruit. But if you cease to live in faith and fail to bring forth fruit, you will be cut off, just as the natural branches were cut off. A great deal of preaching today speaks only about the goodness of God and not at all about His severity. Yet it is like a coin with two sides. One side is goodness; the other side is severity. If you deface one side of a coin, the coin becomes valueless. If we present a message about God that speaks only of His goodness and not also of His severity, it has no value. We must be faithful to God. | 2 |
| 32. | **They will be grafted in again.**<br><br>What a positive statement! Israel is not excluded forever. | 1 |
| 33. | **Contrary to nature**<br><br>This description gives us pause for thought. In horticulture, the principle of grafting involves joining a fruitful, cultivated branch with wild rootstock, so that the vigorous sap of the uncultivated stock (which is barely fruitful) can flow through the fruitful branch and bring forth good fruit. Paul's depiction is of the opposite—wild branches being grafted into a cultivated tree. Paul is saying that bringing the cultivated branches back into their own tree will be so much easier. | 1 |
| 34. | **The fullness of the Gentiles has come in**<br><br>It has never been a total hardening. Again, there have been Jews in every generation who have acknowledged Jesus as their Messiah. So, the hardening that has happened to Israel has always been only partial. Wherever the Bible speaks about God's rejection of Israel, it always follows with a word like *until*. In other words, it is not permanent. | 1 |

| Question | Answer | Points |
|---|---|---|
| 35. | **All of it**<br><br>We have already dealt with the fact that when we talk about "all" Israel, we are speaking of *"the Israel of God"* (Galatians 6:16). This term refers to the believing people of Israel—not merely the natural descendants of Abraham, Isaac, and Jacob but the children of the promise who are also grafted into (or back into) the olive tree by faith. | 1 |
| 36. | **On the basis of God's covenant\* with them**<br><br>God has made a covenant commitment that the Redeemer (or Deliverer) will come to Israel and take away the people's sins, and the whole nation of believing Israel will be saved. | 1 |
| 37. | **Irrevocable**<br><br>To *revoke* something is to change or reverse it. The word *irrevocable* refers to the opposite of this—it describes something that is unchangeable or irreversible. We often hear the last phrase of the passage, *"the gifts and the calling of God are irrevocable,"* quoted with reference to spiritual gifts and ministries, and this is appropriate. But bear in mind that it is said initially about God's gift and calling to the people of Israel. Those two things are irrevocable. Nothing is ever going to cancel them. | 1 |
| 38. | Mercy<br><br>The mercy we have received, despite our disobedience, is ultimately to bring about God's mercy for Israel. Do you remember that the lives of Christians are meant to provoke Israel to jealousy? It is the same idea here—that through the mercy shown to us, they may also obtain mercy. | 1 |
| 39. | **God**<br><br>What an astonishing statement! God has us all penned in the prison of disobedience. Whether we are Jews or Gentiles, Russians or Americans or Chinese, we are all disobedient. God has shut us in there in order that He might show mercy. Isn't that just like God? | 1 |
| 40. | **Unsearchable**<br><br>Do not deceive yourself: you cannot understand all the judgments of God. You do not know all the ways in which God works. Just accept that fact and trust Him. He knows what He is doing even when you do not. | 1 |
| 41. | **Glory**<br><br>Jesus said, *"I am the Alpha and the Omega, the Beginning and the End"* (Revelation 21:6). When we receive this revelation, only one response is appropriate: to worship Jesus and give Him the glory due His name. | 1 |
| | Check your written memory work. If your memory work is word-perfect, 4 points for each verse. (1 point off for each mistake in a verse. If there are more than three mistakes, do not mark any points for that verse.) | 12 |
| | Total Points | ____/63 |

Fill in the total points for lesson 21 on the "Tally Sheet for Each Lesson" on page 254.

# LESSON 22 ANSWERS

| Question | Answer | Points |
|---|---|---|
| 1. | **What Paul previously said is foundational to what is coming next.**<br><br>When you find a *therefore* in the Bible, you need to find out what it is "there for." It always indicates a logical connection with what has gone before. This *"therefore"* in the first verse of Romans 12 is connected with all the preceding eleven chapters, where Paul has wonderfully unfolded the divine plan for mankind to be reckoned righteous* with God, to come back into a relationship with Him, and to receive the full provision of Jesus's sacrifice on the cross. All this has been unfolded as only the Holy Spirit speaking through Paul could do.<br><br>But God does not stop there. Now the issue is, how can we live it out? What does it mean in our lives day by day? That is why this *"therefore"* is there. In the light of all that God has done and provided for us, what should our response be? | No points |
| 2. | **Our bodies (as a living sacrifice, holy, acceptable to Him)**<br><br>The response God asks of us is that we present our bodies as living sacrifices. God is not asking something theological—not something that sounds mystical or intellectually stimulating. No, He says, "I want your body. I want that earthen vessel in which you live. That is what I am asking for. And I am not going to be satisfied with anything less. I want you to present your body as a sacrifice—a living sacrifice—on My altar of service." | 1 |
| 3. | **A living sacrifice**<br><br>Paul is saying, "Just as with the former animal sacrifices, God wants you to place your body on His altar—but do not kill it. Present it alive." It is a living sacrifice. Paul calls this your reasonable—or, we might say, logical—service.<br><br>The Greek word for *"service"* is the term always used of the service of the priest in the tabernacle or temple. We ourselves become priests through our faith in Jesus, and one of our primary priestly duties is to present our bodies on God's altar as living sacrifices. | 1 |
| 4. | **He has set them apart for Himself.**<br><br>In the old covenant*, anybody who brought an animal for sacrifice to God no longer owned that animal. Once it touched the altar, the animal was set apart to the Lord. In the same way, when you place your body on God's altar, from that time onward, you no longer own it; your body belongs to God.<br><br>Is God interested only in your body? Is He not interested in your spirit and soul? God is clever. When He gets your body, He gets the contents—the whole thing. And, again, He is not going to settle for less. You can limp along as a half-committed Christian and stand in church next to a lot of people just like you. But you will never know the satisfaction and joy and freedom of the Christian life until you have made that commitment. | 1 |
| 5. | a. **conformed**<br><br>There are two Greek words for "world"—*cosmos*, meaning "order" or "world," and *aion*, meaning "age," which gives us the English word *eon*. Most Bible versions, including the *New King James Version*, translate the word in this verse as *"world"*: *"Do not be conformed to this world."* But the Greek word Paul uses here is not *world*, a kind of social system, but *age*, a time concept; so, the distinction between *world* and *age* has been obscured.<br><br>We are living in a certain age, a certain period of time, and Paul is saying, "Do not be conformed to this time period." We are not to live like people who belong in time at all. We don't. We belong to eternity. Christians who try to live as if they still belong in this age live in a state of confusion..<br><br>b. **transformed**<br><br>Notice that God does not change us from the outside in; He changes us from the inside out, starting with our mind. He changes the way we think. Then, that changes the way we live. | 5 |

| Question | Answer | Points |
|---|---|---|
| 5. (cont.) | Religion does the opposite. It starts with the outside—what we wear, what we eat, what we drink, where we go—and tries to make us good by changing the external. That does not work. God's method works. Again, He changes us from the inside. He changes the way we think. Once we are changed in the way we think, we will be changed in the way we live. As I indicated earlier, we cannot think wrong and live right, and we cannot think right and live wrong. | |

**c. good; acceptable; perfect**

Millions of Christians who have been born again have not yet discovered God's will for their lives. They are floundering, trying to lead good lives but having no real motivation or vision. Proverbs 29:18 says that without vision, people *"cast off restraint."* That is why many Christians are undisciplined; they have cast off restraint because they do not have a vision.

Yet the more you find out God's will in experience, the better it gets. When you start with God's will, it is *good*. He wants the best for you. Are you sure of that? He does! Then, it is *acceptable*. The better you know it, the more you enjoy it. Finally, it is *perfect*. It covers every area of your personality and every detail of your life. His will covers the food you eat, the clothes you wear, the people you meet, and the places you go. Once you have discovered God's perfect will, there is no detail in your life that is not covered.

| 6. | a. **highly** | 3 |

Paul warns us not to think of ourselves more highly than we ought to think. Faith and pride are incompatible. That is a truth that runs throughout the Bible. There is a kind of substitute faith that is arrogant and boastful, but it is not the faith of the New Testament.

**b. soberly**

In Jesus's earthly ministry, the two people He praised the most for their faith were individuals who thought of themselves as unworthy. The Roman centurion said to Jesus, "I'm not worthy that you should come under my roof." What did Jesus say about him? "I have not found anyone in Israel* with such great faith." (See Matthew 8:5–13.) And the Syro-Phoenician woman, when Jesus talked to her about being "a little dog," replied, "True, Lord, I am a little dog—but all I want is a crumb." What did Jesus say to her? "Woman, great is your faith. Have what you want. Help yourself." (See, for example, Matthew 15:21–28.) So, the two humblest people were those with the most faith. This leads to our next question concerning what we do with the measure of faith God has given us.

**c. faith**

God has allotted to you a specific measure of faith. He relates to each of us individually. We do not all have the same faith or even the same kind of faith. Even preachers or ministers do not all have the same faith. Some preachers have great faith for healing; some do not. But God deals to each servant of His a specific measure of faith, which we should learn to exercise fully.

| 7. | a. **One body** | 3 |

Each of us is designed to be part of the body of Christ. Once more, we can function effectively only when we have found our place and are fulfilling our calling. The longer I live the Christian life, the more I realize how much I need the body of Christ. And, occasionally, when I begin to feel a little self-sufficient, God allows things to happen that show me I need my fellow Christians. I need to be in the body of Christ, functioning as part of the body.

If you are frustrated, wondering why things are not going well for you, consider whether you have found your place in the body of Christ. Perhaps you have faith but do not know what to do with it.

**b. No**

The cause of much frustration among believers is that they are trying to be the wrong part of the body of Christ, trying to fulfill a function for which God has not given them the faith. We all find our faith being tested, but if you are always struggling to have faith, it is almost a certain sign that you are not in your right place in the body.

| Question | Answer | Points |
|---|---|---|
| | c. **Christ**<br><br>Do you remember that, in Romans 6:3–4, we learned that we are *"baptized into Christ"*? Our place in the body of Christ is not made available to us until we have died to ourselves and have become alive to God in Christ Jesus. | |
| 8. | **Gifts**<br><br>The Greek word for "gifts" is *charismata*, and the Greek word for "grace" is *charis*. *Charismata* is a derivative of the word for grace. The charismatic gifts are grace gifts—gifts you cannot earn. God has given you a particular place in the body of Christ, and He will equip you with the gifts you need to function in that place. | 1 |
| 9. | a. **prophecy**<br><br>Many people, when they begin to prophesy, see exciting results, and their minds get puffed up. They go beyond their proportion of faith and start to say things that are not from God, creating a lot of confusion.<br><br>I have had much prophecy given over me, and I praise God for it. But I do not go to somebody as one would go to a fortune-teller to find out what is going to happen next, because sometimes you get fortune-telling and not prophecy. The two are very close. There is just a razor's-edge division between the true prophetic gift and a divining (occult) spirit.<br><br>b. **ministry (or serving)**<br><br>Ministry, or serving, is an art. When you are serving a person, you do not do things the way you think you ought to do them but the way the person wants them done, whether you think that way is right or not. To adjust your thinking to the thinking of another person and do things the way they want—that is a gift and not something you can really work out yourself.<br><br>Since the word *deacon* is the translation of the Greek word for *"servant,"* such ministry or serving could be deaconship. I have often thought that certain churches would be different if they called the board of deacons "the board of servants," since that is what they should be.<br><br>c. **teaching**<br><br>James 3:1 says that no one should be a teacher unless God calls them, because teachers will be judged more strictly. So, if you are not called to teach, stay out of it. I know God has specifically called me to be a teacher of the Scriptures because I cannot help but teach. You could stand me on my head in a corner, and I would start teaching. It is just in me!<br><br>d. **exhortation**<br><br>Many people have the wonderful gift of exhorting—but that gift is not teaching. "To exhort" means "to stimulate," "to encourage," "to admonish," and "to stir up." Admonition can include severe warning and even rebuke. However, exhortation does not include condemnation. Do not become a teacher if you are called to be an exhorter. Stick to your "profession."<br><br>e. **giving**<br><br>Do you realize there is a ministry of giving? It is a ministry, a gift. If this is your particular gifting, do it with liberality and simplicity. Do not make a big deal out of the fact that you are giving. And be very, very careful not to try to manipulate others by your giving.<br><br>f. **leading**<br><br>The Greek word translated "leads" in Romans 12:8 means "to stand out in front." In 1 Timothy 3:5, Paul says that if a man cannot *"rule"* (or *"manage"* NIV, NASB) his own family, he cannot manage the church of God. The word Paul uses for *"leads"* in Romans 12:8 is the same one he uses for *"rule"* in 1 Timothy 3:5. It means to be a leader—"out in front." It means "to take responsibility for." It also means to be a protector—to stand between the people you lead and the forces that oppose them. That is the ministry of leading. Without leadership, any operation just founders. Leadership is one essential for any kind of real success. | 7 |

| Question | Answer | Points |
|---|---|---|
| 9. (cont.) | **g. showing mercy**<br><br>We have this beautiful ministry listed at the end: showing mercy. How we need that ministry. During WWII, when I was hospitalized in Egypt for about one year, there was a dear, seventy-five-year-old lady, a Salvation Army brigadier, who took a very difficult journey all the way from Cairo to El Balla to visit me in the hospital. And that visit transformed my life. It initiated something totally new in me in terms of showing mercy that has continued to this day. How I thank God for a lady of that age who would make the sacrifice to visit an unknown British soldier in a hospital. That is the ministry of showing mercy, and everything in my ministry from that time onward has to be partly credited to her. | |
| 10. | **a. wisdom**<br><br>**b. knowledge**<br><br>**c. faith**<br><br>**d. healings**<br><br>**e. miracles**<br><br>**f. spirits**<br><br>**g. tongues**<br><br>**h. interpretation**<br><br>**i. apostles**<br><br>**j. prophets**<br><br>**k. teachers**<br><br>**l. helps**<br><br>**m. administrations**<br><br>**n. evangelists**<br><br>**o. pastors**<br><br>To the twenty-two gifts in Romans, 1 Corinthians, and Ephesians, we might add four additional *charismata* that are either stated or implied as gifts in the New Testament: righteousness* (see Romans 5:15–17), eternal life (see Romans 6:23), celibacy (see 1 Corinthians 7:5–7), and miraculous intervention (see 2 Corinthians 1:8–11).<br><br>It is not sensible to pray for gifts in the abstract: "Lord, give me this or that gift." Rather, seek out your place in the body of Christ, and then you will know what gifts you need, and God will begin to give them to you or show you how to exercise the ones you already have. Again, when you need gifts for your job in the body, God will not leave you unequipped. | 15 |
| 11. | **Love**<br><br>As we go through these final chapters of Romans, we see again and again that the fountainhead of all Christian living is sincere love, without hypocrisy. Everything flows out of love. Paul is not laying out a set of rules you have to follow; he is offering guidance on how to direct the love that God has put into your heart. | 1 |
| 12. | **a. heart**<br><br>**b. conscience**<br><br>**c. faith**<br><br>Love is the goal of our instruction. Is this true of you? Is *"love from a pure heart, from a good conscience, and from sincere faith"* what you are aiming for? In this passage, Paul goes on to say that anything in the church that does not ultimately produce love is a waste of time and is misapplied effort. | 3 |

| Question | Answer | Points |
|---|---|---|
| 13. | **evil; good** | 2 |
| | Hate evil; love good. There is no neutrality. Many people, including Christians, have no appreciation for the reality that they are in the middle of a spiritual war. They have the idea that there is a place of neutrality where they can live that isn't particularly intentional toward good but is also not evil. That place doesn't exist. We must choose good because there can be no compromise with evil from those who truly love the Lord. (See also Psalm 45:7; 97:10.) | |
| 14. | **love; preference** | 2 |
| | Be affectionate and devoted to one another and prefer one another in honor. Give more honor to other people than you seek for yourself. | |
| | I used to wonder how I could honor a person I didn't think was as good as I was! But then I heard Paul say that those who compare themselves among themselves (see 2 Corinthians 10:12) and measure themselves by other people (like the Pharisee in Luke 18:9–14) are unwise. I realized there is only one standard: Jesus. When I measure myself by Him, it is easier to prefer other people. | |
| 15. | a. *"not lagging in diligence"* | 2 |
| | b. *"fervent in spirit"* | |
| | A few Bible versions translate *"lagging in diligence"* as *"lazy."* Search the Bible and see if you can find one good word about laziness. It is condemned much more severely than drunkenness. The strange thing is, we will tolerate lazy people in our churches far more easily than we will drunkards. Do you know any people who are too lazy to read their Bibles, too lazy to pray, or too lazy to visit those unable to come to church or to take the good news of Jesus to those who haven't heard? According to the Roman Catholic Church, laziness is a deadly sin. | |
| 16. | **The Lord** | 1 |
| | The second part of verse 11 exhorts us to serve the Lord with passionate dedication. I love this statement of William Booth's oldest daughter, Catherine Booth-Clibborn: "Christ loved us passionately, and loves to be loved passionately." There is very little passion in the church today. Let me ask you, "Do you love the Lord with passionate devotion?" | |
| 17. | **hope; patient; prayer** | 3 |
| | This speaks of an existence that is settled in the Lord, of someone who is cheerfully optimistic and believes in God's sovereignty despite any circumstances, who holds out under pressure, and who loves to pray. | |
| 18. | **saints; hospitality** | 2 |
| | I translate this phrase as "sharing with fellow believers and practicing hospitality." Hospitality is a ministry. If God has blessed you with it, cultivate it as a ministry and use it for the glory of God. Remember that Jesus said, in effect, "Don't invite your friends or the rich for a meal; invite the poor, the blind, the people who can't pay you back." (See Luke 14:12–13.) Then, He gave this wonderful promise: *"You shall be repaid at the resurrection of the just* [righteous]" (Luke 14:14). If you get your reward now, you receive nothing then. If you forfeit your reward now, you will have it waiting for you in the next age. | |
| 19. | **persecute; curse** | 2 |
| | How easy do you find it to bless those who hurt you? I have had to come to the discipline of regularly forgiving people who have been unkind or uncharitable toward me, and blessing them. It has lifted me to a new level. I say, "Lord, I forgive them. And having forgiven them, I bless them in Your name." So, when we are cursed, what do we do? We bless. It may not change the attitude of the person who is cursing, but it will ensure our own spiritual purity. | |

| Question | Answer | Points |
|---|---|---|
| 20. | **rejoice; weep**<br><br>Be equally sympathetic with those who rejoice and with those who weep. If we have trouble with this instruction, the problem is our self-centeredness. We cannot fully rejoice with those who rejoice and weep with those who weep until we have been delivered from being self-centered. (If you want a sure recipe for unhappiness, cultivate self-centeredness. I guarantee that you will be unhappy!) | 2 |
| 21. | **mind; humble; wise**<br><br>Here is my translation of verse 16: "Live in harmony; be humble, not conceited or arrogant, and, above all, avoid pride." Proverbs 13:10 says that when pride comes, contention starts. The greatest single cause of quarrels and disunity is pride. | 3 |
| 22. | **evil**<br><br>Jesus says, *"But whoever slaps you on your right cheek, turn the other to him also"* (Matthew 5:39). The natural reaction is to hit them back, but the spiritual response is to turn the other cheek. First Peter 3:9 says, *"Not returning evil for evil or insult for insult, but giving a blessing instead; for you were called for the very purpose that you might inherit a blessing"* (NASB95).<br><br>In 1 Corinthians 4:12, speaking about the apostles, Paul says, *"We toil, working with our own hands; when we are reviled, we bless; when we are persecuted, we endure"* (NASB95).<br><br>I believe that, basically, we have to overcome the negative by the positive. When somebody curses or reviles you, bless them, even though you may not do it out loud. Take a positive attitude, and keep your own spirit clear. | 1 |
| 23. | **possible; peaceably**<br><br>You cannot have peace with everybody; some people will not make peace. But as far as it lies in your power, make peace and keep peace with everybody. It will do your digestive system good! (Do you know how many times our stomachs get tied up in knots because we have become resentful, bitter, unforgiving?) As we have seen, the word for "peace" in Hebrew, *shalom*, is a beautiful word. It means "completeness." When you give out peace, you receive peace. Remember *who* is our peace. (See Ephesians 2:14.) | 2 |
| 24. | **wrath; Vengeance**<br><br>Paul is making a strong statement: "Make room for the wrath of God." If you do not avenge yourself, God will avenge you. Which would you rather face: another person's vengeance or God's vengeance? If God takes over that person's case, that is frightening. So, when you are wronged by someone, you cannot do anything more sobering than step back and say, "I won't avenge that wrong. God is going to deal with you." | 2 |
| 25. | **evil; good**<br><br>Respond in the opposite spirit. That is the teaching of Loren Cunningham, founder of Youth With A Mission. Here are just a few examples: Meet hatred with love. Meet bitterness with sweetness. Meet anger with gentleness. Never meet a bad person on his or her own level.<br><br>And Paul says, *"Overcome evil with good."* The only thing powerful enough to overcome evil is good. But it *is* powerful enough. So, either we will be overcome by evil or we will overcome evil. Heaven is made for overcomers of evil. | 2 |
|  | Check your written memory work. If your memory work is word-perfect, 4 points for each verse. (1 point off for each mistake in a verse. If there are more than three mistakes, do not mark any points for that verse.) | 8 |
|  | Total Points | ____/75 |

Fill in the total points for lesson 22 on the "Tally Sheet for Each Lesson" on page 254.

# LESSON 23 ANSWERS

| Question | Answer | Points |
|---|---|---|
| 1. | **a. Submission** | 8 |

Submission is a very important trait for believers that has no substitute. Many people seem to think that submission makes them weak, but that is only true if they submit to the wrong things. Jesus was submissive to the Father and became obedient to death on a cross. In Ephesians 5:21, we are exhorted to "[submit] *to one another in the fear of God.*"

**b. The Lord's**

*Sake* is a word that can be used in Christian circles without being properly understood. To get the right understanding, we could substitute *benefit*, *purpose*, or *glory*. The point is that our primary reason for submission to authority is that it honors the Lord.

**c. Good**

Paul keeps returning to this theme of doing good and repaying good for evil. This has to be one of the results of the grace that we walk in—that we glorify God and fulfill His will by doing good.

**d. Using liberty as a cloak for vice**

In the earlier chapters of the book of Romans, Paul addresses numerous anticipated questions from skeptical readers. Here he makes a similar maneuver and stops any idea that Christians can use their freedom to hide any wickedness within.

**e. Honor; Love; Fear; Honor**

Some cultures have lost sight of these principles, but they are nonetheless biblical. I would like to highlight the third and fourth statements because I feel they are lost to so much of society. Again, I know of no other attitude that brings more blessing than the fear of God, and Scripture is full of references to it. Note also this statement of Peter: *"Honor the king."* This is a foreign concept to so many believers due to their varying forms of government, but to me it says two things. First, we should honor earthly kings and governments. Second, it is a reminder that Jesus is the King of kings and that His kingdom is the everlasting kingdom.

| 2. | **a. Subject** | 3 |
|---|---|---|

**b. It is God.**

**c. God appoints them.**

*"There is no authority,"* Paul says categorically, *"except from God."* That is a breathtaking statement when you consider that Paul made it in the time of the Roman Empire, which had crucified Jesus and was later to execute him, the author of this epistle*. The authorities that exist—in Paul's time as much as today—are established by God.

| 3. | **Jesus** | 1 |
|---|---|---|

Following His resurrection, Jesus was clear about the fact that all authority had been given to Him. It is logical, therefore, that He is the source of authority, and He is the One who appoints those in government.

| 4. | **head** | 1 |
|---|---|---|

All authority in the universe, then, has been delegated by God the Father to Jesus Christ the Son. Paul wrote these words—and Peter wrote the words we previously read—in the light of understanding that all authority ultimately is in the hands of Jesus.

| Question | Answer | Points |
|---|---|---|
| 5. | **Judgment** | 1 |
| | Our first reaction is to think Paul means the one who resists *righteous\** authority—but that is not what he says. He says that the one who resists *any* governmental authority resists the ordinance of God and will receive judgment. Paul goes on to say in Romans 13:3 that *"rulers are not a terror to good works,"* but we also know that this is not always the case because, in these latter days, some laws are *against* goodness and godliness. The notes in the answer for question 18 below will provide some additional guidance and balance regarding this seeming contradiction. | |
| 6. | **What is good** | 1 |
| | As long as your conscience is clear and you do what is right, Paul says there is no reason to be afraid. | |
| 7. | **God's minister** | 1 |
| | In place of the word *minister*, which gives a cloudy impression, it is clearer to use the word *servant*, which is what the Greek word translated *"minister"* means. I also prefer translations like the one in the *New American Standard Bible* that use the pronoun *it* to describe the authority, as in *"For it is a servant of God…"* (Romans 13:4 NASB). Paul is not talking about the person who occupies the office but the office itself. It is a minister of God to you for good. | |
| 8. | **wrath; conscience** | 2 |
| | We are to subject ourselves to the governing authorities, then, not merely because we will be dealt with severely if we do not, but also for the sake of conscience. Questions arise about ungodly rulers and laws, and they are legitimate questions. But, as I see it, Paul and Peter are saying the same thing: behind the office of authority is God; and our relationship to the office ultimately depicts our relationship to God. | |
| 9. | **To pay taxes** | 1 |
| | In a certain sense, when you pay taxes, you are paying them to God—God's representative, His agent. Some of you may find this idea hard to receive. It is a truth that Christians have overlooked, but it is very clearly stated in the Bible. | |
| 10. | a. **Taxes** | 4 |
| | b. **Customs** | |
| | c. **Fear** | |
| | d. **Honor** | |
| | This is a clear outline of our responsibilities as citizens of our respective nations. | |
| 11. | **First order of importance (***"First of all"***)** | 1 |
| | In other words, the first thing to focus on in the local church is not preaching; it is prayer. Paul speaks of four different kinds of prayer. With *"supplications,"* we call out to God for mercy. With *"prayers,"* we come to God with petitions for specific requests. And with *"intercessions,"* we stand in the gap on behalf of someone else. *"Giving of thanks"* is self-explanatory. | |
| 12. | **quiet; peaceable; godliness; reverence** | 4 |
| | Ask yourself, "Does the government I live under affect the kind of life I live?" The answer is yes! So, it is enlightened self-interest to pray for the government. If we do not pray for the government, we deserve what we get. | |
| | Christians are more prone to criticize their governments than to pray for them. But Jesus never told us to criticize the government, and the Bible tells us to pray for it. Frankly, in many respects, the offices of government are doing their jobs more faithfully than the Christians who criticize them are doing theirs. Our job is not to criticize; our job is to pray. | |

| Question | Answer | Points |
|---|---|---|
| 13. | *"All men to be saved and to come to the knowledge of the truth."* | 1 |

God places a great responsibility on His church to pray that the government will enable us to live quiet and peaceable lives that include the freedom to proclaim the gospel. I venture to say that if we do not pray, we have no right to expect the kind of government that facilitates the preaching of the gospel.

Our first responsibility as Christians, then, in relation to secular authority, is to be regular and faithful in our prayers for the government. As I see it, this is primarily (but not exclusively) public prayer because, in 1 Timothy 2, Paul is talking about the conduct of a local church.

| | | |
|---|---|---|
| 14. | **They would fight.** | 1 |

Jesus's words contain an important principle: the kingdom of God is never established by carnal weapons. I am not saying we should not use them, or that Christians should not carry arms. That is a personal decision. But I am saying that we do not usher in the kingdom of God with them.

Christians have dual citizenship. We are citizens of the kingdom of God, and we are citizens of a particular country. As citizens of that country, we may be responsible to fight. But God's kingdom is not established by fighting.

| | | |
|---|---|---|
| 15. | **No (It will be established by God's Spirit.)** | 1 |

Scripture gives the name of God as "the Lord of hosts" over two hundred times in the Old Testament. The word *hosts* is not in common usage any longer, but some modern translations make this title for God clearer as "the Lord of heaven's armies." This makes the statement in Zechariah more remarkable because, in spite of having this great power, God will accomplish His will by His Spirit.

| | | |
|---|---|---|
| 16. | **Pilate** | 1 |

Did Pontius Pilate have this authority over Jesus? He certainly did. But he was not the source of his authority. Authority flows downward, and when we are under authority, our authority is derived from what or whom we represent.

| | | |
|---|---|---|
| 17. | **Above** | 1 |

In other words, behind Pilate, who was about to make an unjust decision concerning Him, Jesus saw the authority of His Father.

| | | |
|---|---|---|
| 18. | a. **An angel of the Lord** | 7 |

b. **The temple**

c. **obey**

d. **"Go into all the world and preach the gospel to every creature."**

e. **They beat them.**

f. **Because they were counted worthy to suffer shame for His (Jesus's) name**

g. **No**

Notice that the leaders would not say the name of Jesus but referred to Him as *"this name"* (Acts 5:28). It is interesting that the prejudice goes back this far.

What if a ruler demands that you do something that, as a Christian, you cannot do with a clear conscience? The answer is, you refuse to do it, but you also submit to the consequences. You say, "I won't do that, but you can do whatever you like with me."

| Question | Answer | Points |
|---|---|---|
| 18. (cont.) | It was not a foggy issue. The apostles were determined to obey the Lord. It was not about their gaining something for themselves. So, when they were told they must not preach, they said, "We can't stop! We won't obey you. You can do what you will with us, but, on this issue, we have to obey God rather than man." They did not stage a revolution. They simply submitted to unjust treatment—and, as a result, they were flogged.<br><br>When the issue is clear-cut, we must obey God and, if necessary, disobey human authority. But, when we disobey authority, let us be very sure that obeying God is really what we are doing. | |
| 19. | a. **The blood of the Lamb**<br>b. **The word of our testimony**<br>c. **Not loving our lives to the death**<br><br>I interpret this verse to mean that, for these brothers and sisters mentioned in Revelation, it is more important to do the will of God than to stay alive. They will not be able to use those spiritual weapons—the blood of the Lamb and the word of their testimony—if they do not have that degree of commitment not to *"love their lives to the death."*<br><br>As we previously talked about, Satan is not the least bit scared of uncommitted Christians. You can use all the language and pray all the prayers, and he will laugh in your face. But when you are ready to lay your life on the line, then he treats your prayers with respect. | 3 |
| 20. | **The debt to love one another**<br><br>Do you owe anyone anything? You know what the Bible says about debt: *"The borrower is servant to the lender"* (Proverbs 22:7). Again, when we get into debt, we make ourselves servants of the person or organization we are borrowing from. So, Paul does not want us to owe anyone anything, with one exception: love. | 1 |
| 21. | **The law***<br><br>When we studied Romans 8:3–4 in lesson 12, we dealt with *"the righteous requirement of the law"* (v. 4). Remember Paul's explanation in Galatians 5:14, *"For all the law is fulfilled in one word, even in this: 'You shall love your neighbor as yourself'"*? So, love is *"the righteous requirement of the law."* It is important to be clear about that. We are not required to follow all the details of the law of Moses*. But we are under obligation to love. | 1 |
| 22. | **Love**<br><br>All the commandments are summed up, then, in that one commandment, *"You shall love your neighbor as yourself"* (Romans 13:9). We must not be unclear about how we relate to the law of Moses. We have been set free from all its enactments and regulations, but we are commanded to live out its righteous requirement, which is love. | 1 |
| 23. | **As Jesus has loved us**<br><br>Although God, through Moses, gave Israel* the Ten Commandments (Judaism has 613 commandments), Jesus said, "I'll give you just one commandment." In that one commandment, everything is included. It is so simple. What is that one commandment? Love one another. | 1 |
| 24. | **The perfect law of liberty**<br><br>We have dealt at length with the law of Moses and how it was powerless to bring us into true freedom due to our carnal nature. Here we have a law that is *"perfect"* and brings freedom. The next question will complete the revelation. | 1 |
| 25. | **The royal law**<br><br>This is the royal law, the perfect law of liberty: *"Love your neighbor as yourself."* When that is what motivates you, you live like a king. Nobody orders you about. Nobody can force you to do something, because you always want to do the right thing. It is the law of perfection, the law that is kingly, the law of liberty. | 1 |

| Question | Answer | Points |
|---|---|---|
| 26. | **The son who sleeps in harvest**<br><br>Our churches are full of sons and daughters who are asleep in the harvest. We need to be awakened so that we can take the gospel to *"all nations, tribes, peoples, and tongues"* (Revelation 7:9). | 1 |
| 27. | **The times**<br><br>The question we must ask ourselves is, "Do *I* have an understanding of the times?" When we consider the sin, the evil, and the confusion in the world around us, do we fret, or do we trust in God's sovereignty? In Luke 21:7–28, Jesus tells the disciples many things that will happen as the age draws to a close, and He concludes with an important statement: *"Now when these things begin to happen, look up and lift up your heads, because your redemption draws near"* (v. 28). | 1 |
| 28. | **Awake out of sleep.**<br><br>Too many Christians are not awake and are in danger of sleepwalking to Christ's coming. If we truly appreciate the times in which we live, we will remain alert and intentional, submissive to God's Word and sensitive to His Holy Spirit. We will learn to increasingly walk in the royal law of liberty—love—and eagerly anticipate the Lord's return. I want to see Jesus in His glory and to see His kingdom established on earth because, again, that is the only solution to the innumerable problems of humanity. | 1 |
| 29. | a. **darkness**<br><br>b. **light**<br><br>c. **walk**<br><br>d. **Lord Jesus Christ**<br><br>When we are dead to self and alive to God, we walk differently. We no longer walk in the darkness but in His marvelous light. (See 1 Peter 2:9.) This is a picture of people who are living in excited anticipation of the Lord's return and who express it in holy living. | 6 |
| 30. | **hope; appearing**<br><br>My conviction, as well as my observation, is that the standard of New Testament holiness will never be found in a church that is not anticipating the Lord's return. Looking forward to that *"blessed hope and glorious appearing"* makes people excited and motivates them to live holy lives. | 2 |
| 31. | a. **died**<br><br>b. **life**<br><br>c. **life**<br><br>d. **you**<br><br>We have all that we need in Christ, and we do not need to make any concessions to our fleshly nature. | 4 |
| | Check your written memory work. If your memory work is word-perfect, 4 points for each verse. (1 point off for each mistake in a verse. If there are more than three mistakes, do not mark any points for that verse.) | 8 |
| | Total Points | ____/72 |

Fill in the total points for lesson 23 on the "Tally Sheet for Each Lesson" on page 254.

# LESSON 24 ANSWERS

| Question | Answer | Points |
|---|---|---|
| 1. | **Receive them** | 1 |

If the body of Christ did not receive those who are weak in faith, it would have very few members indeed. The church should be a place of nurturing and maturing, so Paul reminds us to be inviting toward others and not to dispute with them about areas where Christians may have legitimate differences of perspective. As he writes in Ephesians 4:15–16, *"But, speaking the truth in love, [we] may grow up in all things into Him who is the head—Christ…[who] causes growth of the body for the edifying of itself in love."*

| Question | Answer | Points |
|---|---|---|
| 2. | **all things; only vegetables** | 2 |

The reason this person eats only vegetables is not because he is a vegetarian (although that issue could arise) but because he wants to keep *kosher*. The way Orthodox Jews* choose, prepare, and serve their food has to be done in an exact way. You must not mix milk products with meat products. If you have consumed milk, you must wait six hours before you can consume meat. All sorts of foods are excluded. And the food has to be prepared in a special way and be served on special plates. Some of these complex dietary laws are based on the law of Moses*; many more are based on subsequent religious tradition.

| Question | Answer | Points |
|---|---|---|
| 3. | **He has received them.** | 1 |

For Jewish people today, maintaining their heritage as a separate identity is an urgent issue. When the laws of *kashrut* (or keeping kosher) are broken down and the observance of *Shabbat*, or the Sabbath, diminishes, Jewish people quickly mingle with the surrounding Gentile culture and lose their national identity.

Jews from the West have often been almost totally assimilated into Gentile culture. However, when they come to believe in Jesus, and particularly if they visit Israel* or move there, they suddenly discover the importance of their Jewish identity and are concerned about proving they are truly Jews. They tend to pick up all sorts of rules and regulations that they never observed before they came to Jesus. Native-born Israelis, on the other hand—*sabras*, as they are called—have no identity problem. They know they are Jews, so they tend to be careless about the observance of these rules. Thus, here we have two kinds of people, exactly as Paul describes in Romans 14.

| Question | Answer | Points |
|---|---|---|
| 4. | **His own master** | 1 |

Notice that it is important for believers to be under the lordship of Christ, that they serve Him and respect His authority in their lives. In this verse, Paul points out that the real sin is not about eating or not eating or about observing the Sabbath or not observing the Sabbath. The real sin is to criticize your fellow believers.

| Question | Answer | Points |
|---|---|---|
| 5. | **Each of us should be fully convinced in our own mind.** | 1 |

There are some people who believe Christians should set Saturday as their holy day of rest, while many others look to Sunday, the day of the Lord's resurrection, as their Sabbath. We are not called to judge either group.

As I wrote in the introduction to this lesson, the Jewish Sabbath begins on Friday evening at sunset and ends on Saturday evening at sunset, so Paul is not talking about just Saturday. It is a different concept of measuring the days of the week, going back to creation when the evening and the morning were day one. God's day does not begin with dawn; it begins with sunset.

| Question | Answer | Points |
|---|---|---|
| 6. | a. **The handwriting of requirements** | 6 |

We have already seen that the law* has dominion over a person for as long as he or she lives. But when the law has put us to death, that is the last thing it can do to us. In Jesus, we were put to death and have come back to life beyond the cross, free from the demands of the law.

| Question | Answer | Points |
|---|---|---|
| 6. (cont.) | **b. He nailed it to the cross.**<br><br>As we have seen in our study of Romans, Jesus set aside the law of Moses as the requirement for achieving righteousness* with God. Paul says He nailed the law—our certificate of debt consisting of decrees—to the cross. Thus, once we come to the cross in faith, we are freed from the law. It has no more claims over us. We are no longer subject to it. Through the death of Jesus, we have been delivered from its demands.<br><br>**c. disarmed; spectacle; triumphing**<br><br>Paul is teaching us that Jesus, by His death on the cross, took from Satan every weapon that the enemy could use against us. His primary weapon is guilt. As long as Satan can make us feel guilty, he has us where he wants us. But Jesus, by His death on the cross, made provision for us to be set free from guilt, in two directions: for all our past sinful acts and for our future sinful acts as well.<br><br>**d. Judge us**<br><br>Paul does not say, "Do not observe religious rules about diets and holidays." What he does say is, "Do not let anybody judge you about whether you observe them or not." We have been set free from all the requirements of law. If you have friends whose views on certain observances differ from yours, do not quarrel with them. But you can say, "If I were to let you judge me, I'd be disobeying the New Testament, because Colossians 2:16 says, '*So let no one judge you….*'" It is a delicate balance. We all must decide for ourselves how we understand God's will in our lives. | |
| 7. | **The Lord**<br><br>What matters, Paul is saying, is our personal relationship with the Lord. Once we belong to Him, He will never leave us. We are His for time and for eternity. If we live, we live for the Lord; and if we die, we die for the Lord. The Lord is the One to whom we are ultimately responsible. | 1 |
| 8. | **That He might be Lord of both the dead and the living**<br><br>You may have a wonderful marriage partner, but your first relationship is with the Lord. Your relationship with Him, and not your spouse, comes first. If the Lord tarries, a time is coming when you will pass out of time into eternity, and all other relationships will drop off. But the one relationship that will not change is your relationship with Jesus. We need to live our lives now in the light of that awareness. The one thing that is ultimately decisive in time and eternity is your personal relationship with Jesus. | 1 |
| 9. | **Before the judgment seat of Christ**<br><br>It is important to remember that *"there is therefore now no condemnation to those who are in Christ Jesus"* (Romans 8:1). So, the judgment Paul refers to is to assess our service for Jesus in this life. Every Christian will have to stand directly and personally before the Lord Jesus and answer for everything they have done. If we would realize that, Paul says, we would be so busy preparing ourselves that we would not have time to judge others. Those who judge others are not preparing themselves for the judgment seat of Jesus. | 1 |
| 10. | **a. Every knee shall bow to the Lord/God.**<br><br>**b. Every tongue shall confess to God.**<br><br>Bear in mind that there are two main judgments. First, the judgment of believers will take place before the *bema*—the Greek word translated as "*judgment seat*" (of Christ). (See Romans 14:10.) A final judgment will take place later before God's "*great white throne*" (Revelation 20:11). That second judgment, which is of all the resurrected dead, will determine whether we are saved or lost. But the *bema* judgment is the judgment in which Christ judges His people.<br><br>The Greek word for "*confess*," translated in various ways, means "to confess to the uttermost," "to confess everything," "to confess from the bottom of the heart." On that day, you will be able to hide nothing. Everything will be transparent in the eyes of the Lord Jesus. Nothing will be held back—no secrets, no covered-up corners of your life. The whole truth will come out before Jesus. | 2 |

| Question | Answer | Points |
|---|---|---|
| 11. | **Ourselves** | 1 |
| | About whom will I give account to Jesus? Not about my friends. Not about other brothers or sisters in Christ. They will be busy doing that for themselves. There is just one person about whom I must give an account: myself. | |
| 12. | a. **To be well pleasing to the Lord** | 3 |
| | This phrase is reminiscent of the parable of the talents in Matthew 25, where the lord says to two of the servants, *"Well done, good and faithful servant…. Enter into the joy of your lord"* (verses 21, 23). | |
| | b. **Before the judgment seat of Christ** | |
| | You may turn up late for a lot of appointments, but you are going to be on time for this one. This is an appointment none of us is going to miss. | |
| | c. **What we have done, whether good or bad** | |
| | We will have to answer for everything we have done in this life. There are only two categories: good and bad. There is nothing neutral, nothing in between. Everything done for the glory of God, according to the will of God and the Word of God, is good. Everything else is bad. | |
| 13. | **Judge one another anymore** | 1 |
| | Paul has been admonishing us not to judge other believers. I want to suggest to you that judging and criticizing other people destroys you, destroys the people you criticize, and disrupts the body of Christ. But criticizing can be an addiction. If you are addicted to criticism, you will need God's supernatural grace to stop criticizing others. Live your life in view of the fact that you will have to give an account to Jesus for everything you say and do. | |
| 14. | **We are no longer walking in love.** | 1 |
| | The central principle is love. You do not abstain from a certain food because it is forbidden but because if you were to eat it in front of a fellow believer, it might offend them. I would never eat bacon in front of an Orthodox Jewish believer—not because I think there is anything wrong with bacon but because they think there is something wrong with it and may still regard it with abhorrence. | |
| 15. | **No** | 1 |
| | Paul says, *"There is nothing unclean of itself."* But if a person thinks something is unclean and eats it anyway, it defiles them. | |
| 16. | **The things that come out of us** | 1 |
| | Nothing we take in through the mouth can defile us. But what comes out of our mouth—that is what defiles us. The disciples did not understand what Jesus was saying here. When they questioned Him about it, He explained His meaning, as we read about in the next question. | |
| 17. | **The heart** | 1 |
| | We must lay hold of two important principles here. First, from that time onward, on the authority of Jesus, there has been no such thing as a food that is unclean in itself. But, subjectively, a food may be unclean. For example, some people shudder at the thought of eating eels. But, for the Danes, an eel is a delicacy. If you do not feel good about eating eels, you don't have to. But don't criticize the Dane who does. | |
| | Second, the heart is a source of potential defilement. Proverbs 4:23 puts it succinctly: *"Keep your heart with all diligence, for out of it spring the issues of life."* | |
| 18. | a. **The word of God** | 2 |
| | b. **Prayer** | |
| | In many parts of the world, praying over your food is not a mere formality, because you may not know what you are eating. But if you have the faith—if you *"believe and know the truth,"* as Paul says in verse 3—the food is already sanctified by the Word of God, and it can be sanctified from food poisoning and other things by your prayer. But be sure you have the faith. | |

| Question | Answer | Points |
|---|---|---|
| 19. | **Destroy them**<br><br>When Paul looked out on humanity, whether Jew or Gentile, he saw people for whom Jesus died. He related to people on that basis. We need to have the same vision. | 1 |
| 20. | **Letting our good be spoken of as evil**<br><br>Do not expose yourself to unnecessary criticism. This is a wise practice, not only from the point of view of maintaining healthy relationships but also because, when you are criticized, negative spiritual forces from the enemy are released against you, and you need to guard your heart, mind, and spirit. Why expose yourself to those forces unnecessarily?<br><br>This requires wisdom because we should also not be drawn into arguments and counteraccusations. One of the proclamations I make at least once a day begins with Isaiah 54:17, and I personalize it as follows: *"No weapon formed against* [me] *shall prosper, and every tongue which rises against* [me] *in judgment* [I] *shall condemn. This is the heritage of the servants of the* Lord, *and* [my] *righteousness is from* [You]." | 1 |
| 21. | a. **Righteousness**<br>b. **Peace**<br>c. **Joy**<br><br>Being in the kingdom of God is not a question of what we eat or drink but of three elements that make up the kingdom: righteousness, peace, and joy—all in the Holy Spirit.<br><br>Outside the Holy Spirit, all we have are laws, rules, and religion. It takes the Holy Spirit to bring the kingdom of God into a life or situation. Again, when the Spirit is allowed to have His way, He will produce three results: righteousness, peace, and joy. Notice that the first result is righteousness; the second, peace; and the third, joy. | 3 |
| 22. | **They shall be filled.**<br><br>Jesus does not specify those who hunger for peace or joy or healing or prosperity. Many Christians hunger and thirst for healing or prosperity, but not many hunger and thirst for righteousness. Yet the blessing is on those who hunger and thirst for righteousness. Once you have entered into righteousness, peace and joy will follow as natural consequences. | 1 |
| 23. | **None**<br><br>Wickedness and peace cannot coexist because the essential condition for peace is righteousness. Are you in the kingdom of God right now? Are you enjoying righteousness, peace, and joy in the Holy Spirit? If not, regardless of what denomination you may belong to, you are not enjoying your full inheritance in the kingdom of God because righteousness, peace, and joy in the Holy Spirit are the boundaries of the kingdom of God. | 1 |
| 24. | a. **They are acceptable to God.**<br>b. **They are approved by men.**<br><br>I became a Christian while serving in the British Army. Though I had hoped that God would release me from my army service, He did not. He chose to leave me with my cursing, blaspheming, ungodly fellow British soldiers for nearly five years. And yet, when I was discharged, my rating was "exemplary"—the highest rating the British Army gives. I say that not to boast but to demonstrate what Paul said: when you serve God in righteousness, peace, and joy, you are accepted by God and approved by men. | 2 |
| 25. | **Food**<br><br>What concerns Paul most is the work of God, the body of Christ. Let us always do what builds up the body, even if it means personal sacrifice. | 1 |

| Question | Answer | Points |
|---|---|---|
| 26. | **stumbles; offended; made weak** | 3 |
| | The issue is not what you are eating or drinking but whether you are building up your brother or sister in Christ or breaking down their faith. You may feel perfectly free to do what is listed in that verse, but do not do it in front of people who would be offended by it. | |
| 27. | **As sin** | 1 |
| | That is a searching statement, isn't it? There is only one basis for righteous* living, and that is faith. If you are not doing something out of faith, don't do it. Whatever is not based on faith is sin. | |
| | Check your written memory work. If your memory work is word-perfect, 4 points for each verse. (1 point off for each mistake in a verse. If there are more than three mistakes, do not mark any points for that verse.) | 4 |
| | Total Points | ____/46 |

Fill in the total points for lesson 24 on the "Tally Sheet for Each Lesson" on page 254.

# LESSON 25 ANSWERS

| Question | Answer | Points |
|---|---|---|
| 1. | **Those who are strong**<br><br>The measure of spiritual strength is not how much you are able to do; it is how much you are able to lift others up. | 1 |
| 2. | a. **Twelve foundations**<br><br>b. **The names of the twelve apostles of the Lamb**<br><br>According to Revelation 21:14, in the New Jerusalem, the names of the apostles are in the foundation—at the bottom. So, spiritual strength does not mean holding everybody down and dictating to them. It means being able to hold up those who are not as strong as you are. | 2 |
| 3. | **Because it leads to edification**<br><br>The word *edification* means "building up." The word *edifice* refers to a building, particularly a large or massive structure. The secret strength of a large structure lies underground, in its foundation. It is the foundation that determines what the size and weight of that structure can be in order to be safely supported. When we edify others, we support them and build them up. | 1 |
| 4. | **Christ**<br><br>Jesus brought upon Himself the reproaches of those who hated God, because He lived for God. We, too, must be prepared to bring reproach on ourselves when we live for God. In Romans 14, we learned that the one who serves Christ in righteousness*, peace, and joy is acceptable to God and approved by men. But there are times when we will come up against people's strong disapproval and reproach, and we shouldn't be surprised by it because Jesus walked the same path. | 1 |
| 5. | **Those things that please Him (His Father)**<br><br>In the previous verse, John 8:28, Jesus makes another clear statement: *"I do nothing of Myself."* Unfortunately, even as Christians, we are often given to doing as we please, but that is not Jesus's example. He did not live for Himself but for the Father. *Self-sacrifice* is almost a dirty word in this age of corpulent Christianity, but it is the only way that brings glory to God. | 1 |
| 6. | **Our learning/instruction (that we through the patience and comfort of the Scriptures might have hope)**<br><br>When Paul refers to *"whatever things were written,"* he means whatever is in the Scriptures. The word *Scripture* literally means "that which is written." And that is a limitation. God has spoken many, many words that are not in the Bible. But the Bible contains the words that God chose to have recorded in writing for our benefit, and we always need to remember that everything in the Bible is for the profit of man. The Scriptures contain everything we really need to know to find the best way in life and to make a safe journey through this world to eternity with God. | 1 |
| 7. | **patience; comfort; hope**<br><br>The Scriptures have been given for our benefit so that *"through the patience ["perseverance" NASB] and comfort ["encouragement" NIV, NASB] of the Scriptures [we] might have hope."* It is wonderful to be comforted and encouraged, but remember that the Scriptures encourage only those who persevere. It is not enough to believe; you must keep on believing. Your faith will be tested; you will go through trials. And the Scriptures will bless you if you persevere. | 3 |
| 8. | **Patiently endure**<br><br>Remember that, for about twenty-five years, Abraham's faith was tested. He endured patiently, holding on to God's promise of a son who would be his heir. And *"after he had patiently endured, he obtained the promise."*<br><br>Some people say that faith is all you need. I do not agree. You need faith *and* patience. Together, they are undefeatable. | 1 |

| Question | Answer | Points |
|---|---|---|
| 9. | **Endurance**<br><br>I have said many times that the only way to gain perseverance or endurance is to endure. In Acts 14:22, we read that Paul and Barnabas *"strengthen[ed] the souls of the disciples, exhorting them to continue in the faith, and saying, 'We must through many tribulations enter the kingdom of God.'"* | 1 |
| 10. | **To be like-minded toward one another**<br><br>This is Paul's objective. He is writing not simply to produce individual believers. He has urged us to put the interests of the body of Christ before our own personal opinions and convictions. He has warned us about various areas that would hinder our harmony. And here is his aim: to produce a body of believers that can function in unity and harmony so that, regardless of our personal differences, we may focus on the Lord's goodness and, together, glorify and praise the Lord Jesus Christ. | 1 |
| 11. | **mind; mouth**<br><br>That is what the church should be—a body of people with one purpose: to *"glorify the God and Father of our Lord Jesus Christ."* All preaching and all teaching and every activity should have that as its goal. | 2 |
| 12. | **Receive one another (just as Christ also received us)**<br><br>That is a challenging phrase: *"just as Christ also received ["accepted" NIV, NASB] us"*! Christ did not wait for us to get straightened out and cleaned off before He accepted us. He accepted us just the way we were, and then He began to change us. The only solution for people whose problem is rejection is acceptance. You cannot say, "Once you get straightened out, I'll acknowledge you as a fellow believer." We have to take people where they are, just as God took us where we were, without waiting for them to be perfect. Everybody has problems; but if there is one place people should find acceptance, it is in the body of Christ | 1 |
| 13. | a. **The circumcision**<br><br>Paul's statement that *"Christ has become a servant to the circumcision"* means that He came first as a servant to the Jewish people to confirm all the promises God made to them over the centuries.<br><br>b. **The fathers**<br><br>*"The fathers"* refers to the patriarchs, whom we discussed to some extent in lesson 17 under the theme of "Children of Promise." In New Testament Greek, there is a very close similarity between the words *father* and *family*. The Greek word for "father" is *pater*; the word for "family" is *patria*—directly derived from the word for "father." All the way from Noah, through Abraham, Isaac, Jacob (Israel*), and his sons, Scripture refers to these heads of families as the "patriarchs" or "fathers."<br><br>c. **By glorifying God for His mercy**<br><br>Jesus also came to bring mercy to the Gentiles*—"the nations" who had no promises and no previous history of God's covenants and dealings—so that they *"might glorify God for His mercy."* In Galatians 2:7, Paul speaks about *"the gospel for the circumcised"*—the gospel for the Jewish people—and *"the gospel for the uncircumcised"*—the gospel for the Gentiles. There are not two different gospels; there is just one gospel (though it is presented differently depending on people's heritage), and it centers on the person of the Lord Jesus Christ and His death, resurrection, and ascension. | 3 |
| 14. | a. **thanks; sing**<br><br>b. **Rejoice**<br><br>c. **Praise/Laud the Lord**<br><br>d. **They will hope in Him.**<br><br>Do you see the progression? David (as a foreshadowing of Christ) is witness to God's great deliverance. The Gentiles receive the revelation with rejoicing; they begin to praise the Lord for themselves and to put their hope in the Messiah. | 5 |

| Question | Answer | Points |
|---|---|---|
| 14. (cont.) | Ultimately, the only way to relate to God is through covenant* with Him. God does not relate to us permanently on any other basis. Gentiles who trust in Jesus for salvation and believe in His atoning death and resurrection have become God's people because they have a covenant relationship with Him through faith in Jesus. And the people of Israel, even though they are largely still outside the grace of God, are still a people of God, because He made an unbreakable covenant with them. Often, because of ignorance or arrogance, Christians approach the Bible without seeing this perspective. | |
| 15. | **hope; joy; peace; hope; power**<br><br>According to Romans 15:13, you can abound in hope only by the power of the Holy Spirit. The Holy Spirit is the greatest optimist! And when He comes in, even though you may have been the worst pessimist, you begin to become an optimist.<br><br>This would be a great verse to proclaim out loud, personalizing it by substituting *"you"* with "me" and "I." As you declare it phrase by phrase, it will be registered in heaven and stand to your account: *"Now may the God of hope fill* [me] *with all joy and peace in believing, that* [I] *may abound in hope by the power of the Holy Spirit."* Amen. | 5 |
| 16. | a.  **Goodness**<br><br>b.  **All knowledge**<br><br>Paul is writing to a church he has never visited, although he knows many people there, and he has been giving them a lot of teaching, some of which has been pretty strict. So, in Romans 15:14–16, he almost apologizes for all that teaching. At the same time, he reminds the believers that he is the apostle to the Gentiles and that teaching is his job. He models the tact many of us need! | 2 |
| 17. | **The Gentiles**<br><br>What a sense of responsibility! What a view of his ministry! Paul is saying, "God has committed this task to me to help everybody know the message of the gospel in such a way that it includes not merely the Jewish people but also the Gentiles." | 1 |
| 18. | **The Gentiles**<br><br>Paul compares himself to a priest in the old covenant* offering up a sacrifice to God—except that his offering is not just a little lamb or even a bullock but *"the offering of the Gentiles,"* the whole Gentile church. | 1 |
| 19. | **The Holy Spirit**<br><br>Every sacrifice had to meet certain conditions, and Paul is praying that the church would be sanctified by the Holy Spirit, set apart, holy and acceptable to God. | 1 |
| 20. | **Boasting/glorying in things pertaining to God**<br><br>It is legitimate to boast, provided you boast about the right things—not about yourself but about things that pertain to God. | 1 |
| 21. | **cross**<br><br>Our "old man" likes to boast in ways that seek to imply our own importance, value, and superiority, but that old carnal nature died with Christ on Calvary. All we have to boast about now is what God has done in us and through us as new creations in Christ so that He gets all the glory. | 1 |
| 22. | **Obedience (to the gospel)**<br><br>Paul is not talking about his own accomplishments but about what *"Christ has…accomplished through me."* The ultimate purpose of his work is this: to bring the Gentiles into obedience to the Word of God through faith. | 1 |

| Question | Answer | Points |
|---|---|---|
| 23. | a. **word; deed** | 5 |
| | b. **signs; wonders** | |
| | c. **Spirit** | |
| | Paul says, "I haven't preached in word only, but my word has been attested to by supernatural signs and miracles. I have fully preached the gospel." The purpose of this "full preaching" is to make the Gentiles obedient—not just to be nominal or "head" believers, but to be believers who are committed from the heart to the Lord Jesus Christ and to the truth of His Word. | |
| | The only way you will gain a "heart certainty" that the gospel is true, and that it is really for you, is if you have a personal experience of the supernatural power of God. No one else can do that for you. It can come only from God. And when it comes, you will know for sure that it came from heaven. | |
| 24. | a. **His crucifixion** | 4 |
| | This verse takes us back to the heart of the gospel: Christ died, Christ was buried, and Christ rose from the dead. Paul's setting aside of human wisdom is especially notable because he tells us in the previous chapter that "*Jews request a sign, and Greeks seek after wisdom*" (1 Corinthians 1:22), and that Christ crucified is "*foolishness*" to the Greeks (verse 23), "*but to those who are called,…Christ* [is] *the power of God and the wisdom of God*" (verse 24). | |
| | b. **Spirit; power** | |
| | The Holy Spirit is invisible, but His presence can be demonstrated by what He does. The preaching of the gospel with power needs to be restored in the church if we are to bring in the full harvest. Words on their own won't do the job. | |
| | c. **In the power of God** | |
| | Human wisdom changes with every generation. All the philosophical theories I examined when I was a student and a professor are now out-of-date. But the Word of God and the power of God never change. | |
| | One of the disasters of the contemporary church is that the cross has been displaced from being the center of focus, and all sorts of gimmicks have been put in its place. The Holy Spirit is not interested in gimmicks. Much of the church is on top and God is underneath, but it takes only a simple, time-tested message with a manifestation of the Holy Spirit to right the situation. | |
| 25. | **To those who were as yet unreached** | 1 |
| | That is apostolic motivation! I believe the key word for every apostle is *go*. When Jesus gave His final orders to His apostles before His ascension, the key word was *go*: "Go and preach the gospel," and "Go into every nation." (See Mark 16:15; Matthew 28:19.) An apostle is not some super-pastor circulating among established churches. An apostle has a vision for the unreached. And God bears supernatural testimony through those who have such a vision. | |
| 26. | **No** | 1 |
| | "*No longer having a place in these parts*"—what a remarkable statement! Paul indicates he has reached everybody between Jerusalem and Rome. At the time he writes this epistle* to the Romans, he is in Corinth. He tells the Romans that he is going to Jerusalem to deliver the monetary gift to the believers there, given by the believers in Macedonia and Achaia, and then he is going to Spain. But, on his way, he plans to stop off and see them in Rome. | |
| 27. | **In the fullness of the blessing of the gospel of Christ** | 1 |
| | Recall that in Romans 1:10, Paul prays that he "*may find a way in the will of God to come to you*" in Rome. How does God answer? By allowing Paul to be taken as a prisoner in chains through a fourteen-day storm and a shipwreck. But several miraculous things happen along the way. Further, the book of Acts closes with these words: "*Then Paul dwelt two whole years in his own rented house* [in Rome], *and received all who came to him, preaching the kingdom of God and teaching the things which concern the Lord Jesus Christ with all confidence, no one forbidding him*" (Acts 28:30–31). | |

| Question | Answer | Points |
|---|---|---|
| 28. | ***"I beg you"***<br><br>The Greek term Paul uses in Romans 15:30 that is translated as *"strive"*—where he asks the church at Rome to *"strive together with me in prayers to God for me"*—is the term from which we get the modern English word *agonize*. It is also the word we read in literature for "contest" in the ancient Olympic Games. Such a request presents a challenge to intercessors. Do you know what it is like to strive, to agonize, to go through a conflict in prayer on behalf of a servant of God? | 1 |
| 29. | **Hopefully, your answer is "Yes."**<br><br>I cannot overemphasize the importance of intercession in accomplishing the purposes of God. There is no higher ministry than that of intercession. But many people called to intercession do not feel they are doing enough because they are not out front on a platform, so they give up this ministry of prayer. If that is your situation, don't do that. God needs you. The servants of God in the ministry need you.<br><br>Intercessors, be willing to strive together to fight, to wrestle with, the powers that seek to destroy movements and leaders in ministry. Without intercession, the ultimate victory cannot be won. | No points |
| 30. | **Peace**<br><br>You already know that *shalom* is the Hebrew word for "peace." It is also the Hebrew greeting. But, as we discussed earlier, it is much more than what we understand by "peace" in English. *Shalom* is related to a word that means "completeness" or "perfection." You can enter into the meaning of *shalom* with words like *harmony*, *wholeness*, and *completeness*, and with the phrase *every account settled*. A verb formed from the word *shalom* means "to pay in full." We can have completeness because everything for our lives has been paid in full, and we can be whole in Jesus Christ. That is peace. | 1 |
| 31. | a. **Phoebe**<br><br>Phoebe was the sister in the Lord who carried this letter to Rome. She was a deacon of the church in Cenchrea, a port town in southern Greece near Corinth, where Paul was staying when he wrote this epistle. Remember that, because there was no postal service at that time, for a letter to be delivered, someone had to personally take it to its intended recipient. Apart from Phoebe's faithfulness, we may never have had the epistle to the Romans. God trusted this woman with the supreme task of transporting this letter.<br><br>b.<br>    **i. Priscilla**<br>    **ii. Aquila**<br><br>Priscilla and Aquila were two of Paul's longtime friends who had been in all sorts of trouble with him for the sake of the gospel. Paul first met them and worked with them in Corinth (see Acts 18:1–3), and he traveled with them (see Acts 18:18). They are also mentioned in 1 Corinthians 16:19 and 2 Timothy 4:19, where Priscilla is referred to as "Prisca."<br><br>c.<br>    **i. Andronicus**<br>    **ii. Junia**<br><br>There is something about being in trouble with other people or enduring hardship together with them that builds the relationship in a unique way.<br><br>d.<br>    **i. Mary**<br>    **ii. Tryphena**<br>    **iii. Tryphosa**<br>    **iv. Persis**<br><br>It is typical of Paul that he singles out the women who have worked hard. In Proverbs 31, from verse 10 onward, we read about the qualities of the *"virtuous wife,"* including the distinction that *"she…willingly works with her hands"* (verse 13). | 12 |

| Question | Answer | Points |
|---|---|---|
| 31. (cont.) | **e. Timothy**<br><br>Timothy is remarkable in that Paul refers to him as his *"beloved and faithful son in the Lord"* (1 Corinthians 4:17). Two of Paul's letters to Timothy are part of the Bible, and, in both of them, Paul reiterates this idea of spiritual sonship regarding Timothy.<br><br>**f. Tertius**<br><br>In lesson 22, we briefly touched on the gift of administration. Again, without the giftings of people like Phoebe and Tertius—people who have served as couriers, scribes, translators, and librarians—we might not have the letter to the Romans in our possession today. Let's encourage people in their giftings and not diminish their importance in God's work.<br><br>**g. Gaius**<br><br>In the person of Gaius, we need to acknowledge another seldom recognized gift—the gift of hospitality. As I wrote in lesson 1, in the church where I first agreed to follow Jesus, I probably would have walked out of that place after the service and never gone back again, but an elderly couple who kept a boardinghouse near the church invited my fellow soldier and me back for supper. Because of that act of hospitality, the Lord was able to get my attention. So, again, that is a very simple, personal example of the importance of exercising this gift of hospitality in the ministry. | |
| 32. | **Those who cause divisions and offenses**<br><br>The apostle Jude, in verse 19 of his epistle, describes those who cause divisions as *"sensual"* (carnal or soulish). Remembering that the soul includes the mind, the will, and the emotions, it is easy to see that divisions are often caused by those who exalt the mind over the Spirit. In fact, that is Jude's conclusion: such divisive people are *"not having the Spirit."* | 1 |
| 33. | **a. good**<br><br>**b. evil**<br><br>Having purity of heart and mind is highly esteemed in Scripture. In Matthew 5:8, Jesus says, *"Blessed are the pure in heart, for they shall see God."* Hebrews 10:22 talks about *"having our hearts sprinkled from an evil conscience."* God invites us into a cleansing process so that we can be transformed into the likeness of Jesus. | 2 |
| 34. | **Under our feet**<br><br>We have already noted the fact that, within three centuries of its birth, the church of Jesus Christ defeated the Roman Empire. Without the apparatus of modern technology, media, and propaganda, the church dethroned one of the most powerful empires in human history. But Paul's statement in Romans 16:20 is also a promise to the end-time church. Satan will be crushed beneath the feet of the church of Jesus Christ (because the feet are the lowest and the last) before our feet finally take off for a better place. So be encouraged! | 1 |
| | Check your written memory work. If your memory work is word-perfect, 4 points for each verse. (1 point off for each mistake in a verse. If there are more than three mistakes, do not mark any points for that verse.) | 8 |
| | Total Points | ____/75 |

Fill in the total points for lesson 25 on the "Tally Sheet for Each Lesson" on page 254.

# TALLY SHEET FOR EACH LESSON

| Lesson | Lesson Title | Points |
|---|---|---|
| 1 | Prelude to the Book of Romans | ____/42 |
| 2 | Stage 1: God's Self-Revelation: Man's Rejection and Its Consequences | ____/56 |
| 3 | Stage 2: Moral Knowledge and Personal Responsibility | ____/39 |
| 4 | Stage 3: Accountability to God | ____/46 |
| 5 | Stage 4: God's Provision of Righteousness | ____/39 |
| 6 | Stage 5: Justification by Faith, Not Works | ____/38 |
| 7 | Stage 6: Five Experiential Results of Being Justified by Faith | ____/50 |
| 8 | Stage 7: Comparison Between Adam and Jesus | ____/48 |
| 9 | Stage 8: God's Solution for the Old Man: Execution | ____/38 |
| 10 | Stage 9: How to Apply God's Solution for the Old Man in Our Lives | ____/27 |
| 11 | Stage 10: The Believer's Relationship to Law | ____/48 |
| 12 | The Destination: The Spirit-Filled Life, Part 1 | ____/46 |
| 13 | The Destination: The Spirit-Filled Life, Part 2 | ____/40 |
| 14 | The Destination: The Spirit-Filled Life, Part 3 | ____/52 |
| 15 | The Destination: The Spirit-Filled Life, Part 4 | ____/51 |
| 16 | The Destiny of Israel and the Church, Part 1: God's Sovereignty or Humanism? | ____/31 |

| Lesson | Lesson Title | Points |
|--------|-------------|--------|
| 17 | The Destiny of Israel and the Church, Part 2: Children of Promise | _____/30 |
| 18 | The Destiny of Israel and the Church, Part 3: Is Israel Now the Church? | _____/39 |
| 19 | The Destiny of Israel and the Church, Part 4: God's Mercy | _____/45 |
| 20 | The Destiny of Israel and the Church, Part 5: Salvation Through Messiah | _____/40 |
| 21 | The Destiny of Israel and the Church, Part 6: All Israel Will Be Saved | _____/63 |
| 22 | Living Out Your Faith Under Pressure, Part 1 | _____/75 |
| 23 | Living Out Your Faith Under Pressure, Part 2 | _____/72 |
| 24 | Living Out Your Faith Under Pressure, Part 3 | _____/46 |
| 25 | Living Out Your Faith Under Pressure, Part 4 | _____/75 |
|  | Grand Total Points | _____/1176 |

50 percent or more (588+ points)= Pass

70 percent or more (823+ points)= Very Good

80 percent or more (941+ points)= Excellent

# GLOSSARY

**Atonement/Atoning:** *Atonement* refers to the sacrifice Jesus made on the cross to pay the price for our sins. The word *atonement is* made up of three parts: "at-one-ment." It is in the atonement that God and man are brought together to be "at one." God and man had been separated by man's disobedience, which caused a barrier to their relationship—one of rebellion and sin. But through Jesus's *atoning* sacrifice on the cross, this barrier was broken down, enabling the relationship to be restored.

**Circa:** This word comes from the Latin *circum*, meaning "around." It is used to indicate an approximate date.

**Covenant:** There are two basic words in Scripture for "covenant": the Hebrew word used in the Old Testament is *b'rit* (or *b'rith*); the Greek word used in the New Testament is *diatheke*. These words are regularly translated by two different English terms: *covenant* and *testament*. The concept of covenant is central to the whole of God's revelation to us. It has been suggested that the root meaning of *b'rit* is "to bind," but that meaning is not certain. What is certain, however, is that a covenant is binding. The root meaning of *diatheke* is "to set something out in order." It suggests, therefore, the setting forth of specific terms and conditions. This word has more of a legal association than its Hebrew counterpart. One should not take lightly either entering into a covenant or breaking one. Essentially, a divine covenant expresses a relationship that God Himself sovereignly initiates with human beings out of His own choice and decision. He defines the terms on which He is prepared to enter into that relationship. God never enters into a permanent relationship with anyone apart from a covenant. (See also the entries "New covenant" and "Old covenant.")

**Depravity:** *Depravity* generally refers to wickedness or moral corruption. In a Christian sense, it more specifically refers to the corruption of human nature due to original sin.[3]

**Destiny:** This term refers to where a person will ultimately end up for eternity, determined by how they respond to their calling to salvation in Jesus Christ. The time when God confronts us with this call is the most significant moment of our lives because our whole destiny for time and eternity is at stake.

**Doctrine:** A belief or set of beliefs held by a church, a denomination, or another group. The concepts of doctrine and teaching are closely related because the Latin word *doctrina* means "teaching." By establishing our faith on a solid foundation of sound doctrine, we can build stable, successful Christian lives.

**Epistle:** A book in the New Testament that was originally written by an apostle or another Christian leader as a letter to an individual, a local church, or a general audience of believers.

---

3. Paraphrased from the *Oxford English Dictionary*, s.v. "depravity."

**Gentiles:** "Gentiles" refers to heathen nations, especially people who are not Jewish.

**Hallelujah:** This word literally means "God be praised" or "Praise the Lord." The *jah* at the end of the word refers to the name *Jaweh* or, as it is more commonly spelled, *Yahweh*, which is one of the names of God in the Bible.

**Identification:** "Identification" refers to the concept of linking or associating one person with another. Important examples of this idea from Scripture include Jesus identifying with us and our sin when He died on the cross in our place, and our identifying with Jesus when we believe in Him, die to ourselves, and are buried with Him through baptism so that we can also be raised to new life with Him.

**Israel:** This name can have many related meanings: (1) the land God gave to Abraham and his descendants as an everlasting covenant; (2) Abraham's grandson Jacob, whom God renamed Israel; (3) all twelve tribes, descended from Jacob's sons, until the end of King Solomon's reign; (4) the northern kingdom in contrast to the southern kingdom after Israel divided in the days of King Rehoboam; (5) the Jews after the return from exile in Babylon (such as those depicted in the New Testament); and (6) the modern state of Israel in the Middle East.

**Jews:** Although this designation can be, and is, used to refer to all of the tribes of Israel (and their descendants to the present day), in its narrowest sense, it refers to the tribe of Judah. (See also the entry "Judah.")

**Judah:** *Judah* may variously refer to one of the sons of Jacob (or Israel), to the tribe descended from Judah, or to the southern kingdom in contrast to the northern kingdom after Israel divided in the days of King Rehoboam. Judah is also the tribe of Israel through which the Messiah came. The name *Judah*, or *Yehuda*, means "praise." The word *Jew* is a derivative of this term.

**Justified/Justification:** I describe being justified, or being made righteous, as being "just-as-if-I'd" never sinned. When we receive Jesus's sacrifice for sin as our own, an exchange takes place: because Jesus died our death, we now receive His life. As part of that process, we are justified and made righteous with a righteousness that has never known sin. The term *justification* is a noun form related to the past-tense verb or adjective *justified*. (See also the entry "Righteous/Righteousness.")

**Law:** This term indicates any set of rules, regulations, or statutes. It is important to remember that when the apostle Paul refers to "*the law*" (lowercase) in the book of Romans, the word "the" has been added by translators, which can suggest that he is only referring to the law of Moses, but that is incorrect. There is no law of any kind that can make us righteous; our righteousness can come only through faith in Jesus Christ.

**Law, the:** In this study course, where the term "the Law" is used with a capital *L*, it is synonymous with the capitalized form of "the Law of Moses." (Please refer to the entry "Law of Moses.")

**Law of Moses (usually lowercase, "law of Moses"):** This term generally refers to the laws that God gave to Moses for the people of Israel after He delivered them from Egypt. More specifically, it can refer to the *Pentateuch*, which is a term used for the first five books of the Bible—Genesis to Deuteronomy. In this study course, wherever the term *law* in this phrase is capitalized ("Law of Moses"), it refers specifically to the Pentateuch.

**Legalism:** In a religious sense, this term refers to following law as a means to righteousness. (See also the entry "Law.") The apostle Paul points out that the shortcoming of our trying to attain righteousness by this means is not that the law itself is deficient but that human nature is deficient in being able to follow the whole law. God's alternative is for us to receive righteousness by grace through faith in Jesus Christ.

**Logic:** *Logic* refers to the study or application of correct reasoning. The reasoning of logic usually builds from one point to the next so that, if one thing is true, then we can be confident of certain other facts. For instance, if there is no crack in a cup, we can deduce that the cup will hold a fluid without leaking, and we can thus proceed to fill that cup with a liquid. We depend on logic every day in a multitude of ways.

**Meekness:** This word refers to the quality of being quiet, gentle, or submissive. The noun *meekness* and the adjective *meek* are not to be confused with *weakness* and *weak*.

**New covenant:** When Jesus died on the cross for our sins, He established a new covenant (see also entry for "Covenant") in His blood, so that those who believe in Him can be forgiven of their sins and restored to fellowship with God the Father. He does not require us to follow the law of Moses or any other law to be considered righteous; rather, we must identify with Him in His death, burial, and resurrection. When we do this, we receive new life in Him. The capitalized term *New Covenant* is sometimes used to refer to the second part of the Bible, from Matthew to Revelation, which is commonly called the *New Testament*.

**Old covenant:** Primarily, this term refers to the covenant that God made with Moses and the people of Israel on Mount Sinai. It can also refer to the first part of the Bible, from Genesis to Malachi, which relates significant events in the history of God's dealings with man preceding Jesus's birth. This portion of the Bible is commonly called the *Old Testament* by Christians. In Judaism, it is referred to as the *Tanakh*.

**Prophets, the:** In the Old Testament Scriptures, *the Prophets* refers to the seventeen prophetic books starting with Isaiah and ending with Malachi. These books are further divided into the "Major Prophets" and the "Minor Prophets," although this distinction is based on the length of the books rather than on their importance. A prophet is one who receives a message or messages from God, and while all the men who brought forth the messages contained in the prophetic books were prophets, they are not the only prophets mentioned in the Bible. Deborah, Samuel, Nathan, Elijah, and Elisha were all prophets, but there are no individual books containing their prophecies. Some of their words from God are contained in other books of the Bible.

**Propitiation/Propitiatory:** The Greek word translated "*propitiation*" in Romans 3:25 is the same word that is used in the Greek version of the Old Testament (the Septuagint) for the "mercy seat," the covering of the holy ark of the covenant in the tabernacle and temple. This is a very vivid picture because the ark contained the Ten Commandments, which represented the requirements of the law. Those commandments were flouted and broken by the Israelites. Moreover, the Gentiles, although they did not have the law, were never able to meet the "*righteous requirements of the law*" (Romans 2:26). But Jesus, by His death on the cross, became the Mercy Seat that once and for all covered all the sins that human beings—whether Jews or Gentiles—have committed. *Propitiatory* is the adjective form of *propitiation*.

**Rational/Rationalism:** *Rationalism* is the concept that reason and knowledge triumph over faith and emotion for making decisions and determining actions. The Greeks idolized the human mind. Aristotle's concept of God was of a perfect mind contemplating itself—because nothing less was worthy of its contemplation. Out of this idea, the whole modern philosophy of rationalism has developed. *Rational* is the adjective form used in relation to this philosophy.

**Righteous/Righteousness:** *Righteous* refers to being morally right or justifiable. When we are self-righteous, we seek to justify ourselves by our own merits, but God will never accept our righteousness or its deficient standards. The only righteousness that is acceptable to God is Christ's righteousness, which has never known sin. We receive that righteousness when we accept Jesus as our Savior.

**Sublime:** *Sublime* comes from the Latin term meaning "high" or "elevated." It is used to describe that which is exalted and of outstanding spiritual, moral, or intellectual worth.

**Talmudic:** The *Talmud* is the authoritative body of Jewish tradition made up of two sections: the *Mishna* and the *Gemara*. To describe Paul's thinking as *Talmudic* is to indicate that it is steeped in Jewish thought and tradition.

**Temporal:** *Temporal* derives from *tempus*, which is the Latin word for "time." It refers to those things which relate to time rather than to eternity.

**Watershed:** This word refers to a crucial turning point in a situation. The concept is taken from the place on a mountain (usually a ridge) that marks the point where, if rain falls to one side, it will flow in a certain direction, ultimately ending up in a particular body of water; and if it falls to the other side, it will flow in another direction, ending up in a different body of water.

# APPENDIX: OCCURRENCES OF THE WORDS *ISRAEL* AND *ISRAELITE(S)* IN THE NEW TESTAMENT

This appendix lists the seventy-nine occurrences of the words *Israel* and *Israelite(s)* in the New Testament. References for verses that have been derived from Old Testament sources are indicated.

1. Matthew 2:6:

   *"a Ruler who will shepherd My people Israel"* (cited from Micah 5:2)

2. Matthew 2:20

   *"the land of Israel"*

3. Matthew 2:21

   *"the land of Israel"*

4. Matthew 8:10

   *"not found such great faith, not even in Israel"*

5. Matthew 9:33

   *"never seen like this in Israel"*

6. Matthew 10:6

   *"to the lost sheep of the house of Israel"*

7. Matthew 10:23

   *"not have gone through the cities of Israel before the Son of Man comes"*

8. Matthew 15:24

   *"except to the lost sheep of the house of Israel"*

9. Matthew 15:31

   *"they glorified the God of Israel"*

10. Matthew 19:28

    *"will also sit on twelve thrones, judging the twelve tribes of Israel"*

11. Matthew 27:9

    *"whom they of the children of Israel pierced"* (cited from Zechariah 11:12–13)

12. Matthew 27:42

    *"If He is the King of Israel, let Him now come down"*

13. Mark 12:29

    *"Hear, O Israel"* (cited from Deuteronomy 6:4–5)

14. Mark 15:32

    *"Let the Christ, the King of Israel, descend now from the cross"*

15. Luke 1:16

    *"And he will turn many of the children of Israel"*

16. Luke 1:54

    *"He has helped His servant Israel"* (derived from Isaiah 41:8)

17. Luke 1:68

    *"Blessed is the Lord God of Israel"*

18. Luke 1:80

    *"till the day of his manifestation to Israel"*

19. Luke 2:25

    *"waiting for the Consolation of Israel"*

20. Luke 2:32

    *"A light to bring revelation to the Gentiles, and the glory of Your people Israel"* (cited from Isaiah 49:6)

21. Luke 2:34

"*the fall and rising of many in Israel*"

22. Luke 4:25

"*many widows were in Israel*"

23. Luke 4:27

"*many lepers were in Israel*"

24. Luke 7:9

"*not found such great faith, not even in Israel*"

25. Luke 22:30

"*sit on thrones judging the twelve tribes of Israel*"

26. Luke 24:21

"*He who was going to redeem Israel*"

27. John 1:31

"*that He should be revealed to Israel*"

28. John 1:47

"*an Israelite indeed*" (Jesus referring to Nathanael)

29. John 1:49

"*You are the King of Israel*"

30. John 3:10

"*Are you the teacher of Israel*"

31. John 12:13

"*Blessed is…the King of Israel*"

32. Acts 1:6

"*restore the kingdom to Israel*"

33. Acts 2:22

"*Men of Israel*" (literally, *Israelites*)

34. Acts 2:36

"*Therefore let all the house of Israel know*"

35. Acts 3:12

"*Men of Israel*" (literally, *Israelites*)

36. Acts 4:8

"*Rulers of the people and elders of Israel*"

37. Acts 4:10

"*let it be known to…all the people of Israel*"

38. Acts 4:27

"*with the Gentiles and the people of Israel*"

39. Acts 5:21

"*all the elders of the children of Israel*"

40. Acts 5:31

"*to give repentance to Israel*"

41. Acts 5:35

"*Men of Israel*" (literally, *Israelites*)

42. Acts 7:23

"*to visit his brethren, the children of Israel*"

43. Acts 7:37

"*Moses who said to the children of Israel*"

44. Acts 7:42

"*Did you offer Me…O house of Israel*" (cited from Amos 5:25–27)

45. Acts 9:15

"*to bear My name before Gentiles, kings, and the children of Israel*"

46. Acts 10:36

"*The word which God sent to the children of Israel*"

47. Acts 13:16

"*Men of Israel*" (literally, *Israelites*)

48. Acts 13:17

"*The God of this people Israel*"

49. Acts 13:23

"*God raised up for Israel a Savior*"

50. Acts 13:24

"*the baptism of repentance to all the people of Israel*"

51. Acts 21:28

"*Men of Israel*" (literally, *Israelites*)

52. Acts 28:20

"*for the hope of Israel I am bound*"

53. Romans 9:3–4

"*my countrymen…who are Israelites*"

54./55. Romans 9:6

"*They are not all Israel who are of Israel*"[1]

56. Romans 9:27

"*Isaiah also cries out concerning Israel*"

---

1. This usage restricts the meaning of *Israel* or *Israelite* to only those Israelites who have fulfilled certain spiritual requirements.

57. Romans 9:27

*"Though the number of the children of Israel be as the sand"* (cited from Isaiah 10:22–23)

58. Romans 9:31

*"but Israel, pursuing the law of righteousness"*

59. Romans 10:1

*"my…prayer to God for Israel"*

60. Romans 10:19

*"did Israel not know"*

61. Romans 10:21

*"But to Israel he says"*

62. Romans 11:1

*"For I also am an Israelite"*

63. Romans 11:2

*"he pleads with God against Israel"*

64. Romans 11:7

*"Israel has not obtained what it seeks"*

65. Romans 11:25

*"blindness in part has happened to Israel"*

66. Romans 11:26

*"And so all Israel will be saved"*

67. 1 Corinthians 10:18

*"Observe Israel after the flesh"*

68. 2 Corinthians 3:7

*"the children of Israel could not look steadily at the face of Moses"*

69. 2 Corinthians 3:13

*"the children of Israel could not look steadily at the end"*

70. 2 Corinthians 11:22

*"Are they Israelites? So am I"*

71. Galatians 6:16

*"peace and mercy…upon the Israel of God"*[2]

72. Ephesians 2:12

*"aliens from the commonwealth of Israel"*

73. Philippians 3:5

*"of the stock of Israel"*

74. Hebrews 8:8

*"I will make a new covenant with the house of Israel"*

75. Hebrews 8:10

*"the covenant that I will make with the house of Israel"* (Hebrews 8:8, 10 both cited from Jeremiah 31:31–34)

76. Hebrews 11:22

*"Joseph…made mention of the departure of the children of Israel"*

77. Revelation 2:14

*"Balaam…put a stumbling block before the children of Israel"*

78. Revelation 7:4

*"One hundred and forty-four thousand of all the tribes of the children of Israel"*

79. Revelation 21:12

*"the names of the twelve tribes of the children of Israel"*

---

2. This usage restricts the meaning of *Israel* or *Israelite* to only those Israelites who have fulfilled certain spiritual requirements.

# ABOUT THE AUTHOR

Derek Prince (1915–2003) was born in India of British parents. He was educated as a scholar of Greek and Latin at Eton College and King's College, Cambridge, in England. Upon graduation, he held a fellowship (equivalent to a professorship) in Ancient and Modern Philosophy at King's College. Prince also studied Hebrew, Aramaic, and modern languages at Cambridge and the Hebrew University in Jerusalem. As a student, he was a philosopher and a self-proclaimed agnostic.

While serving in the Royal Army Medical Corps (RAMC) during World War II, Prince began to study the Bible as a philosophical work. Converted through a powerful encounter with Jesus Christ, he was baptized in the Holy Spirit a few days later. Out of this encounter, he formed two conclusions: first, that Jesus Christ is alive; second, that the Bible is a true, relevant, up-to-date book. These conclusions altered the whole course of his life, which he then devoted to studying and teaching the Bible as the Word of God.

Discharged from the army in Jerusalem in 1945, he married Lydia Christensen, founder of a children's home there. Upon their marriage, he immediately became father to Lydia's eight adopted daughters—six Jewish, one Palestinian Arab, and one English. Together, the family saw the rebirth of the state of Israel in 1948. In the late 1950s, they adopted another daughter while Prince was serving as principal of a teachers' training college in Kenya.

In 1963, the Princes immigrated to the United States and pastored a church in Seattle. In 1973, Prince became one of the founders of Intercessors for America. His book *Shaping History through Prayer and Fasting* has awakened Christians around the world to their responsibility to pray for their governments. Many consider underground translations of the book as instrumental in the fall of communist regimes in the USSR, East Germany, and Czechoslovakia.

Lydia Prince died in 1975, and Prince married Ruth Baker (a single mother to three adopted children) in 1978. He met his second wife, like his first wife, while she was serving the Lord in Jerusalem. Ruth died in December 1998 in Jerusalem, where they had lived since 1981.

Until a few years before his own death in 2003 at the age of eighty-eight, Prince persisted in the ministry God had called him to as he traveled the world, imparting God's revealed truth, praying for the sick and afflicted, and sharing his prophetic insights into world events in the light of Scripture. Internationally recognized as a Bible scholar and spiritual patriarch, Derek Prince established a teaching ministry that spanned six continents and more than sixty years. He is the author of more than eighty books, six hundred audio teachings, and one hundred video teachings, many of which have been translated and published in more than one hundred languages. He pioneered teaching on such groundbreaking themes as generational curses, the biblical significance of Israel, and demonology.

Prince's radio program, which began in 1979, has been translated into more than a dozen languages and continues to touch lives. Derek Prince's main gift of explaining the Bible and its teachings in a clear and simple way has helped build a foundation of faith in millions of lives. His nondenominational, nonsectarian approach has made his teaching equally relevant and helpful to people from all racial and religious backgrounds, and his messages are estimated to have reached more than half the globe.

In 2002, he said, "It is my desire—and I believe the Lord's desire—that this ministry continue the work, which God began through me over sixty years ago, until Jesus returns."

Derek Prince Ministries continues to reach out to believers in over 140 countries with Derek's teaching, fulfilling the mandate to keep on "until Jesus returns." This is accomplished through the outreaches of more than forty-five Derek Prince offices around the world, including primary work in Australia, Canada, China, France, Germany, the Netherlands, New Zealand, Norway, Russia, South Africa, Switzerland, the United Kingdom, and the United States. For current information about these and other worldwide locations, visit www.derek-prince.org.